I0795081

The College History Series

UNIVERSITY OF LA VERNE

MARLIN HECKMAN

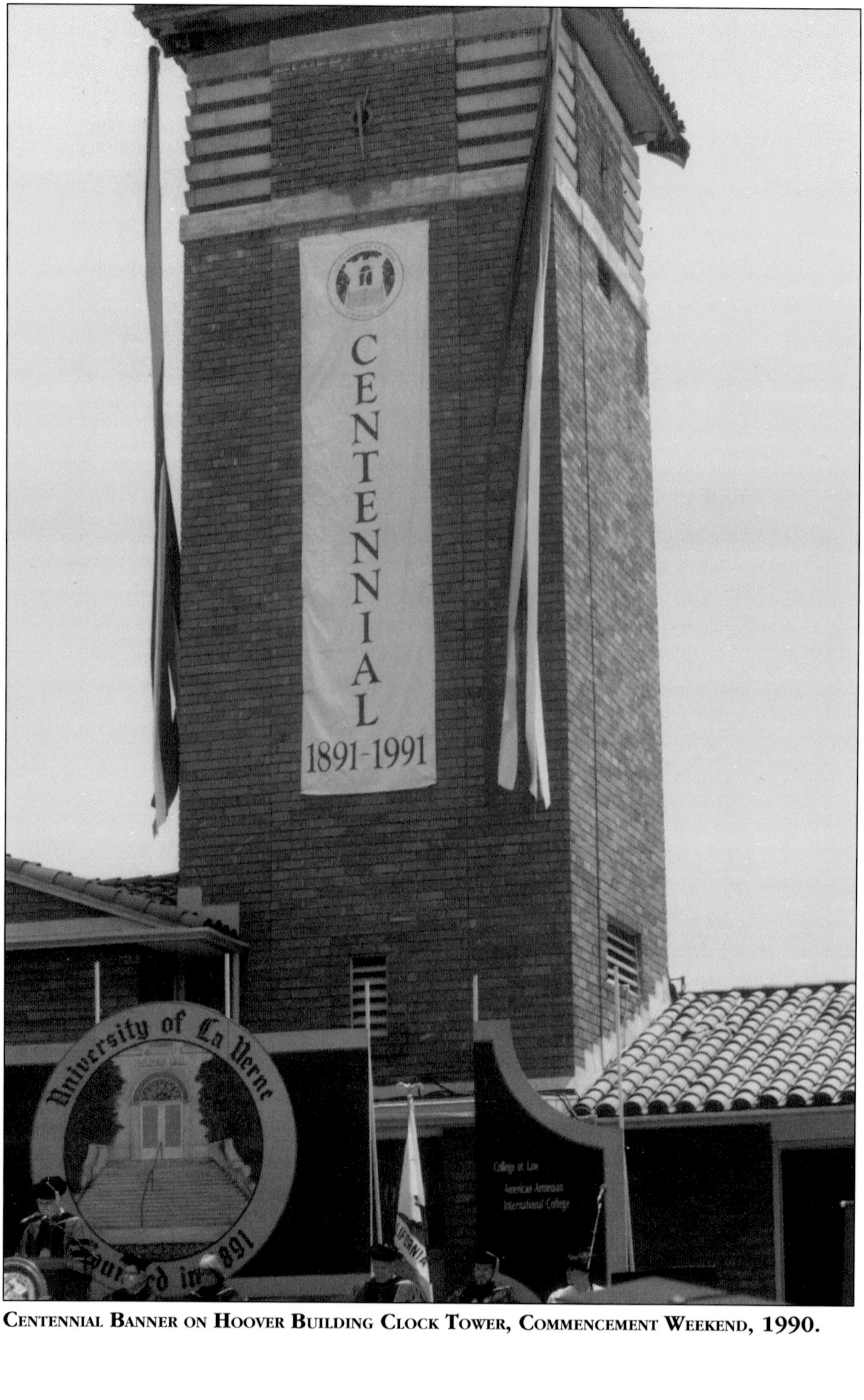

Centennial Banner on Hoover Building Clock Tower, Commencement Weekend, 1990.

The College History Series

UNIVERSITY OF LA VERNE

MARLIN HECKMAN

ARCADIA PUBLISHING

ISBN 978-0-7385-0820-9

Published by Arcadia Publishing
Charleston, South Carolina

Printed in the United States of America

Library of Congress Catalog Card Number: 2001086013

For all general information contact Arcadia Publishing at:
Telephone 843-853-2070
Fax 843-853-0044
E-mail sales@arcadiapublishing.com
For customer service and orders:
Toll-Free 1-888-313-2665

Visit us on the Internet at www.arcadiapublishing.com

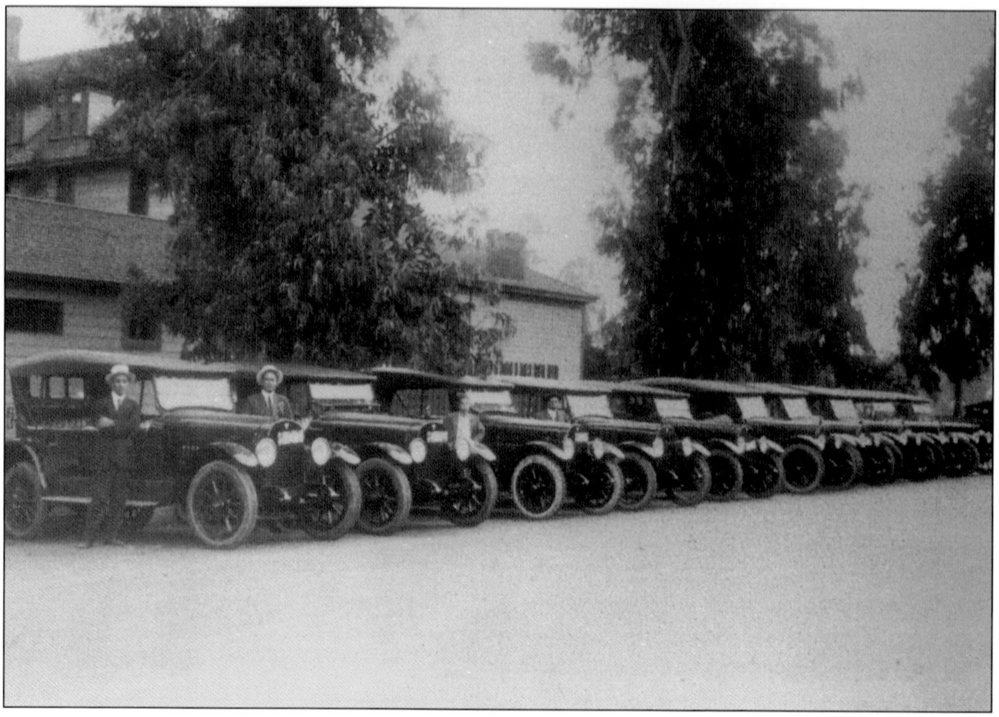

Cars Behind Original College Building. What parking problem?

Contents

ACKNOWLEDGMENTS

Many people have been involved over the years in the preservation of what survives today as the picture files in the University Archives of the Wilson Library Special Collections Department. Alumni and families of alumni have sent pictures and momentos from their hiding places in photo albums and trunks. University publicity department heads and publications advisors have deposited photo files from time to time.

Gladdys E. Muir, longtime history professor at La Verne, began seriously saving material for the archives before the 1930s. For more than a decade, the archive files have been sorted and indexed by E. Louise Larick, who served as librarian at La Verne from 1934 to 1952, and more recently as part-time archivist.

While the current volume is essentially the story of La Verne in pictures, the written history has been preserved in several sources.

Bagley, Mark R. and Marlin L. Heckman, *The ULV Trivia Book, a collection of well-known and some not so well-known facts about the University of La Verne and its predecessors, Lordsburg College, Palmera College & La Verne College.* La Verne, CA: ULV Press, 1988.

Cable, W. Arthur and Homer F. Sanger, *Educational Bluebook of the Church of the Brethren, 1708–1923.* Elgin, IL: General Educational Board of the Church of the Brethren, [1923]. Pp. 70–76.

Eshelman, Matthew M. *A History of the Church of the Brethren* (Southern California and Arizona). Los Angeles: 1917. Pp. 108–117.

Heckman, Marlin L. *The Gem of Lordsburg, the Lordsburg Hotel/College Building, 1887–1927.* La Verne, CA: ULV Press, 1987.

Hogan, Herbert W. *[The Presidency of Stephen C. Morgan, 1985–]* (tentative title). In Press, 2001.

———. and Gladdys E. Muir. *The University of La Verne, a Centennial History, 1891–1991.* La Verne, CA: University of La Verne, 1990.

Muir, Gladdys E. *Settlement of the Brethren on the Pacific Slope, a Study in Colonization.* Elgin, IL: Brethren Publishing House, 1939. Pp. 411–440.

———. *La Verne College, Seventy-five Years of Service.* La Verne, CA: La Verne College, 1967.

Sharp, Solomon Z. *The Educational History of the Church of the Brethren.* Elgin, IL: Brethren Publishing House, 1923. Pp. 183–192.

FOREWORD

Since its founding in 1891 as Lordsburg College, the University of La Verne has enjoyed a colorful history marked by decades of growth and development reflecting the needs of our changing society.

Through each decade, photographers have successfully recorded our generations of students, faculty, staff, and trustees as they have participated in the life of our campus. These pictures reflect a community built on the values of academic excellence and service to others in a highly personalized environment.

The images contained in this unique publication reflect our past and the foundation on which we build our future visions. While the faces and buildings will change, the values that are our foundation will remain the same.

Stephen Morgan

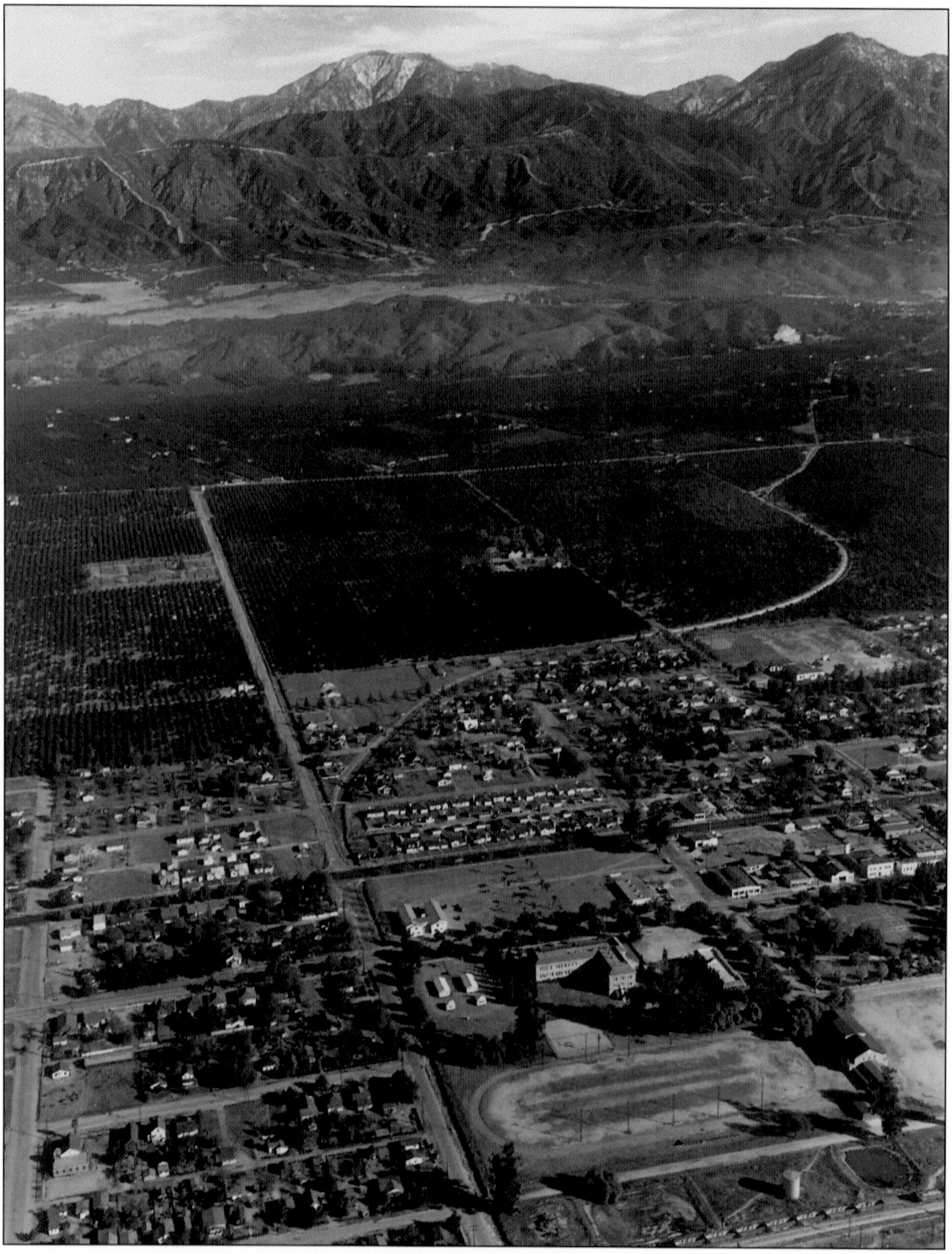

AERIAL VIEW OF LA VERNE CAMPUS AND TOWN IN 1949. Looking north, acres of orange groves surround the town. Mount Baldy rises to 10,000 feet in elevation in the distance.

Introduction

In October 1891, Lordsburg College opened its doors to some 65 students in an unused, land boom hotel in the new town of Lordsburg, California. For the first several years the work was mostly pre-collegiate, and the first bachelor's degree was granted in 1914. Lordsburg College was renamed La Verne College in 1917, and the 1000th degree was granted in 1950. In 1977, the name was changed to the University of La Verne, and there are now more than 40,000 alumni as the University of La Verne approaches 110 years of existence.

The photographs in this volume tell, in both formal and informal ways, the story of the University of La Verne, described in its alma mater as "a dear favored spot, that shall ne'er be forgot." There are pictures here spanning 11 decades. Three photos include 12 of La Verne's 17 presidents. Students and graduates from the 1890s and the 1990s are here. Building pictures range from the earliest, in 1891, to the new law school building, opened in January 2001. Music and sports have always been part of life on the campus from dirt basketball courts to the wooden playing surface in the Supertents and from early musical groups to group practice on electronic pianos. Picnics and food have been integral to campus life. There are signs and traditions that are remembered fondly by many. These pictures will elicit special memories for alumni who attended La Verne in earlier years, while students of more recent generations will perhaps catch a glimpse of life in earlier decades through the stories captured in these photos.

All photographs on these pages are from the University Archives in the Wilson Library of the University of La Verne. The photo archives represent gifts from alumni and friends over the years and historical photo files of various publications. Using yearbooks and other college publications, as well as the memory bank of faculty, staff, and alumni, identification of individuals is as complete as possible.

Marlin L. Heckman
University Librarian

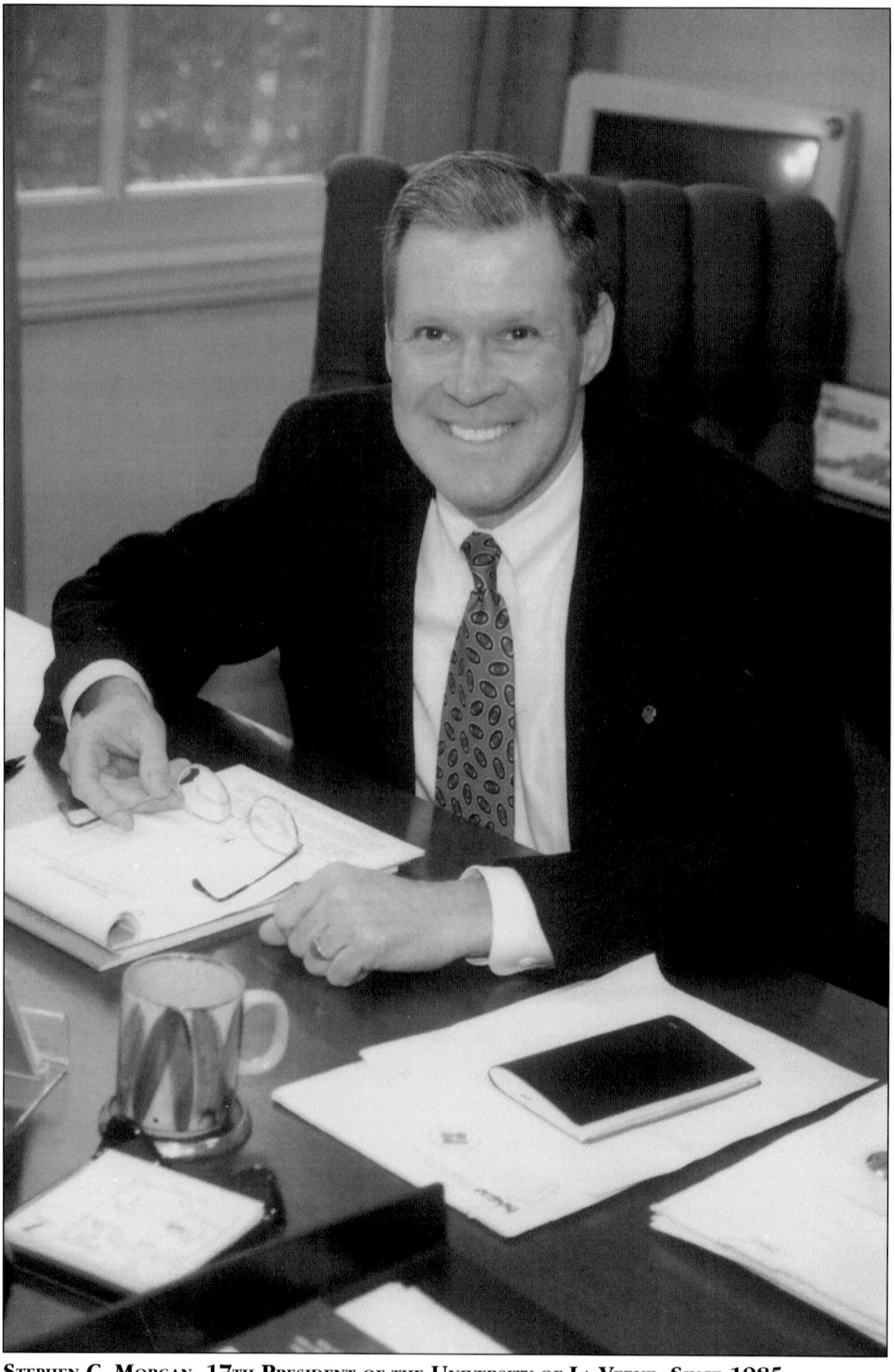

STEPHEN C. MORGAN, 17TH PRESIDENT OF THE UNIVERSITY OF LA VERNE, SINCE 1985.

One

Presidents, Graduates, and Students

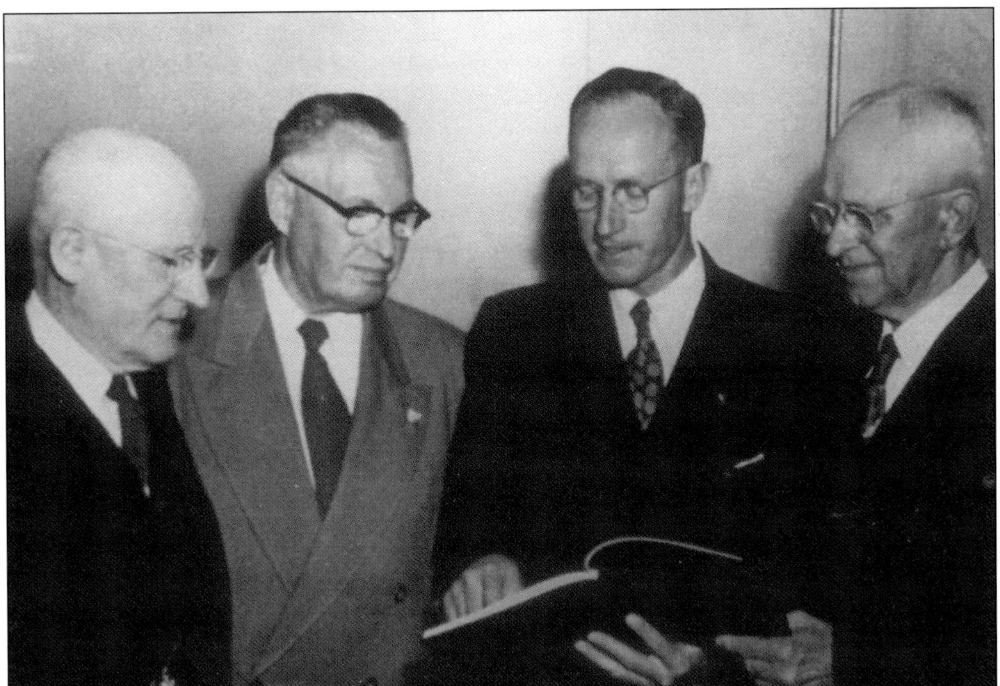

Presidents: C. Ernest Davis (1938–1948), I.V. Funderburgh (1921–1923), Harold D. Fasnacht (1948–1968), Ellis M. Studebaker (1923–1938), ***c.*** **1948.** This picture was possibly taken at Harold Fasnacht's inauguration.

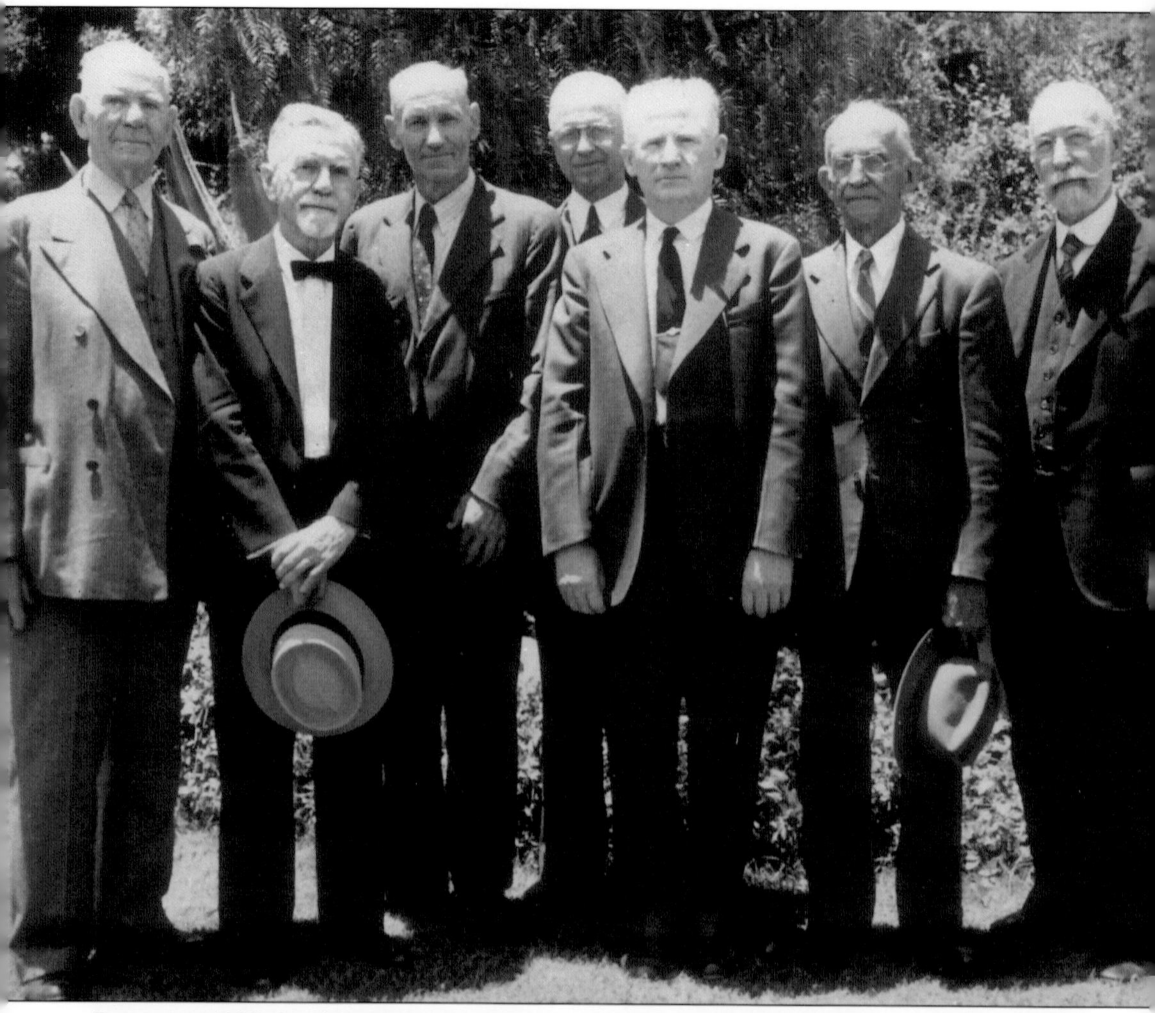

PRESIDENTS: J.M. COX (CHAIRMAN OF THE FACULTY, 1908–1909), EDWARD FRANTZ (1911–1915), W.C. HANAWALT (1902–1908), ELLIS M. STUDEBAKER (1923–1938), C. ERNEST DAVIS (1938–1948), SAMUEL J. MILLER (1915–1921), W.I.T. HOOVER (PRESIDENT 1899–1901, DEAN 1912–1938). This picture was probably taken at the Church of the Brethren Annual Conference in La Verne, 1941, while Davis was president.

Some Interesting Facts about Lordsburg/ La Verne Presidents

	Presidents
1891–1892	S.S. Garst
1892–1899	E.A. Miller
1899	I.N.H. Beahm
1899–1901	W.I.T. Hoover
[1901–1902	College Closed]
1902–1908	W.C. Hanawalt
1908–1909	J.M. Cox (Chairman of the Faculty)
1909–1911	W.F. England
1911–1915	Edward Frantz
1915–1921	S.J. Miller
1921–1923	I.V. Funderburgh
1923	J.B. Emmert
1923–1938	Ellis M. Studebaker
1938–1948	C. Ernest Davis
1948–1968	Harold D. Fasnacht
1968–1975	Leland B. Newcomer
1975–1984	Armen Sarafian
1984–1985	Richard Landis, (Chancellor)
1985–	Stephen C. Morgan

Age at assumption of Presidency

Age	Year	President
27	1891	S.S. Garst, M.D.
30	1892	E.A. Miller
30	1899	W.I.T. Hoover
32	1923	I.V. Funderburgh
33	1902	W.C. Hanawalt
37	1908	J.M. Cox (Chairman of the Faculty)
38	1985	Stephen C. Morgan
40	1899	I.N.H. Beahm
40	1948	Harold D. Fasnacht
43	1911	Edward Frantz
43	1923	Ellis M. Studebaker
45	1938	C. Ernest Davis
48	1968	Leland B. Newcomer
50	1923	J.B. Emmert
52	1915	S.J. Miller
53	1909	W.F. England
55	1975	Armen Sarafian

Years of Service

Less than 1 yr.	Beahm, Emmert, Landis
1 year	Garst, Cox
2 years	England, Hoover, Funderburgh
4 years	Frantz
6 years	Hanawalt, S.J. Miller, Newcomer
7 years	E.A. Miller
10 years	Davis, Sarafian
15 years	Studebaker
20 years	Fasnacht
As of Feb.'01	Stephen C. Morgan 16 years

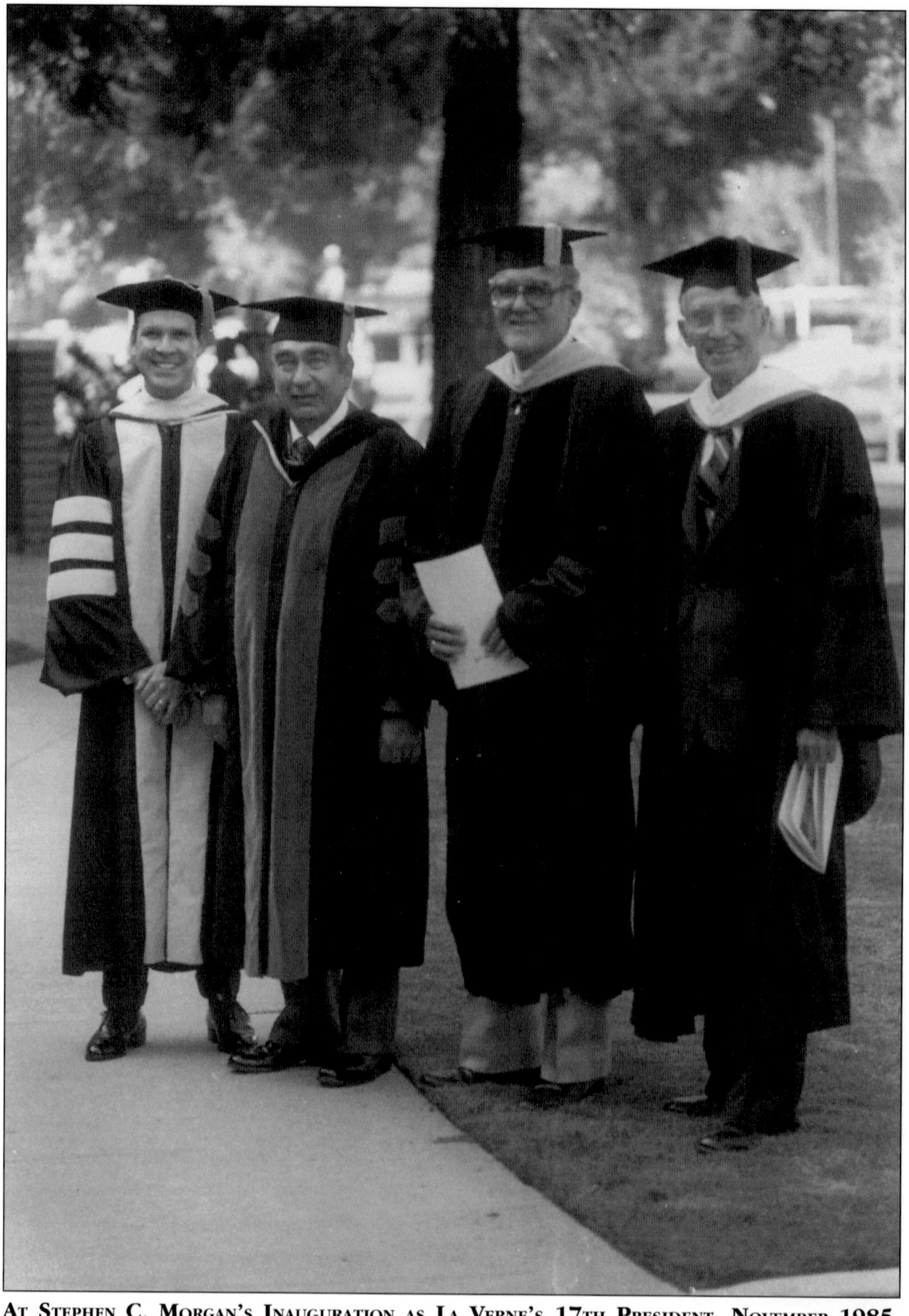

At Stephen C. Morgan's Inauguration as La Verne's 17th President, November 1985. Stephen C. Morgan (1985–), Harold D. Fasnacht (1948–1968), Leland B. Newcomer (1968–1975), Armen Sarafian (1975–1984). In 2001, there is only one living former president, Leland Newcomer.

INAUGURATION DAY, NOVEMBER 1985. Pictured are the proud presidential father, Steve Morgan, and daughter Kesley. (Photographer: Chris Brookhart.)

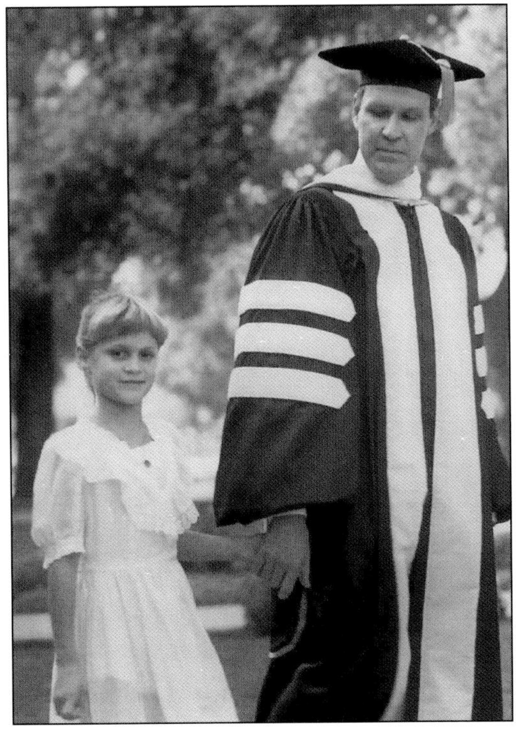

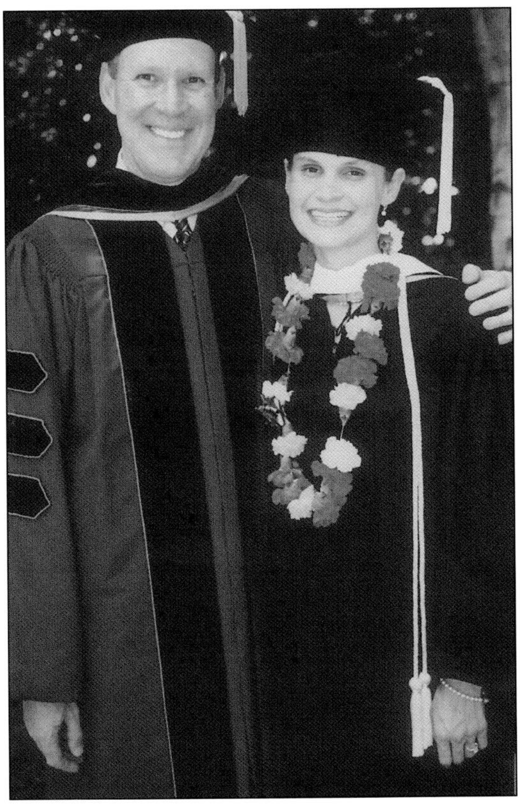

GRADUATION DAY, MAY 2000. Pictured again are presidential father Steve Morgan and graduating daughter, Kesley Morgan Armstrong. Kesley is a fourth generation graduate of La Verne, following great-grandmother Grace Heilman Miller, grandmother Ruth Miller Morgan, and parents Steve and Ann Morgan.

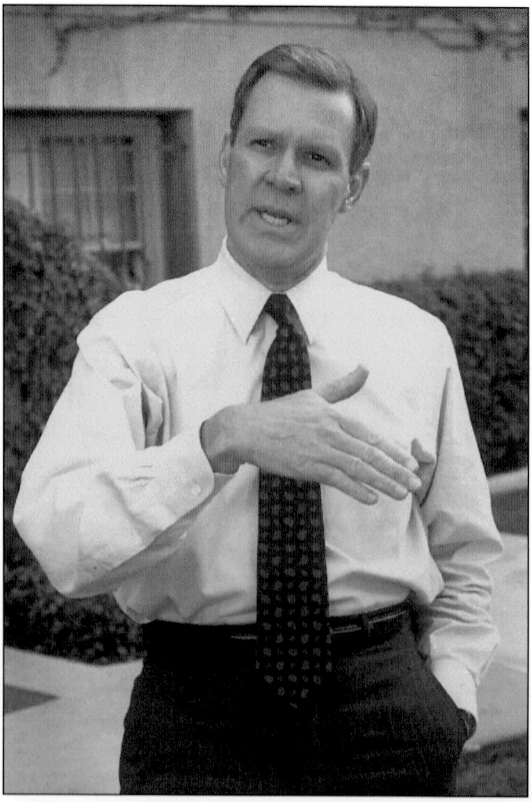

President Steve Morgan, 1992.
(Photographer: Alison David.)

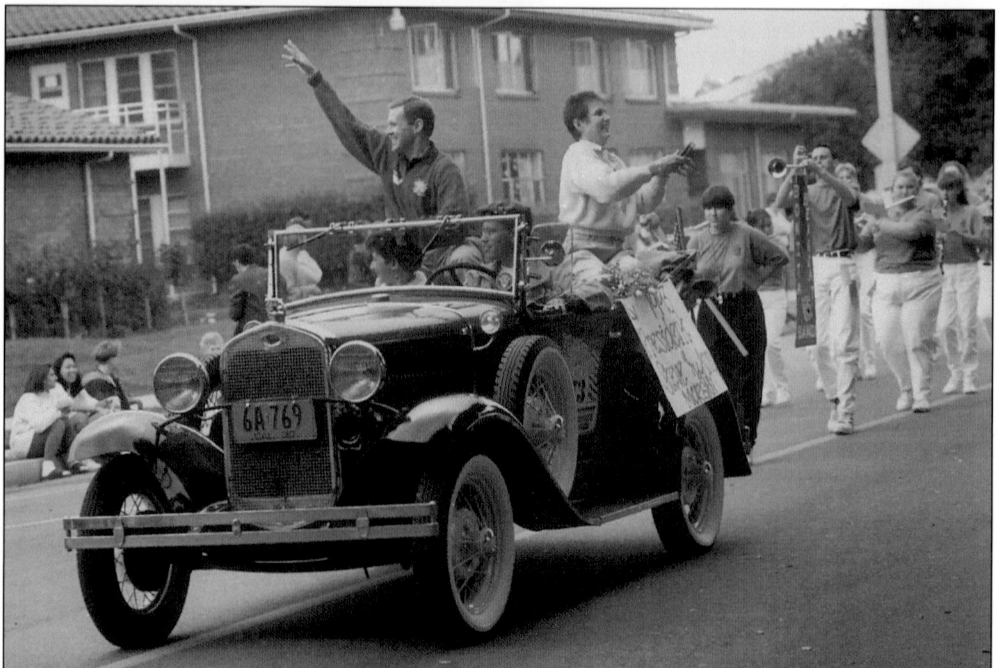

Steve and Ann Morgan in the 1993 Homecoming Parade.

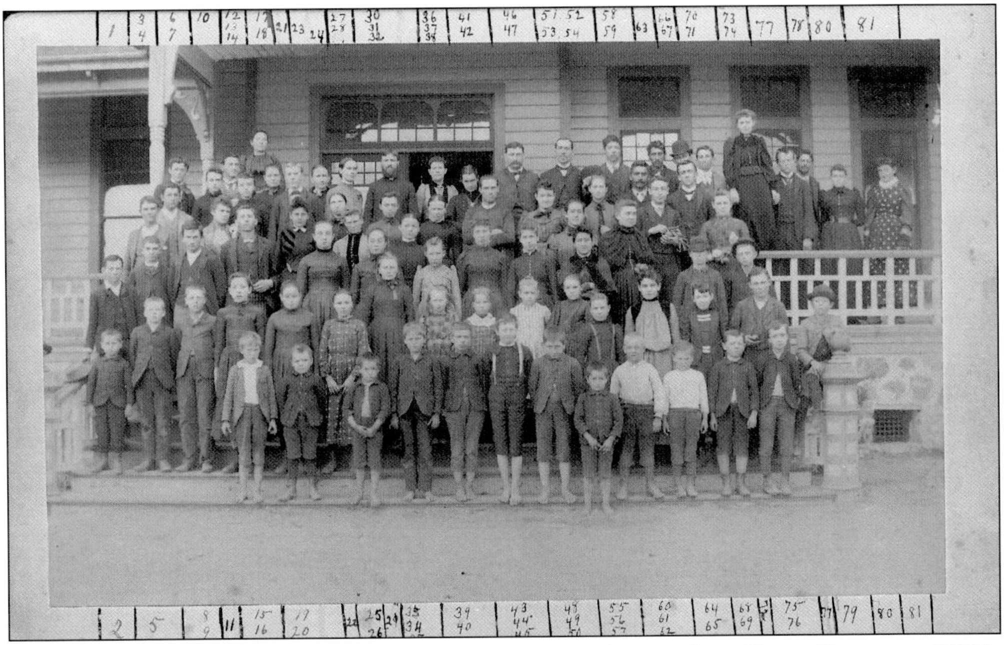

TEACHERS AND STUDENTS (AND A FEW VISITORS) AT THE END OF FIRST TERM, DECEMBER 1891. (Photographer: Hardy, Pomona, California.) List of names, as numbered in sections. Count from top of each section down. – preceding number indicates professor, = indicates visitor.) 1. Richard Rogers, 2. Paul Garst, 3. unidentified, 4. unidentified, 5. Noah Blickenstaff, 6. Forbes Brown, 7. John Neher, 8. Warren Paine, 9. Benj. Horning, 10. Martha Masterson, 11. Kate Stoner (Mount), 12. Wm. Neher, 13. Minnie Masterson, 14. Walter Griggs, 15. Sarah Horning, 16. Peter Hartman Jr., 17. Lillie Lattin, 18. Lottie Flory (Neher), 19. Hannah Blickenstaff, 20. Roy Frantz, 21. C.J. Diamond, 22. Lulu Sharp, 23. Emma Yoder, 24. Mary Flora (McDonough), 25. Katie Blickenstaff, 26. Hattie Hartman, 27. Maggie Nofziger, 28. Mabel Garland, 29. Bertie Neher, 30. Frank Nofziger, 31. Maggie Masterson, 32. Fannie Gibbel, 33. Cora Shively, 34. Nellie Johnson (?), 35. Oscar Hartman, 37. Kate Neher, 38. =Matie Beanblossom, 39. Kennie Johnson, 40. Elias Nair, 41. Mary Robertson, 42. Nicholas Brubaker, 43. =Maggie Worrel (Bartley), 44. Gertrude Flory, 45. Charlie Browning, 46. =Solomon Hendricks, 47. Ella Markey, 48. =Emma Smeltzer (Potter), 49. Ethel Highley, 50. Jesse Neher, 51. –S.S. Garst, 52. Anna Whitmore, 53. Margaret Kuns (Williams), 54. unidentified, 55. Grace Frantz, 56. Sallie Hosfeldt, 57. Harvey Neher, 58. Tom Soto, 59. Ignatia Vejar, 60. Olive Hostetler (Woodruff), 61.unidentified, 62. Harvey Flory, 63. P.L. Soto, 64. Lonnie Yoder (or N.A.), 65. Asa Hartman, 66. Ed Markey, 67. Mahlon Masterson, 68. Alpha Neher, 69. Blanche Rogers, 70. Allesandro Yorba, 71. Jennie Stoner, 72. Levi Shively, 73. Anna Hoffman, 74. Minnie Ullery, 75. Jno. Hartman, 76. Manoah Masterson, 77. Sidney R. McDonough, 78. Porfirio Palomares, 79. Merlie Worrel, 80. Pauline Gubser, 81. Carrie Vejar.

La Verne has had diversity within its student body from the very first year. "The student of California history will particularly be interested in finding on the roster among such Pennsylvania Dutch names as Blickenstaff, Gibble, and Overholtzer, the names of Porfirio Palomares, Ignacio Vejar, and Ramon Vejar, relatives and descendants of the Spanish families who had held the original land grants from Governor Alvarado in 1837." (G.E. Muir, *La Verne College, Seventy-five Years of Service.* La Verne, CA: La Verne College, 1967. p. 8.)

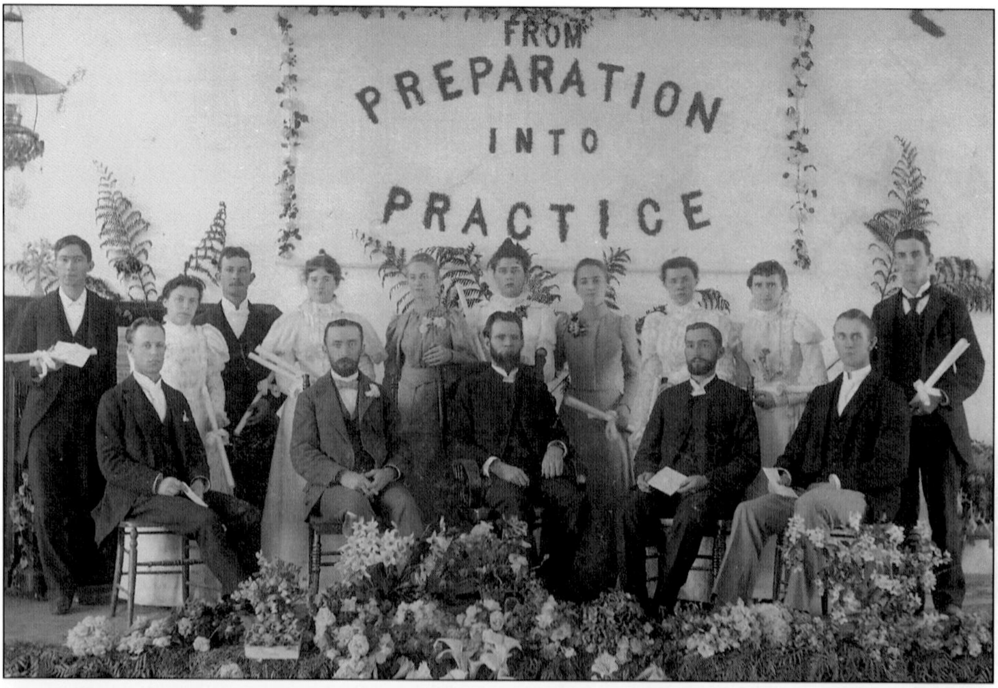

"From Preparation into Practice," the Motto of the Graduating Class of 1896. President E.A. Miller is seated in the middle of the front row. (Photographer: Schwichtenberg, Pomona, Cal.)

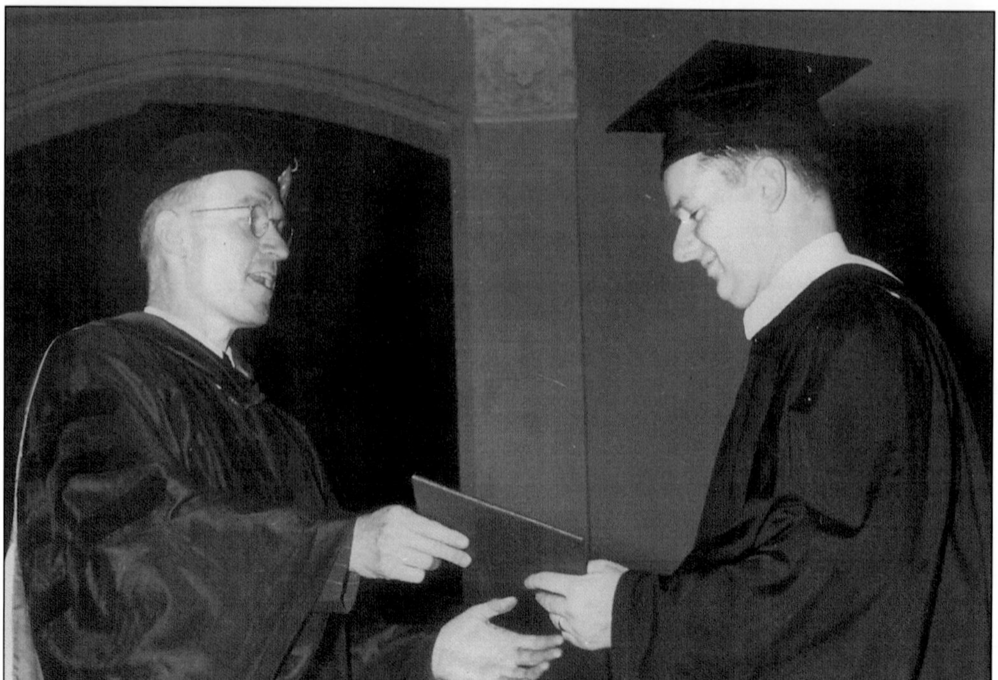

President Harold D. Fasnacht Presenting Diploma to La Verne's 1000th Graduate, Wandell "Stub" Root, in 1950.

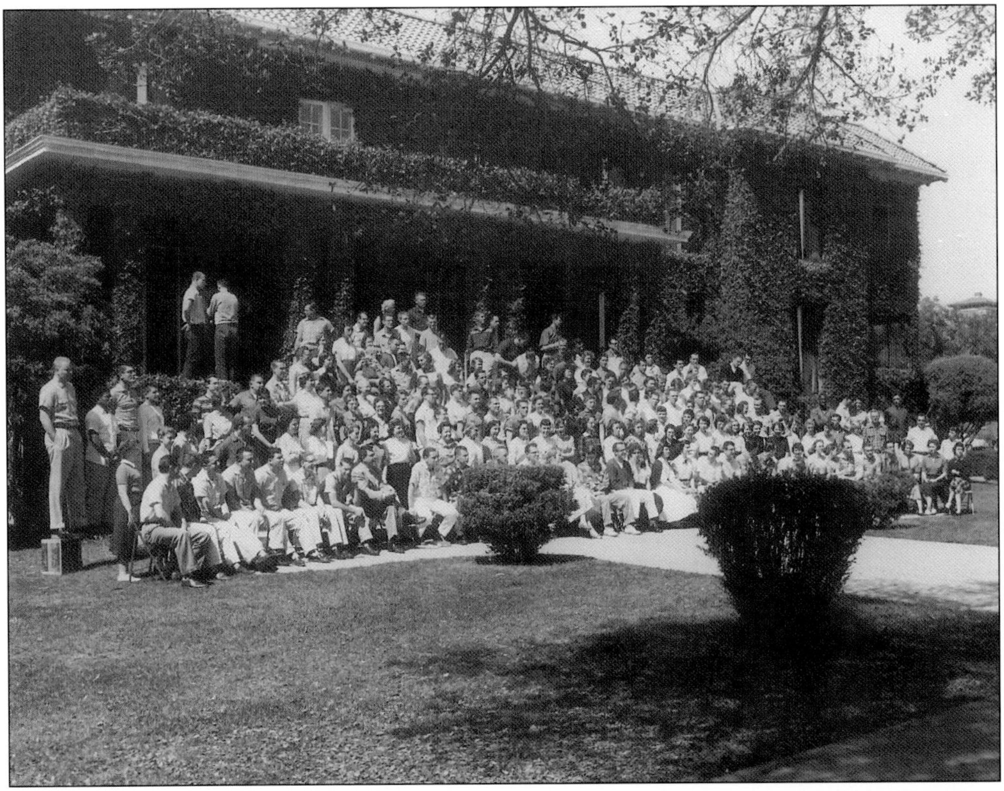

1956 Student Body Awaiting "Formal Photo" on the Steps of Miller Hall. Due to the use of a "moving" camera, the individual standing top left showed up in the formal photo on both the left and right sides of the picture and as a blur in the middle of the picture. He later served many years as a member of the Board of Trustees.

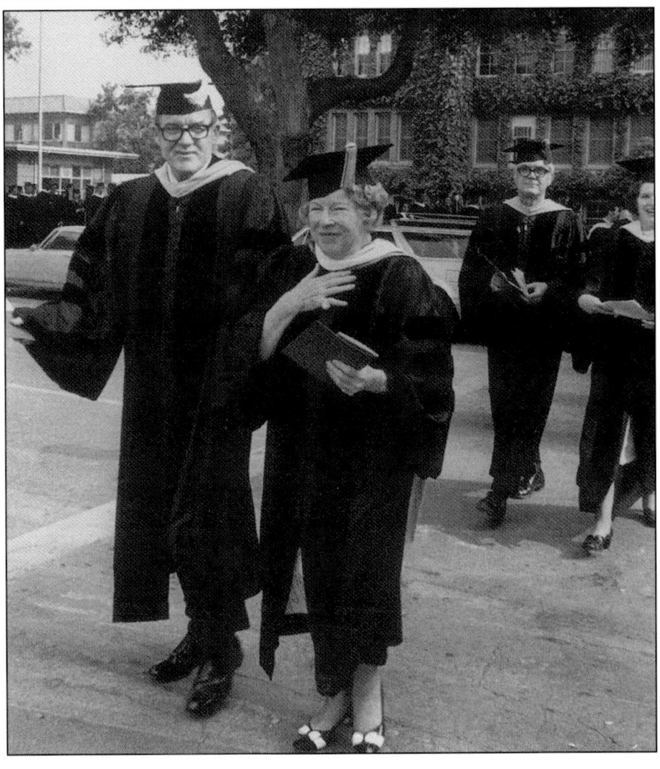

1970s Commencement Procession. Pictured are President Leland Newcomer; Board Chair, Mary La Fetra; Graduate Dean, W. Donald Clague; and Chairman of the Faculty, Margaret Preska.

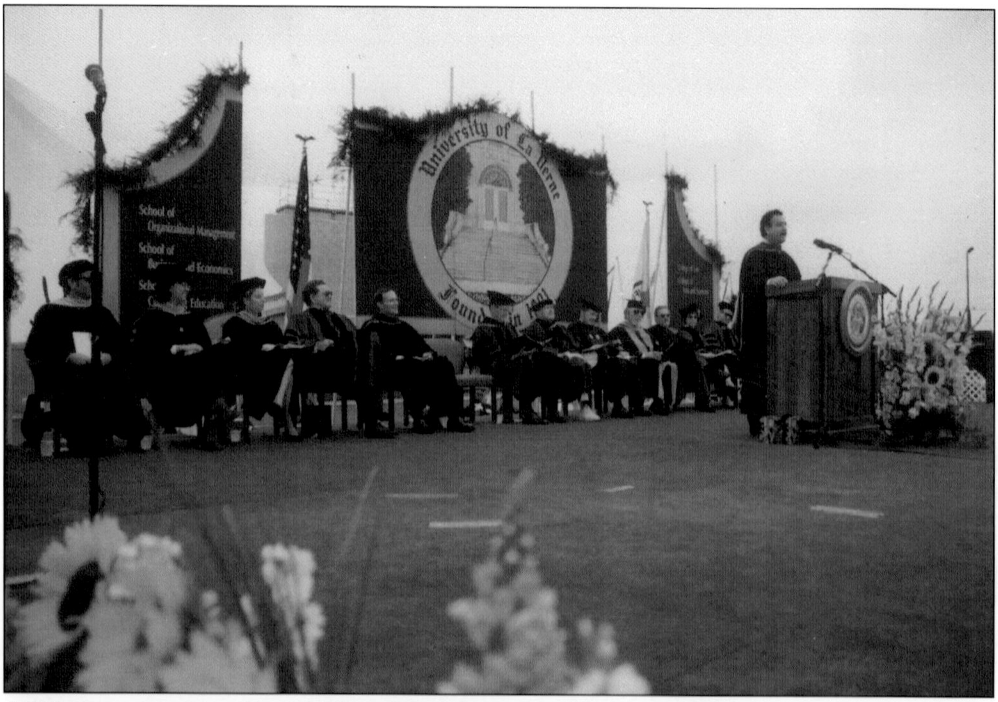

1998 Commencement Speaker, Dr. David Krasnow, Class of 1969.

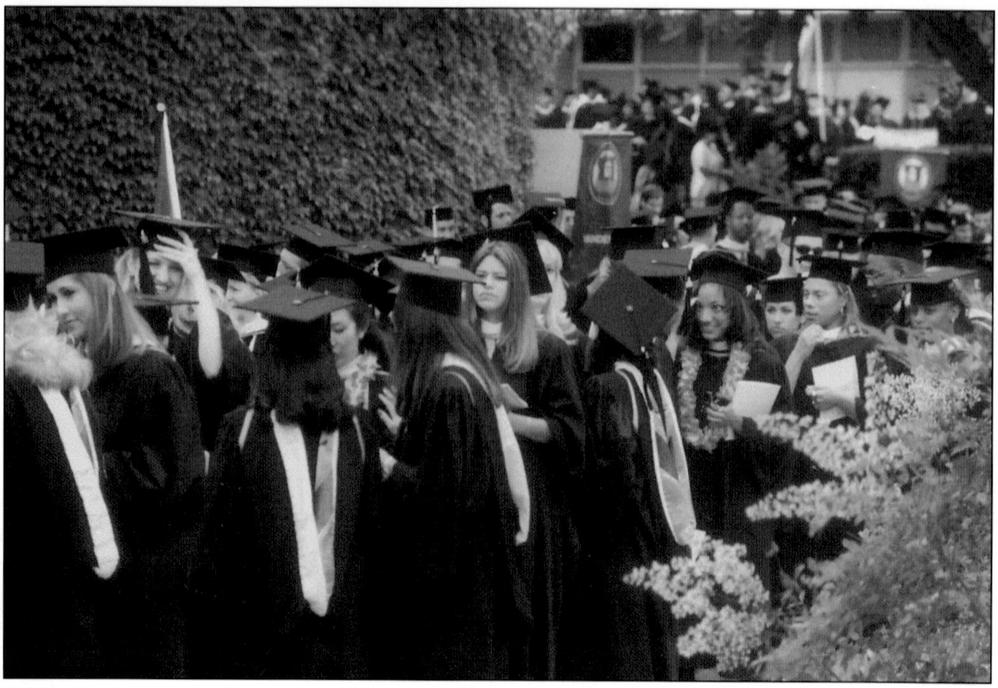

1998 Commencement. Here graduates are lining up for the processional.

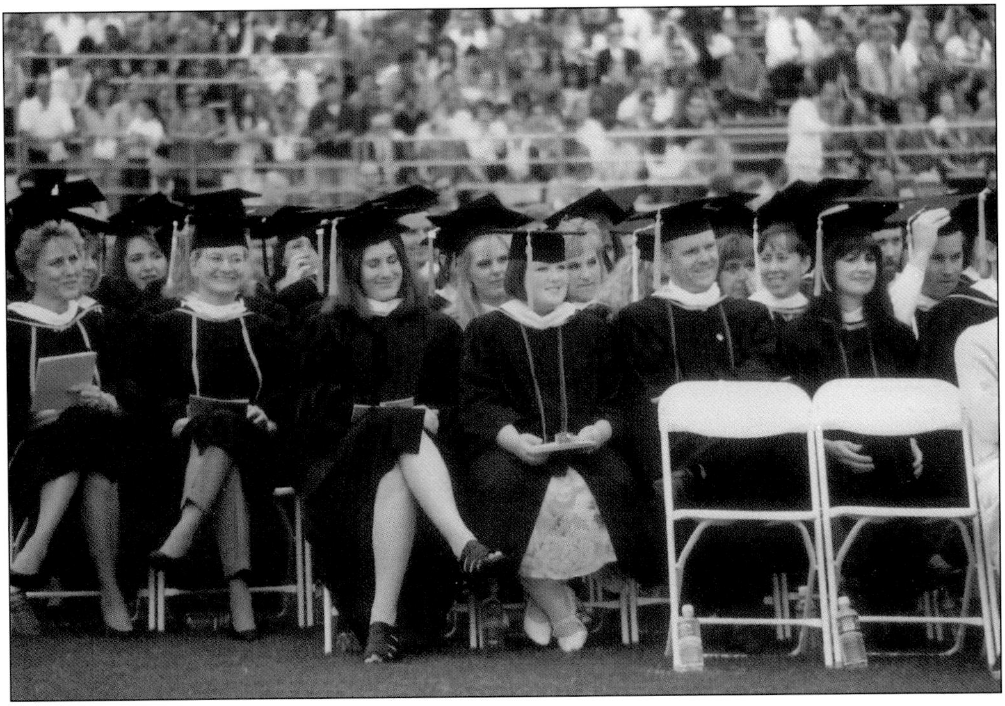

1998 COMMENCEMENT.

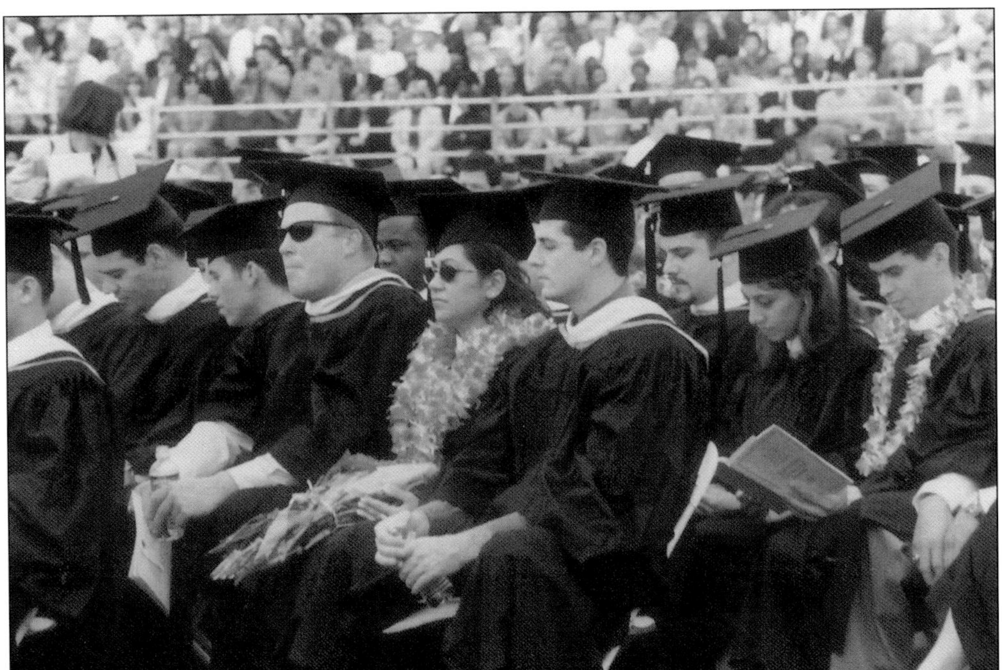

1998 COMMENCEMENT.

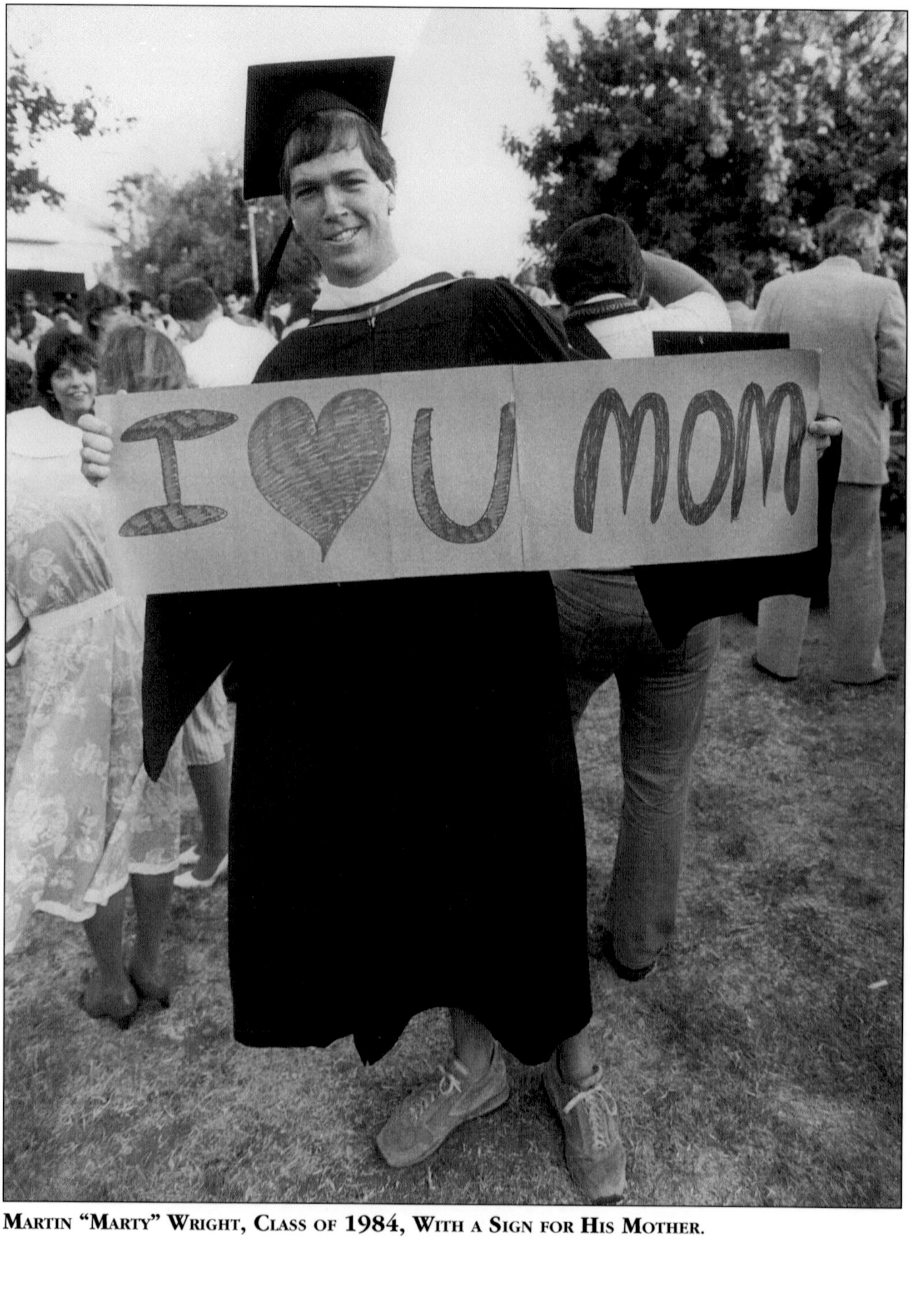

Martin "Marty" Wright, Class of 1984, With a Sign for His Mother.

Two

BUILDINGS 1891–2001

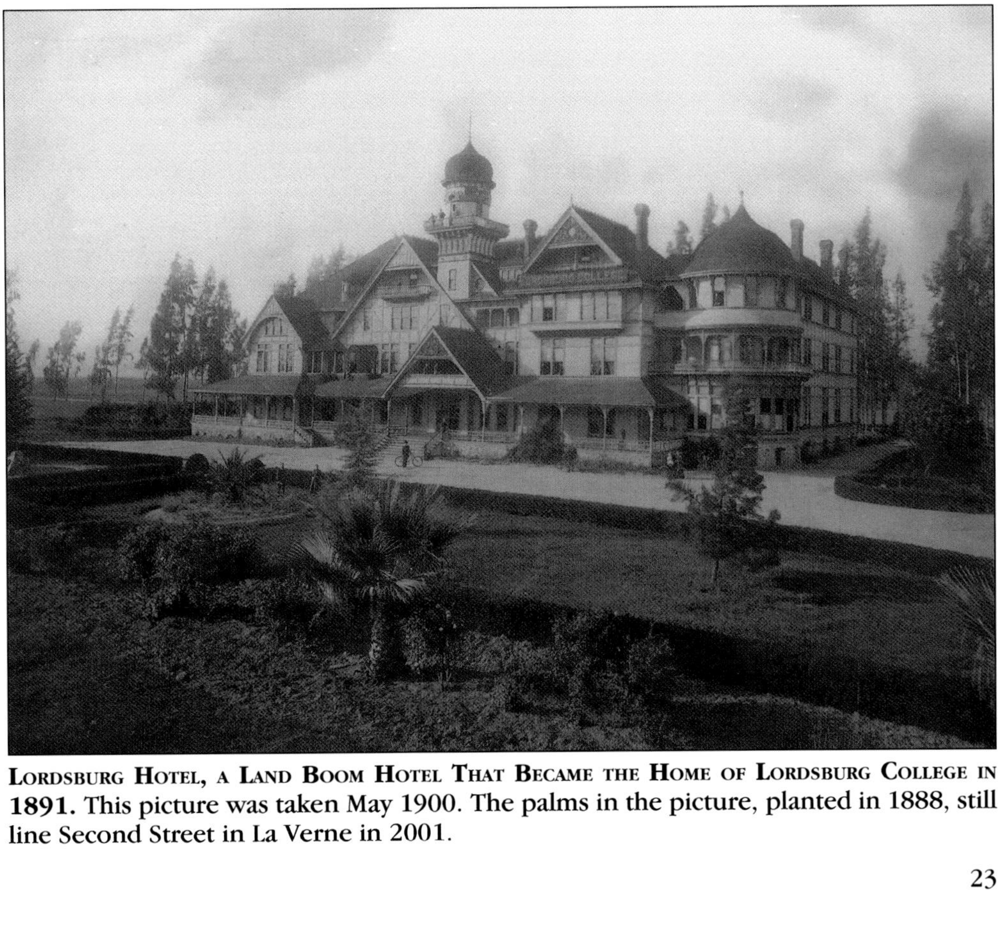

LORDSBURG HOTEL, A LAND BOOM HOTEL THAT BECAME THE HOME OF LORDSBURG COLLEGE IN 1891. This picture was taken May 1900. The palms in the picture, planted in 1888, still line Second Street in La Verne in 2001.

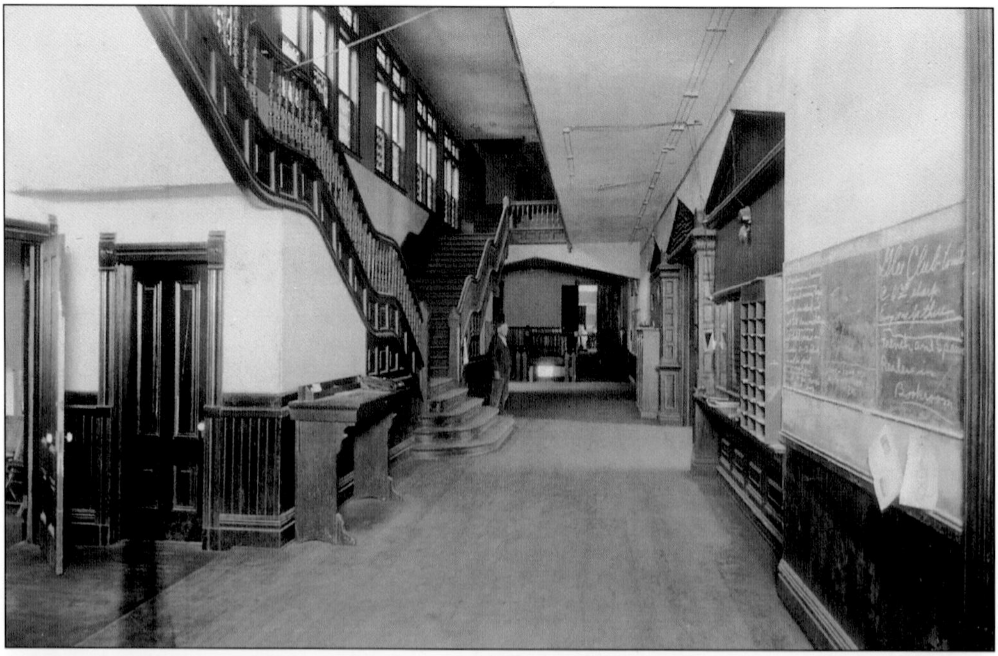

An Interior View of the College Building. The stair railings were made of cherry wood.

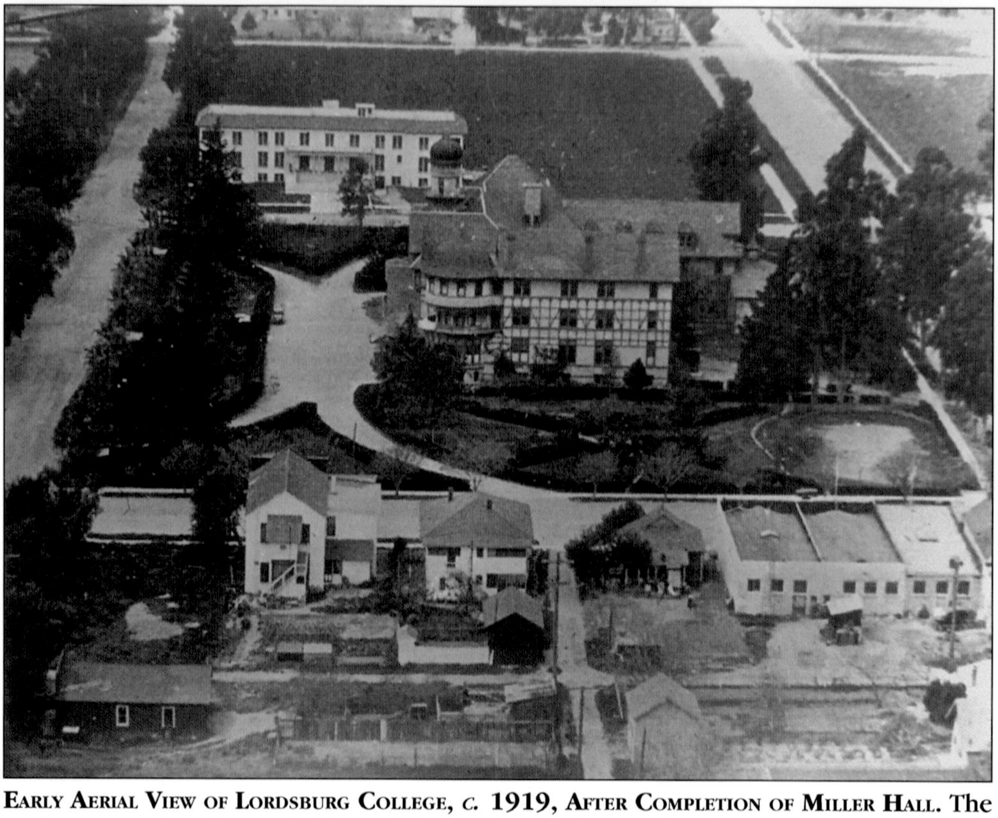

Early Aerial View of Lordsburg College, *c.* 1919, After Completion of Miller Hall. The picture was taken from a balloon. (Photographer: Burton Frasher Sr.)

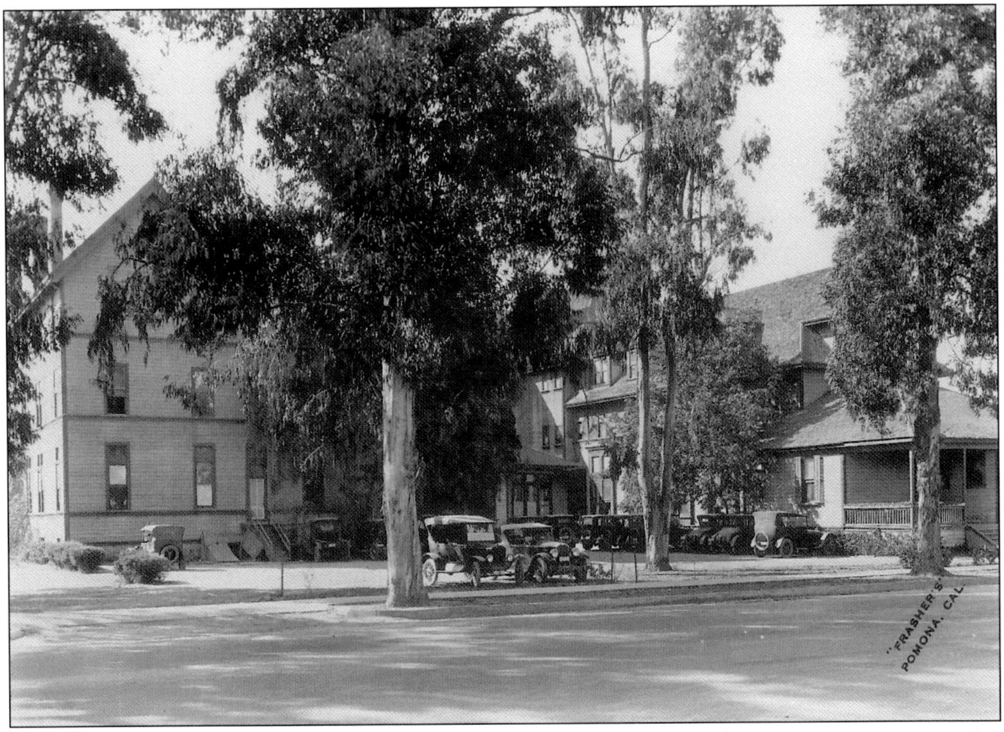

Student and Faculty Parking Behind College Building, 1924. Third Street is in the foreground.

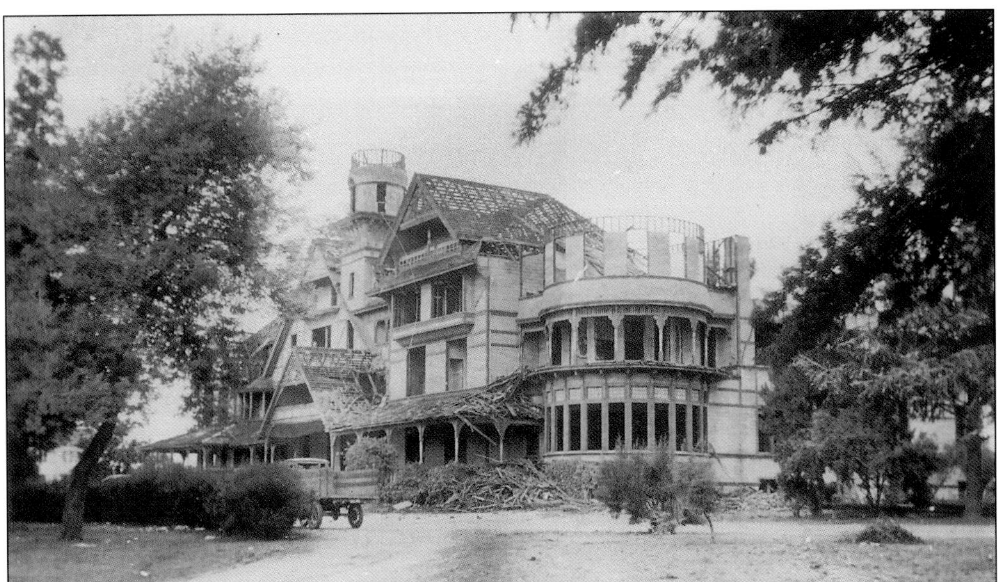

Demolition of the Original College Building in 1927.

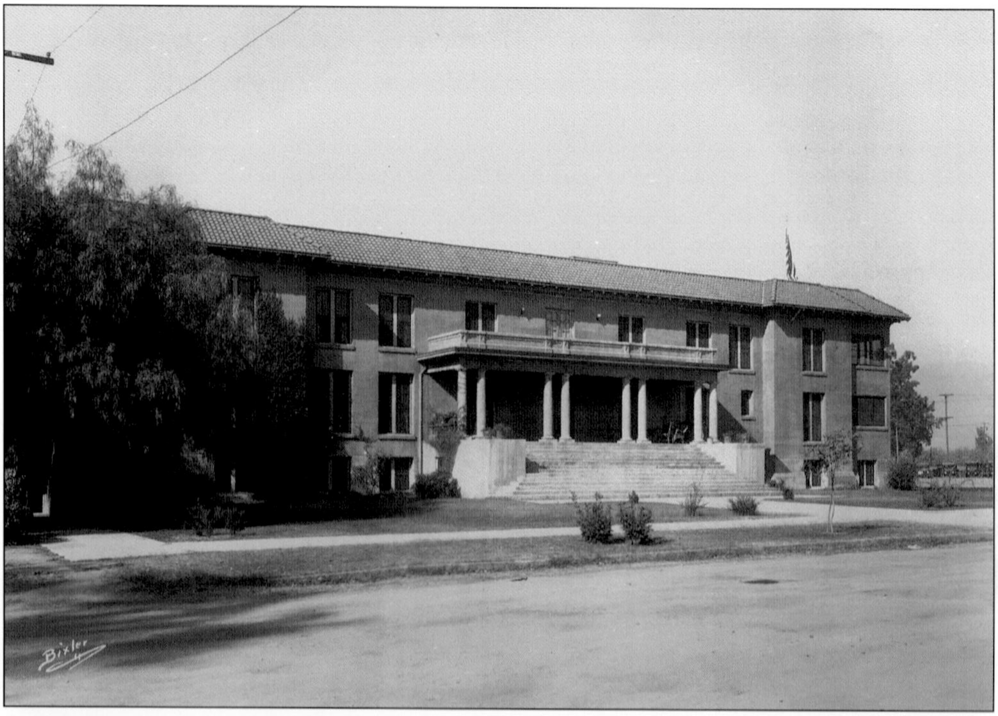

LADIES HALL, BUILT IN 1918–19, LATER NAMED SAMUEL J. MILLER HALL. (Photographer: Bixler.)

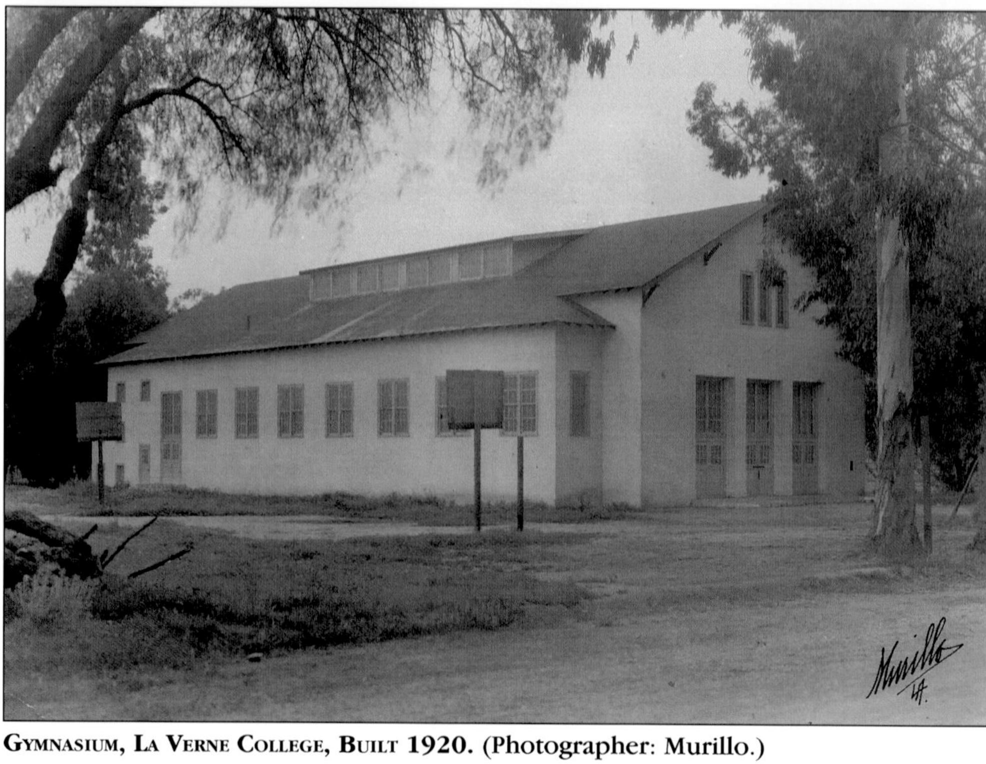

GYMNASIUM, LA VERNE COLLEGE, BUILT 1920. (Photographer: Murillo.)

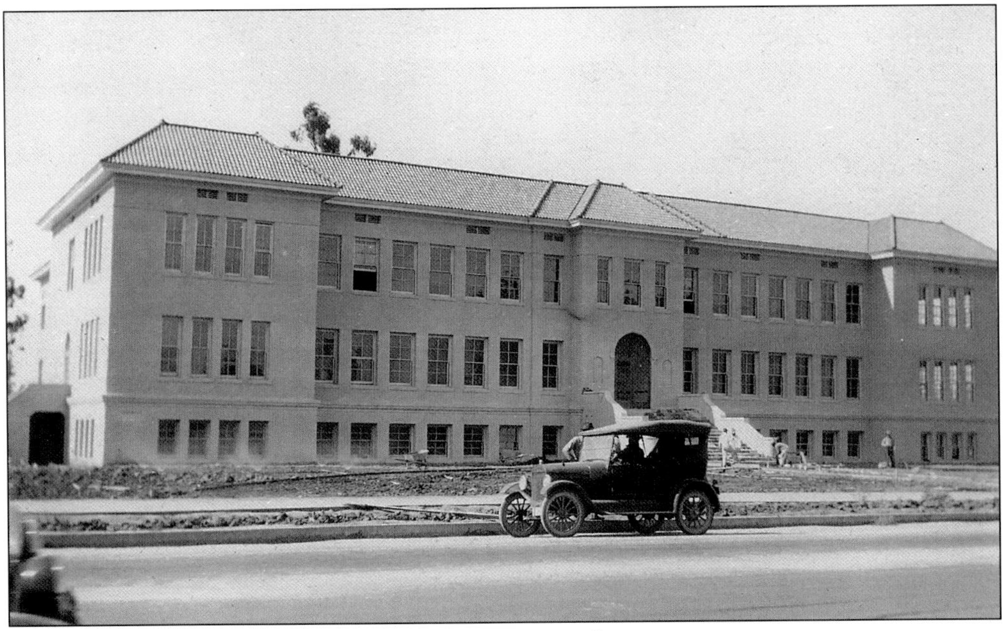

FOUNDERS HALL, ADMINISTRATION BUILDING, BUILT 1926–27.

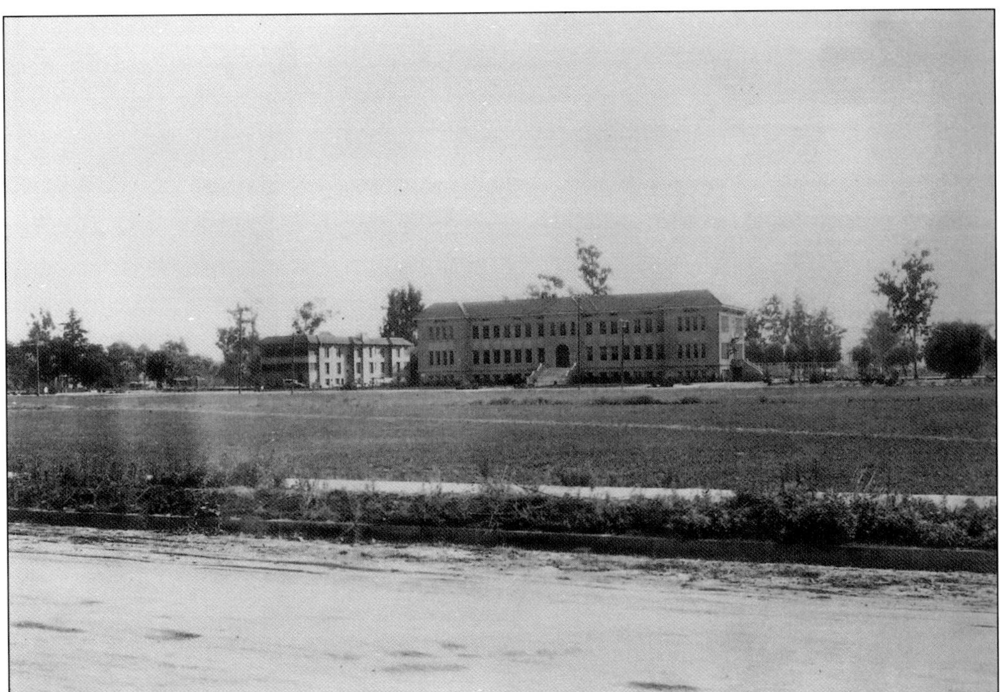

FOUNDERS HALL AND MILLER HALL, LEFT, AS SEEN FROM FOURTH STREET (BONITA AVE.), *c.* 1927.

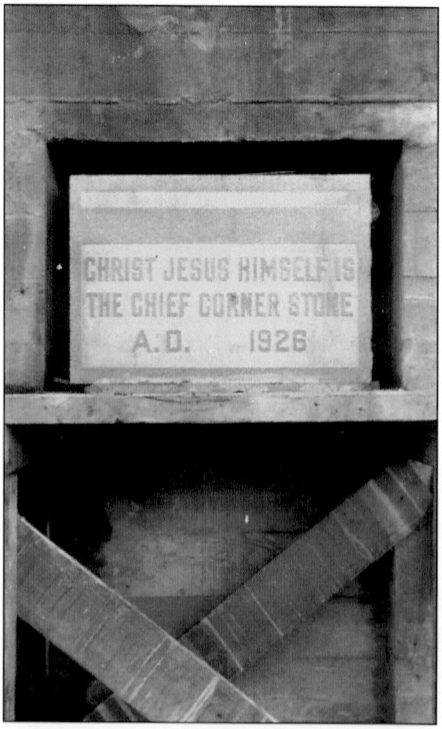

CORNERSTONE FOR FOUNDERS HALL, PLACED IN 1926.

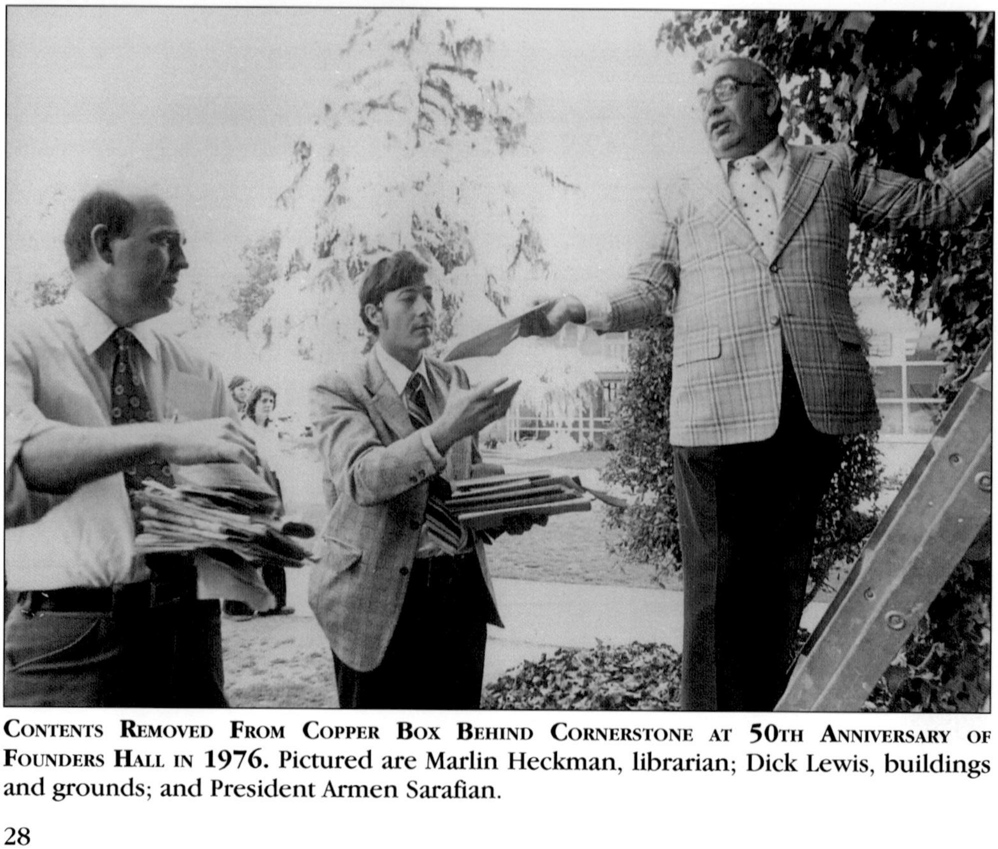

CONTENTS REMOVED FROM COPPER BOX BEHIND CORNERSTONE AT 50TH ANNIVERSARY OF FOUNDERS HALL IN 1976. Pictured are Marlin Heckman, librarian; Dick Lewis, buildings and grounds; and President Armen Sarafian.

Main Stairwell and Banister in Founders Hall. An architect's change-order in the University Archives notes the bumps on the banister were added to keep students from sliding down from the upper floor.

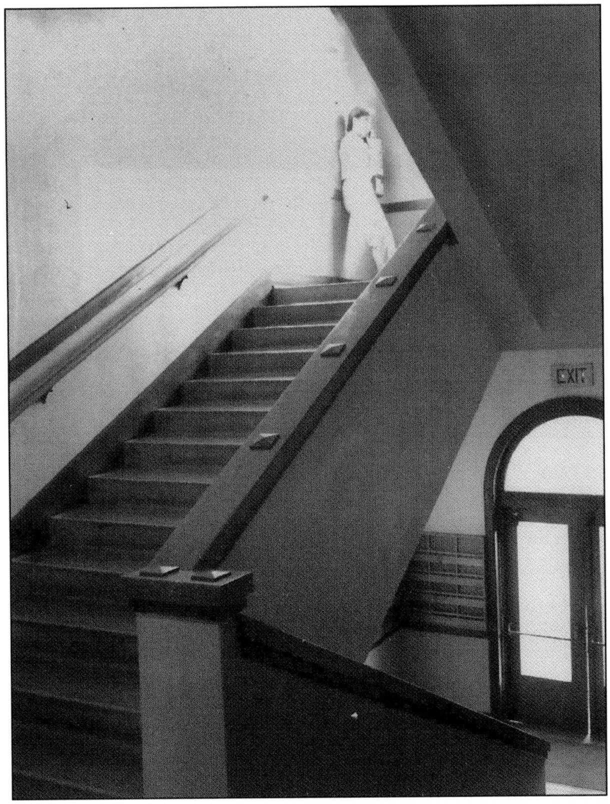

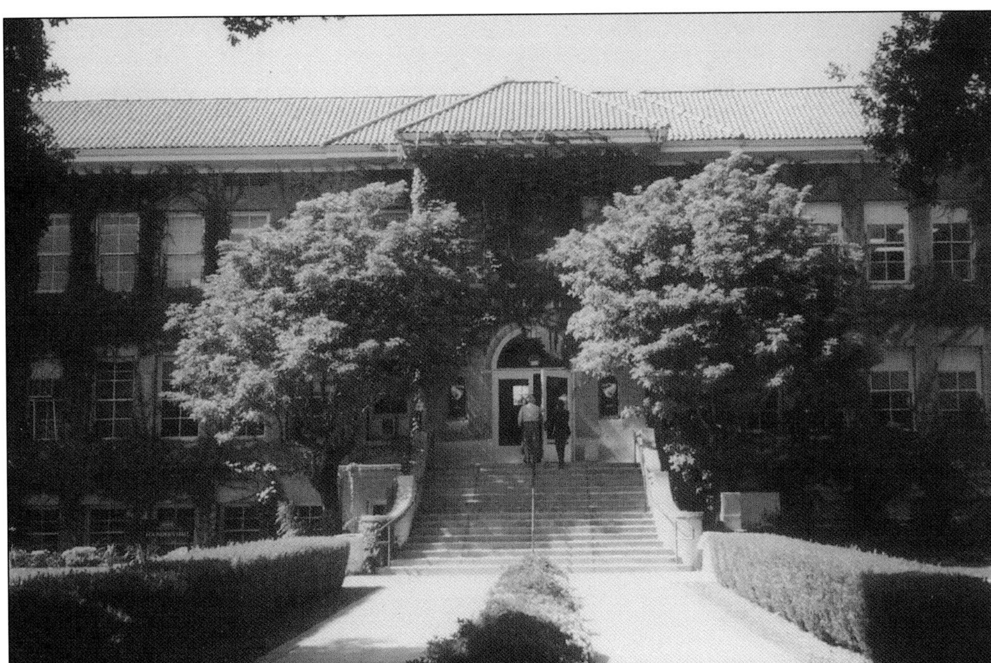

Ivy-Covered Founders Hall, 1990s.

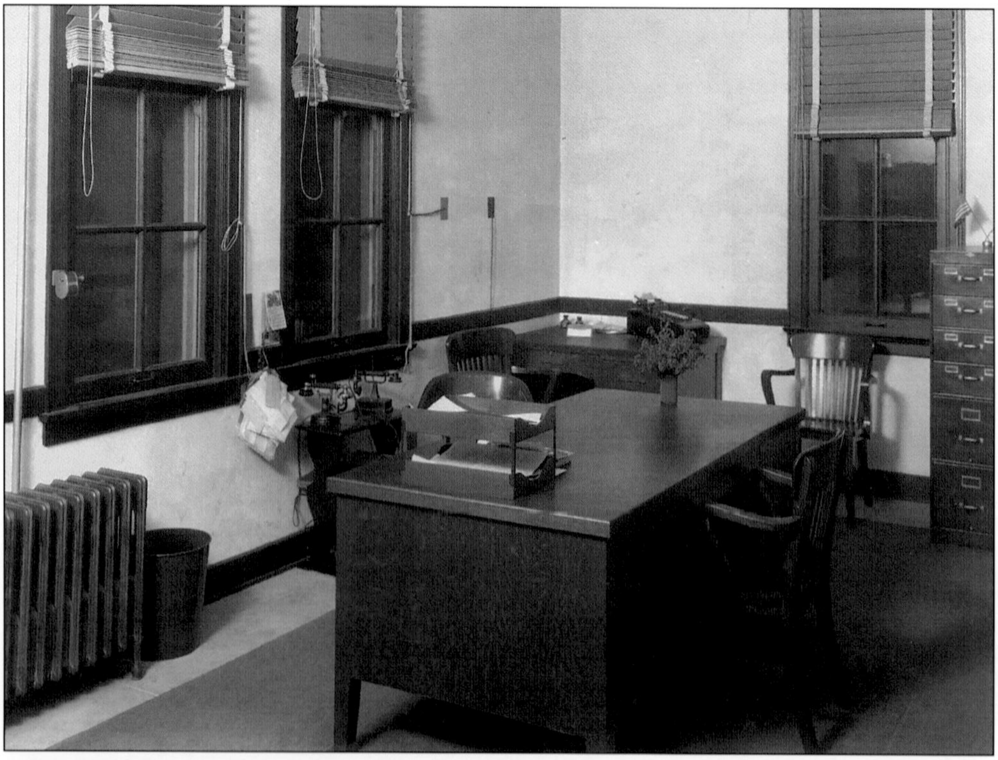

A FOUNDERS HALL OFFICE. IT MUST HAVE BEEN DEDICATION DAY TO HAVE THE DESK SO CLEAN. A "modern" office with calculator, ink bottles, and two telephones.

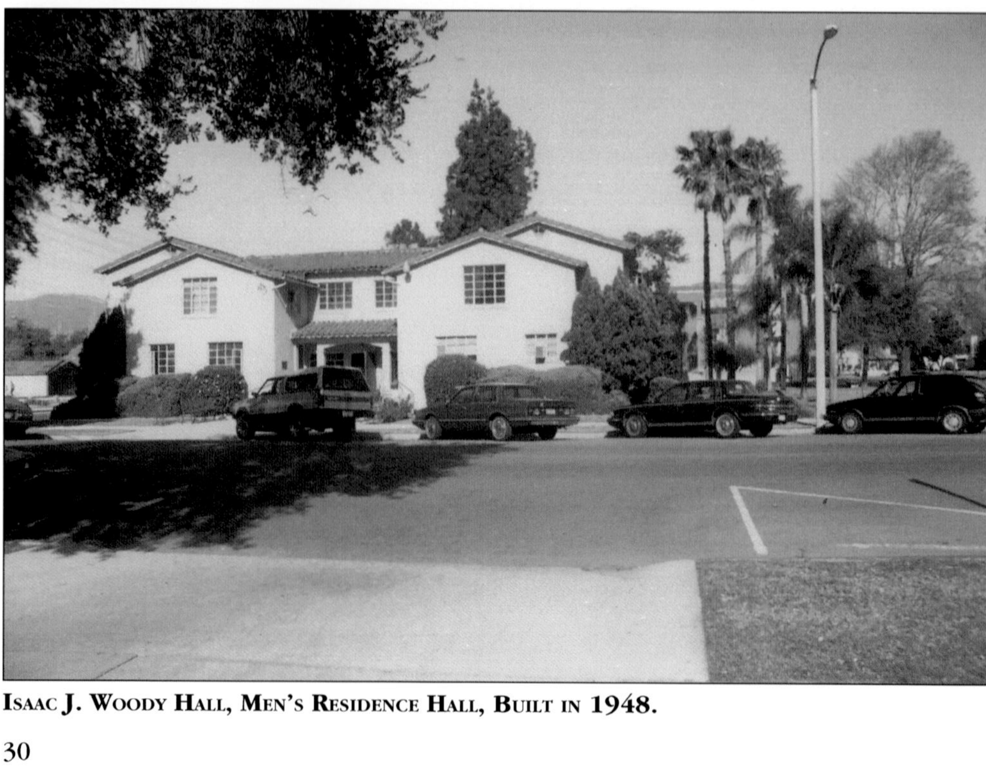

ISAAC J. WOODY HALL, MEN'S RESIDENCE HALL, BUILT IN 1948.

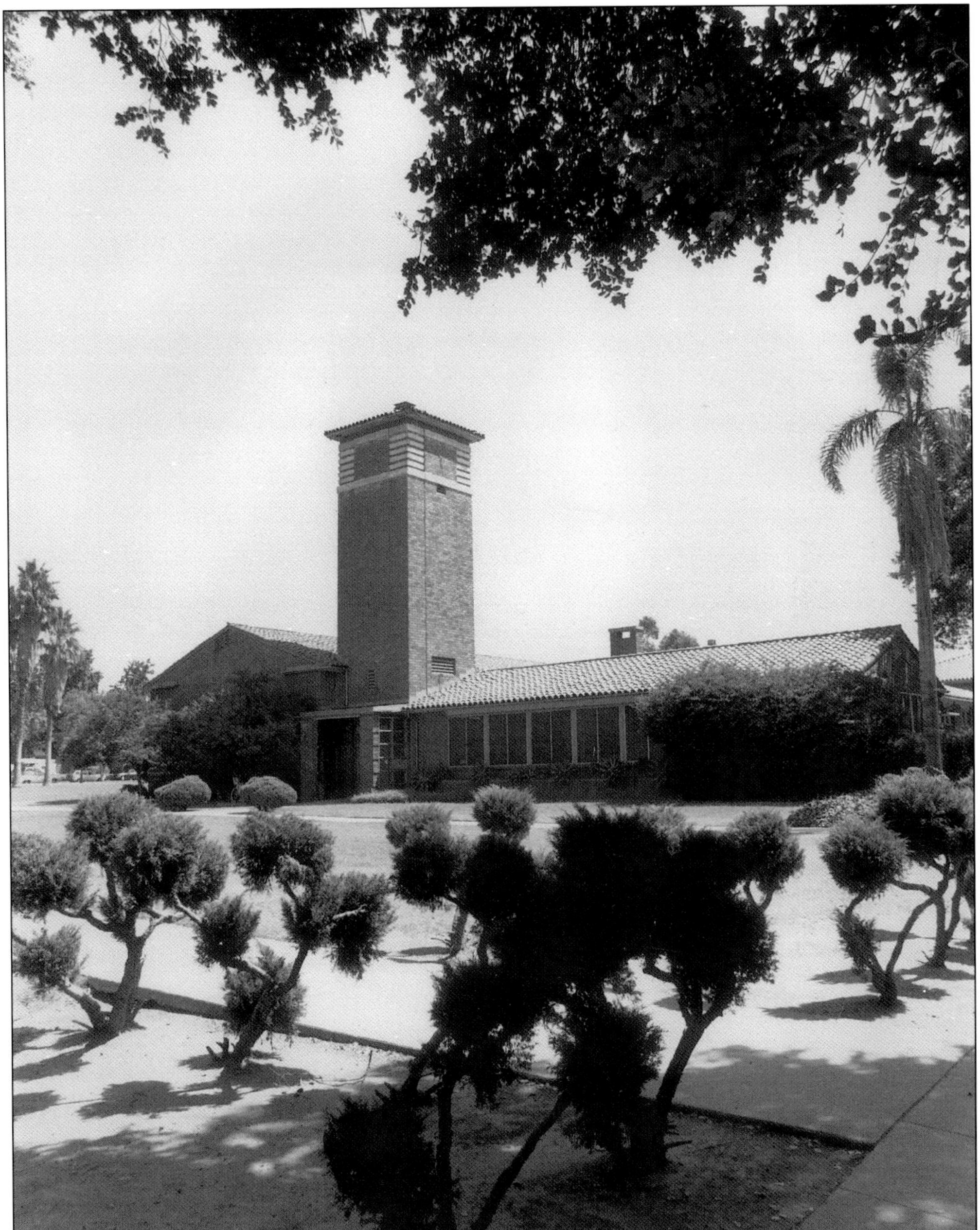

W.I.T. Hoover Memorial Library, Built in 1950–51. It served as the library until 1977, when it became the University of La Verne College of Law. With the move of the law school in January 2001, the Hoover building is being remodeled for the Behavioral Sciences Department, the Office of the Arts and Sciences Dean, and the CAPA program for adult students and several classrooms. Speakers on the clock tower play the alma mater at noon and six o'clock every day.

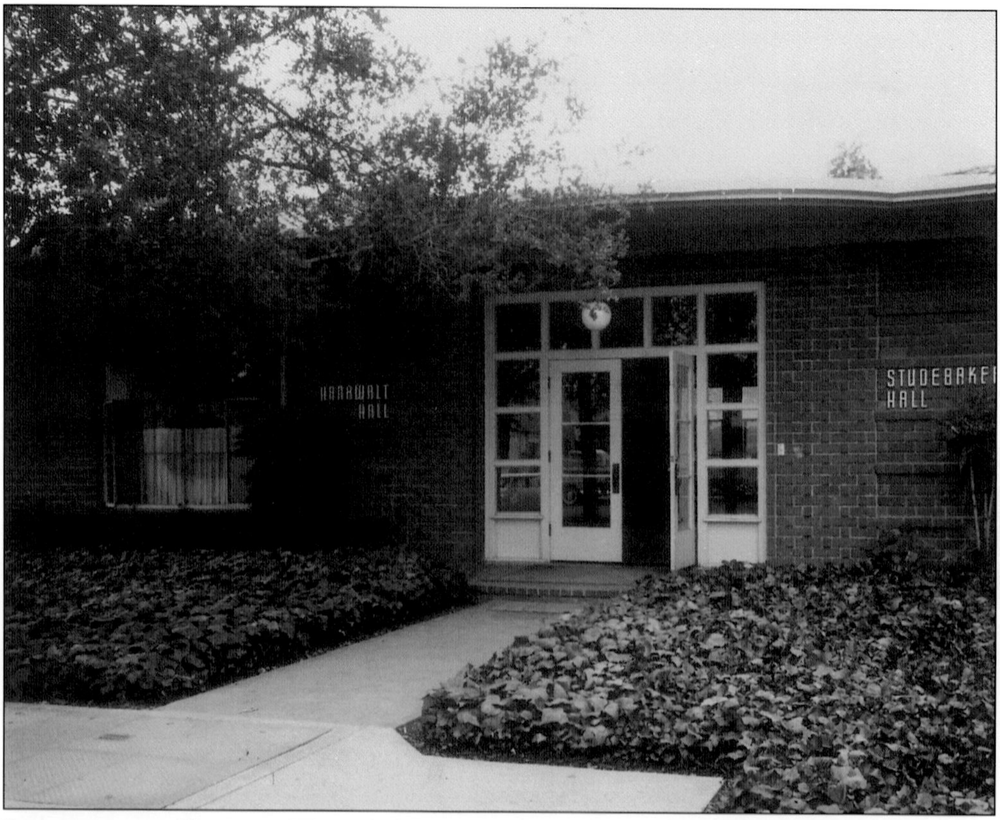

STUDEBAKER AND HANAWALT WOMEN'S RESIDENCE HALLS, BUILT 1956 AND 1957.

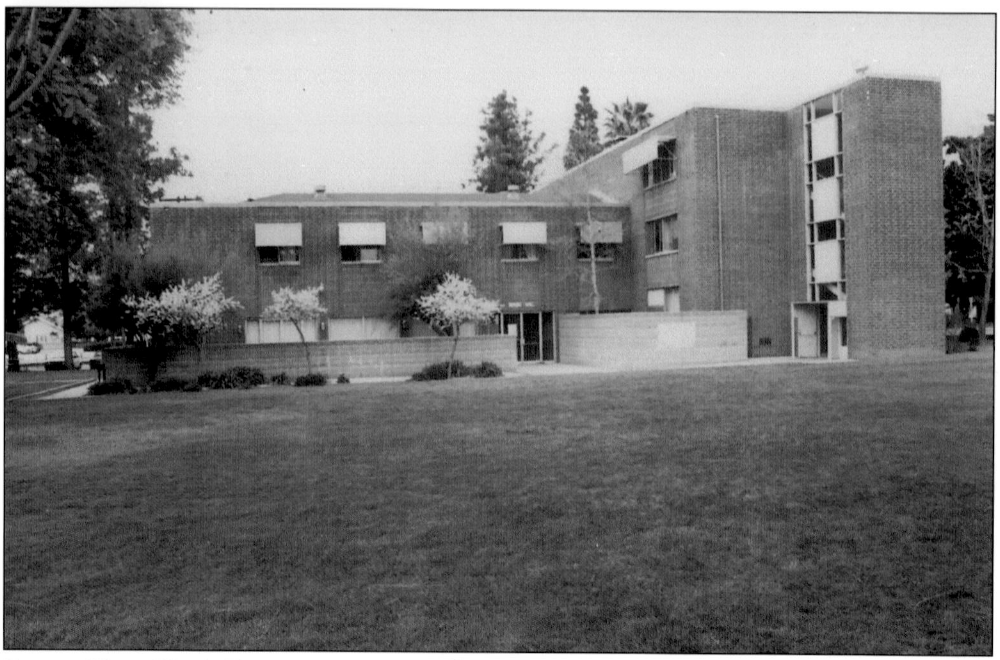

BRANDT HALL, MEN'S RESIDENCE, BUILT 1962.

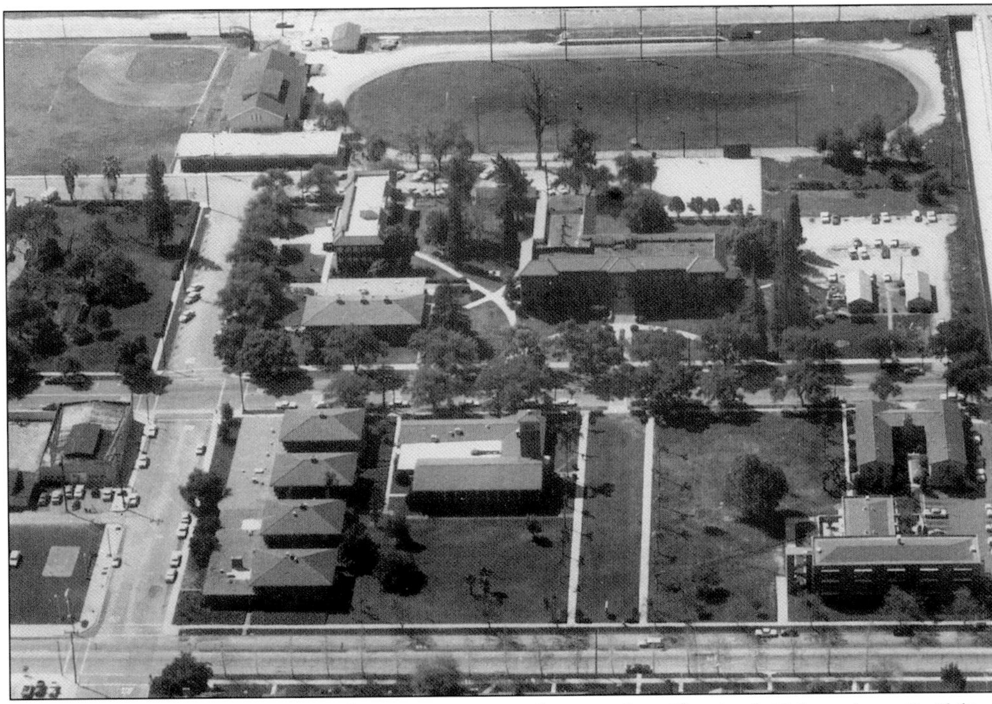

Aerial View of Campus, 1963. This view shows the Physical Education Building (1963), Brandt Hall (1962), and Davenport Dining Hall (1958) as the newest buildings on campus.

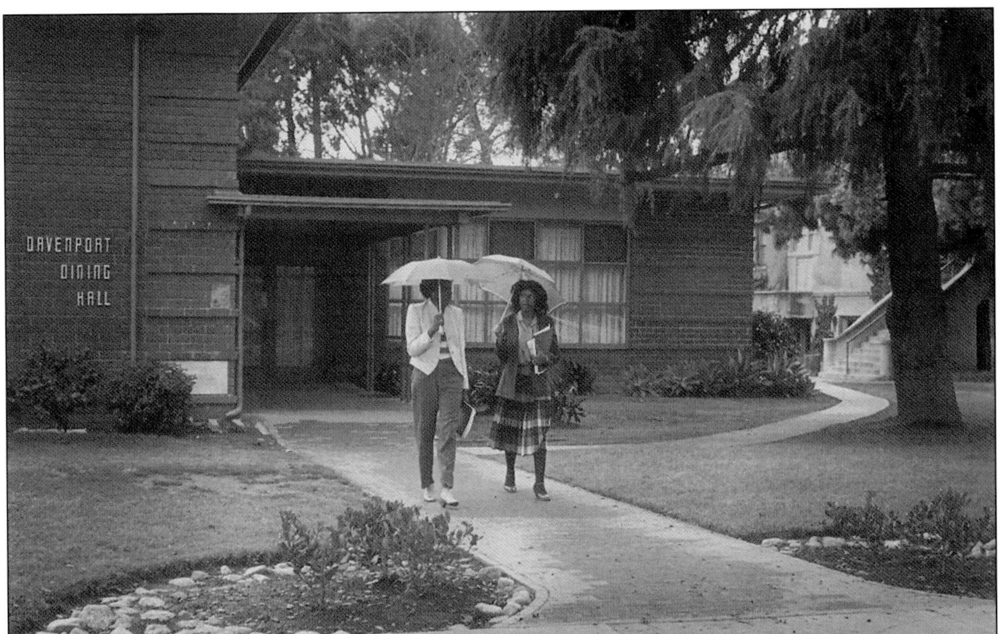

Davenport Dining Hall, Built in 1958. Verna Gillis and Stephanie Barnett were caught in a rainstorm in 1982. (Photographer: Kim Pence.)

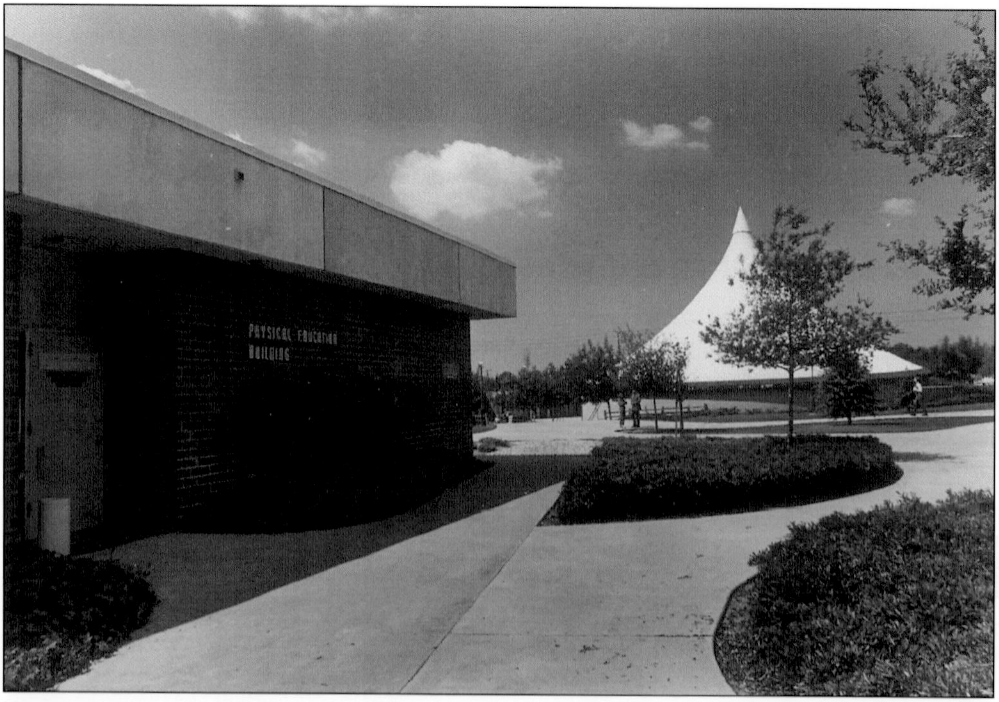

PHYSICAL EDUCATION ADDITION TO GYMNASIUM, BUILT 1963. THE Daily Theater, built 1972–73, can be seen in the distance.

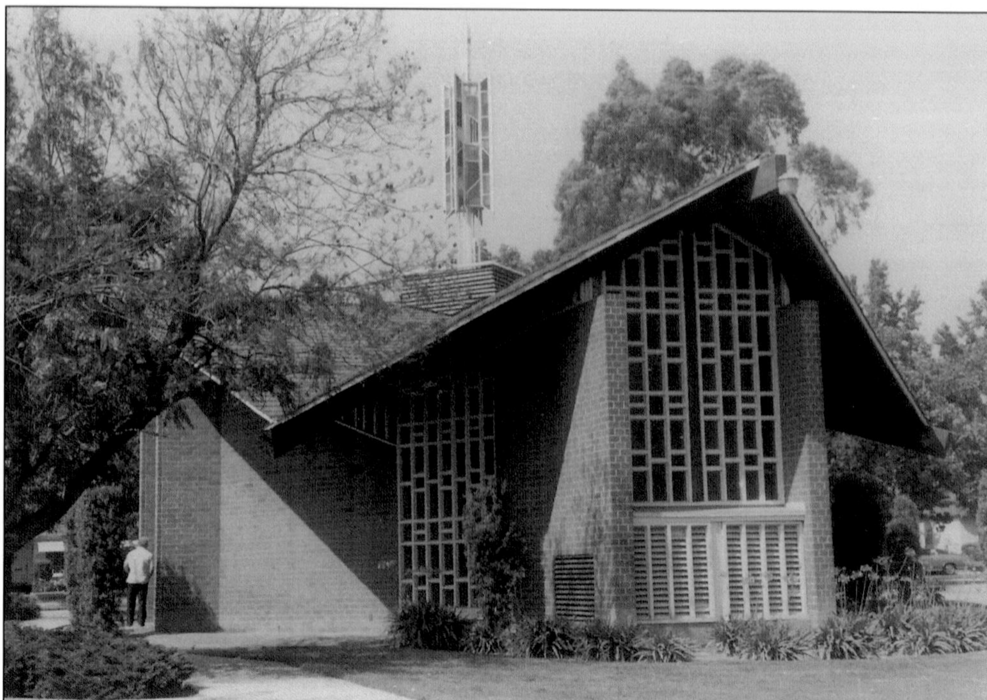

CHAPEL, BUILT 1966.

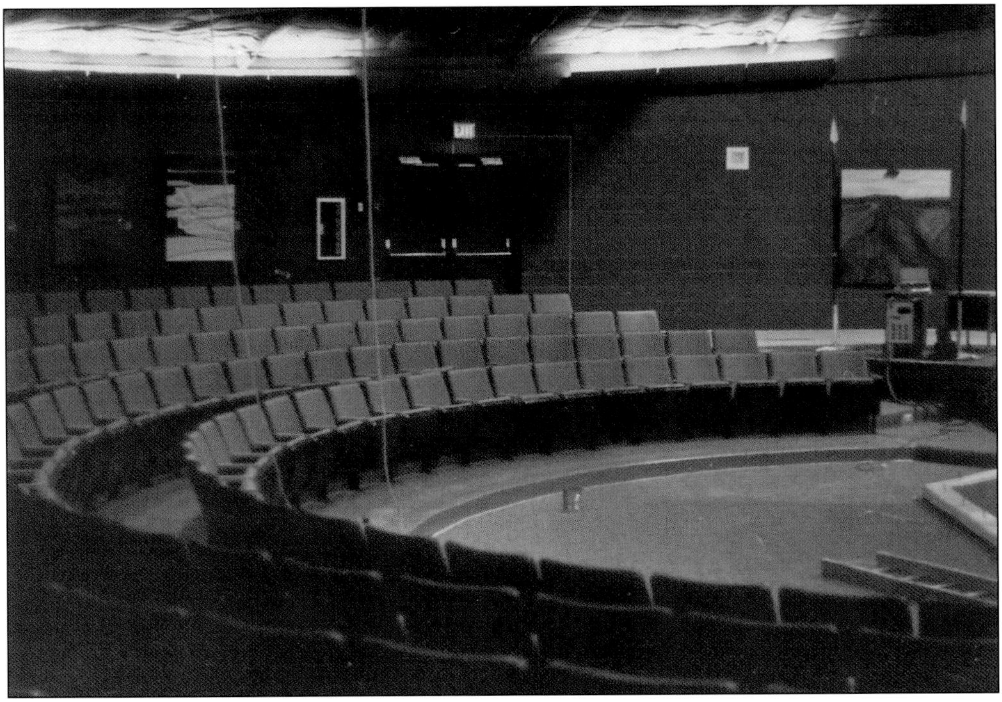

INTERIOR VIEW OF DAILY THEATER.

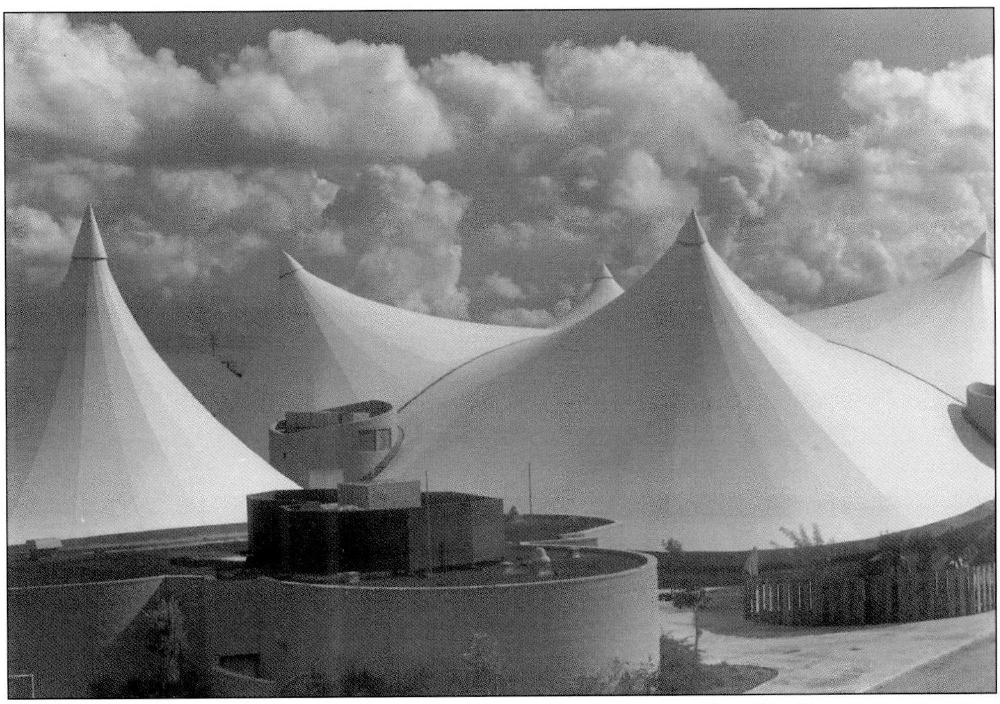

STUDENT CENTER "SUPERTENTS," BUILT 1972–73. The tent is made of Teflon-coated nylon fabric. Interior space includes a sports playing floor on the second level and various student activity spaces on the main floor. The Daily Theater is on the left.

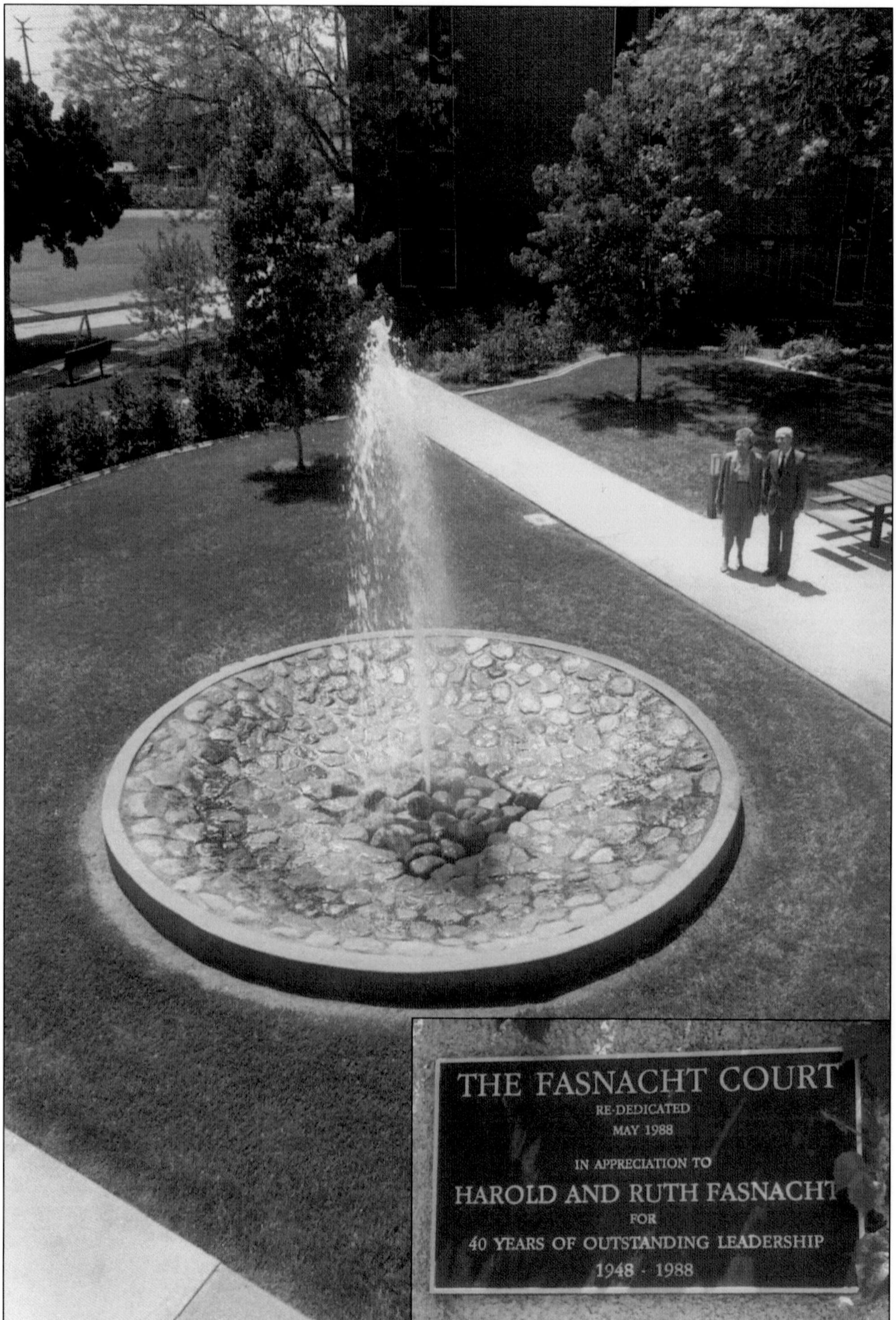

FASNACHT COURT AND FOUNTAIN. The fountain was dedicated in appreciation for 40 years of leadership and given to La Verne by Harold and Ruth Fasnacht.

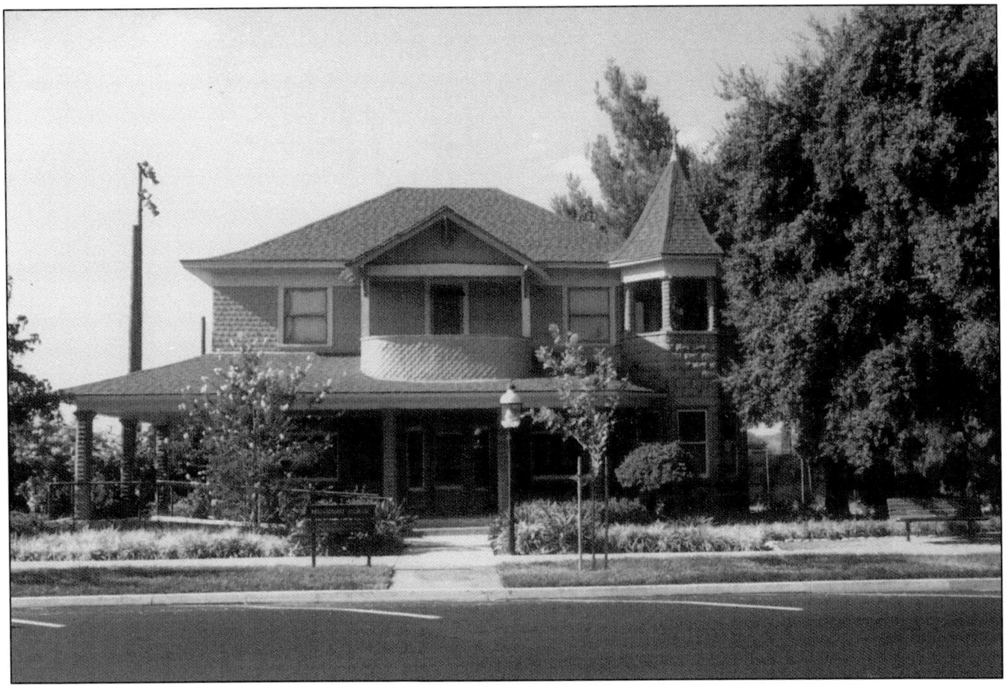

Hanawalt House. This house was built on private property at the edge of the campus in 1908 by President W.C. Hanawalt, after he left the presidency. It was a private home for many years and was sold to La Verne by Hanawalt's widow in the 1960s. It has served as a childcare center and is now used as the university counseling center.

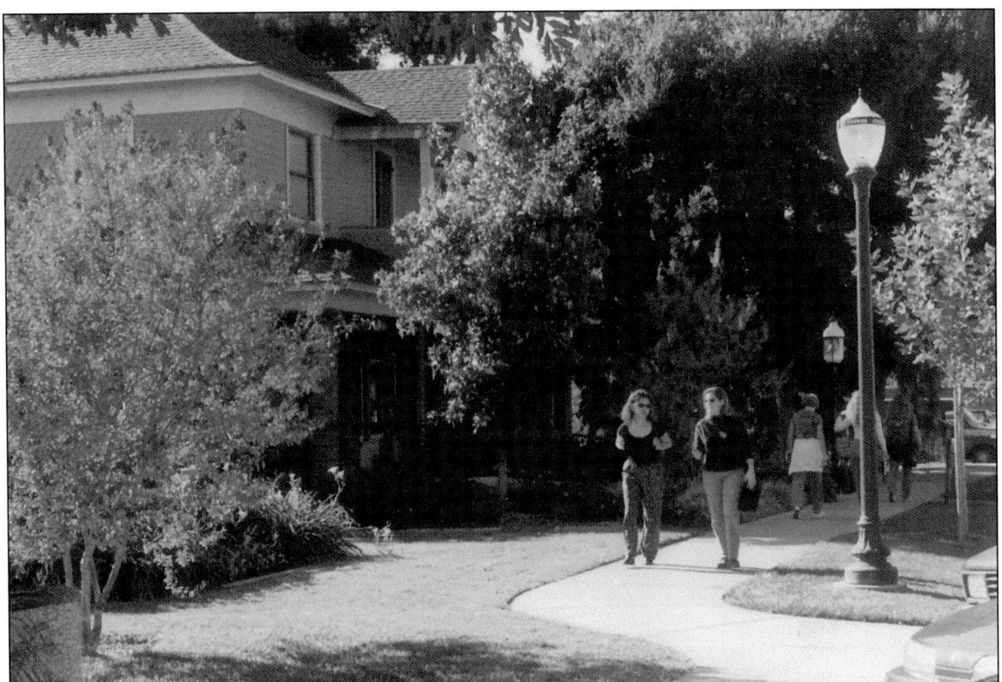

Walkway Along the Front of Hanawalt House.

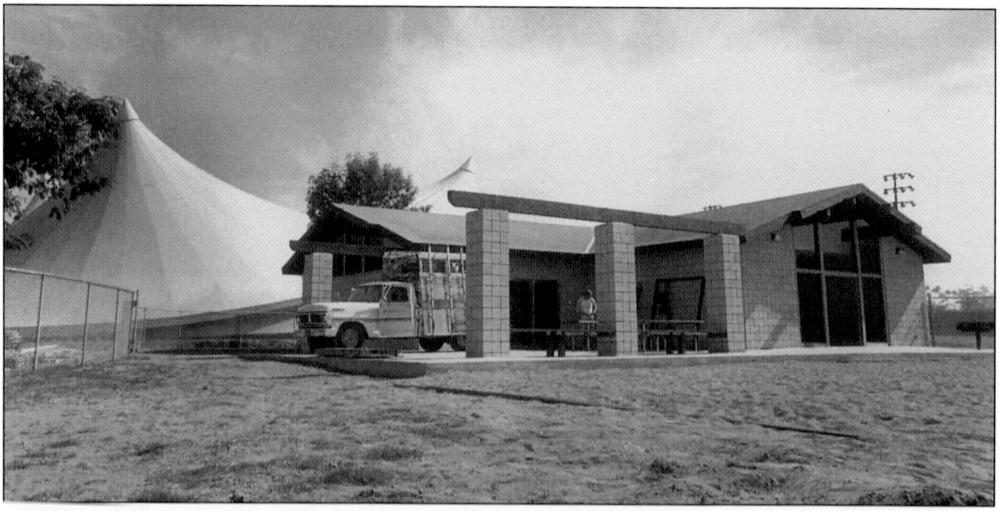

Hanawalt Fitness Center. It was dedicated in 1986 to honor the more than 40–year career of Dwight Hanawalt as coach, dean, and professor at La Verne. (Photographer: Lynda Miller.)

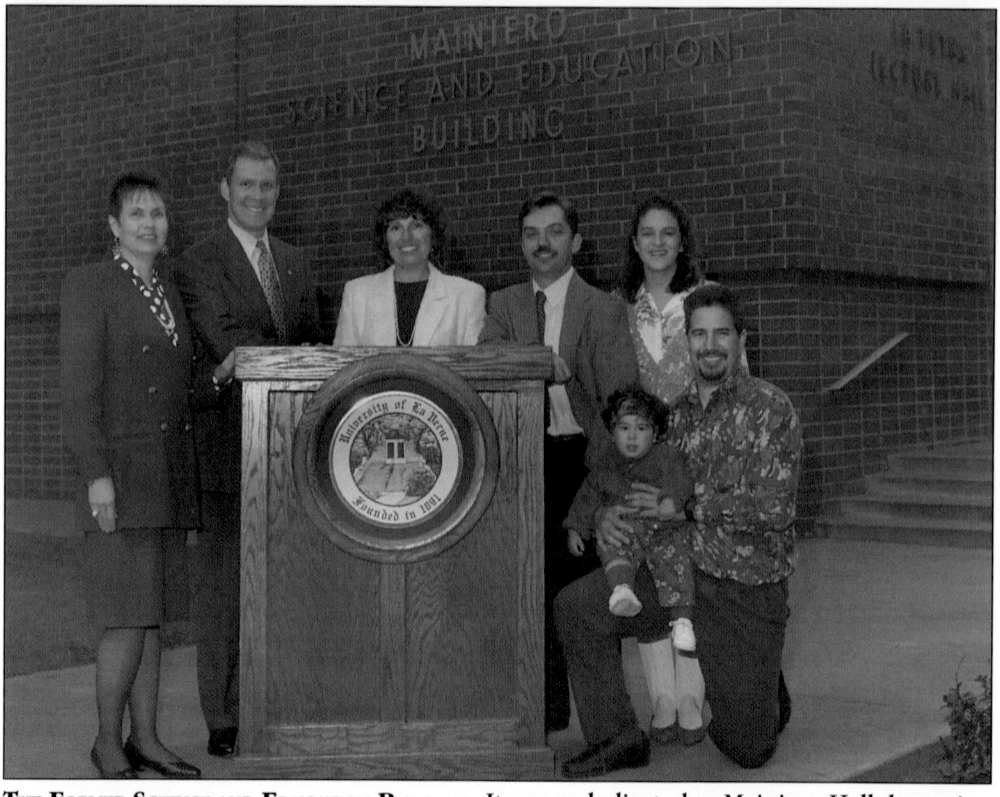

The Former Science and Education Building. It was rededicated as Mainiero Hall, honoring the service of John G. "Skip" Mainiero, following his untimely death in 1993. Ann Morgan, Steve Morgan, Nancy Mainiero, Andy Mainiero, Lisa Rodriguez Mainiero, Ric Maniero, and Allison Fern Mainiero are pictured here March 5, 1994. (Photographer: Professor Gary Colby.)

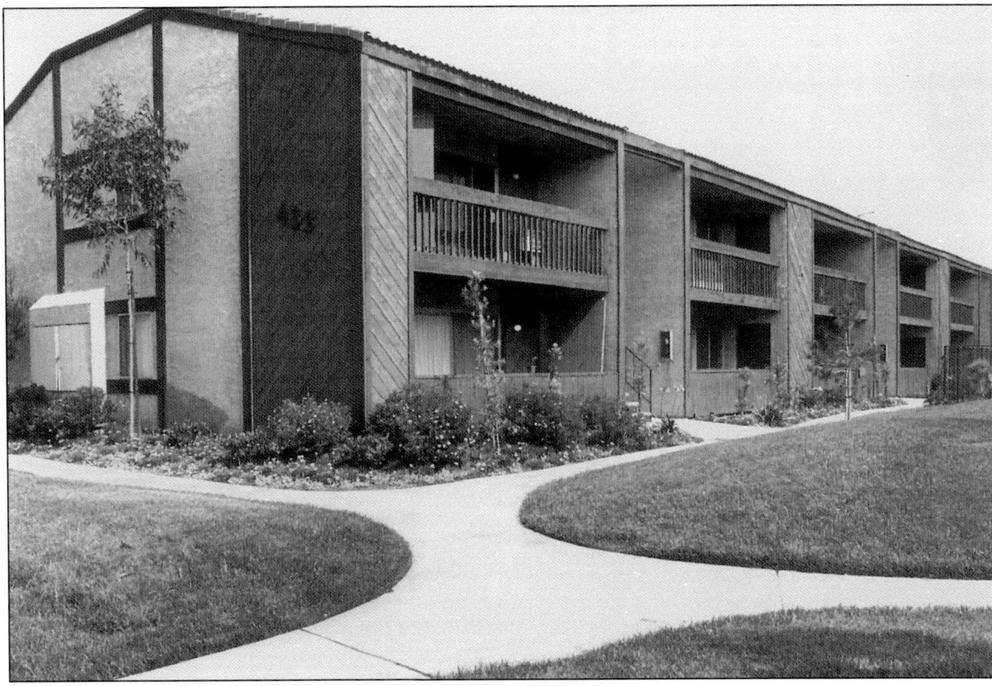

University Woods. This was an apartment complex located a mile off campus in San Dimas, which served as "extra" student housing for a time.

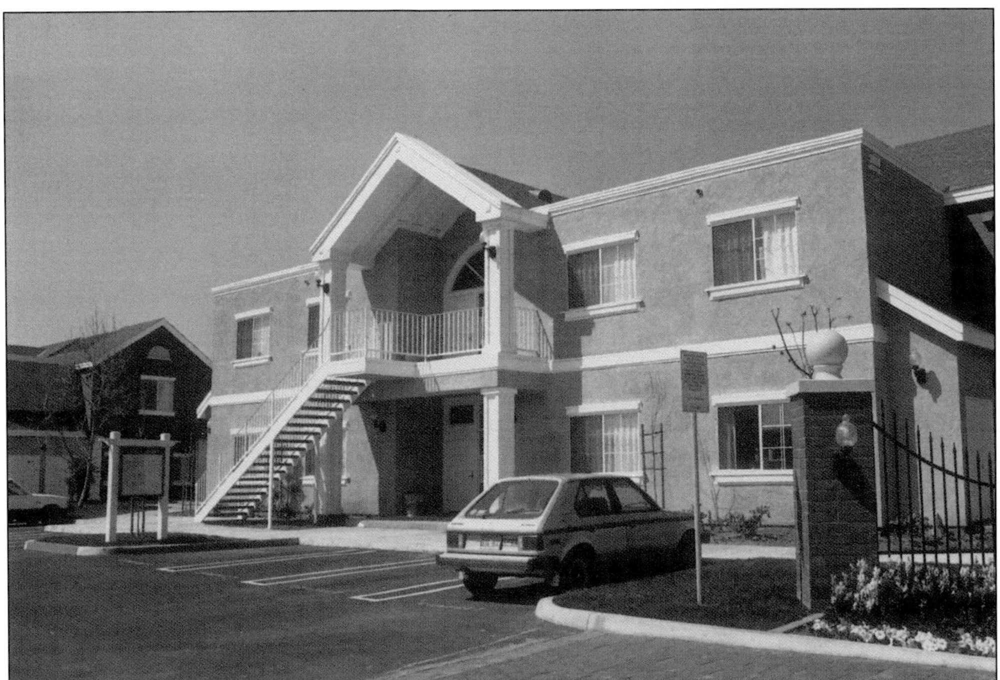

The Oaks, Coed Student Housing, Built 1990. In February 2001, an additional 60 beds were added to the Oaks complex.

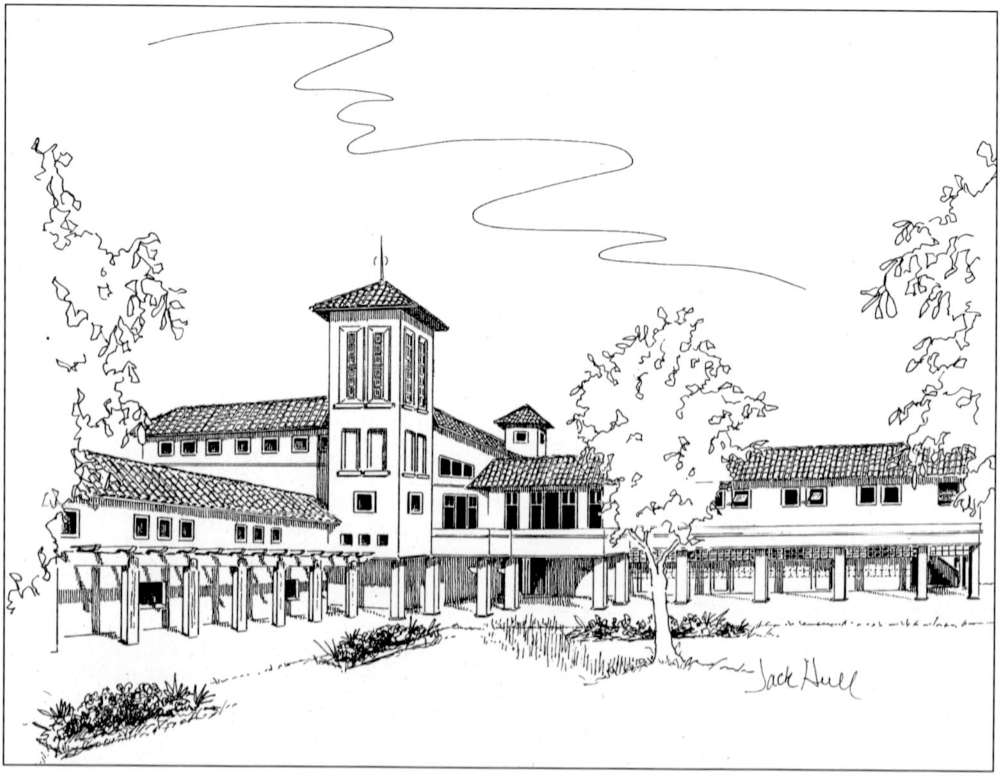

Sketch of Remodeled Wilson Library and Landis Academic Center, 1995. (Sketch by Jack Hull.)

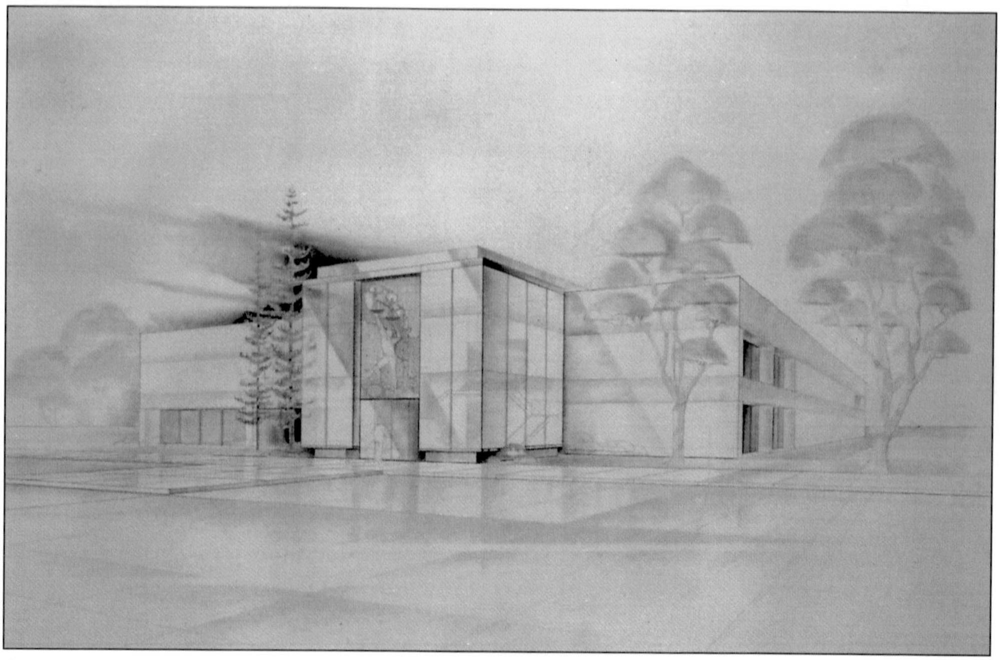

Architect's Rendering of University of La Verne College of Law Building. It opened January 2001 in downtown Ontario, California. (Architect: Rufus Turner.)

Three

Musical Memories

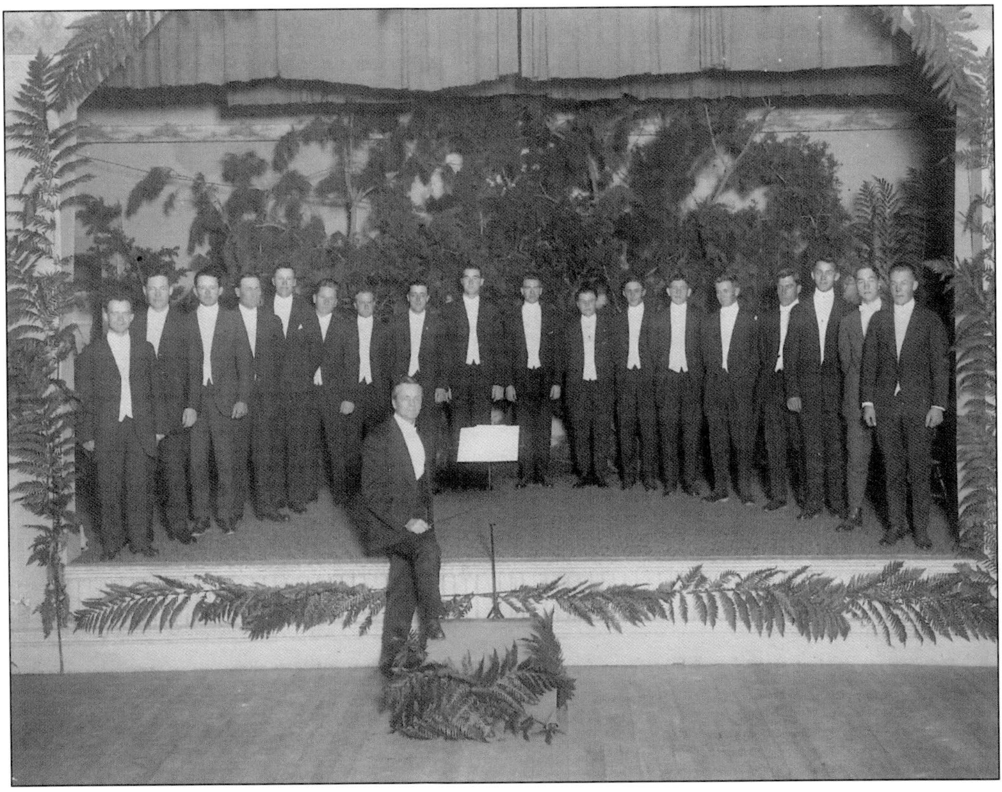

Men's Glee Club, 1913; Professor Benjamin S. Haugh, Director.

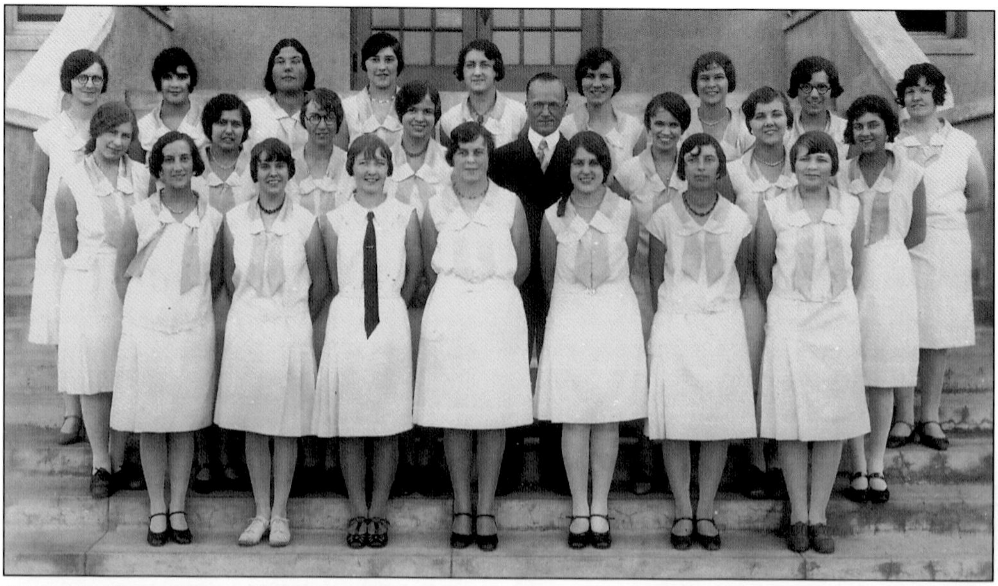

Women's Glee Club, 1929–30; B.S. Haugh, Director. Pictured from left to right are: (front row) unidentified, Arnelia Brubaker, Mary Throne, Flossie Page, Dorothy Page, Anita Bowman, unidentified; (middle row) unidentified, Pearl Niswander, unidentified, Myrtice Butterbaugh, Professor Benjamin Haugh, unidentified, unidentified, Molly Warrington; (back row) Lois Rupert, unidentified, Norma Larick, Evelyn Deardorff, unidentified, Dortha Gans, Mary Platt, unidentified, Grace Brubaker.

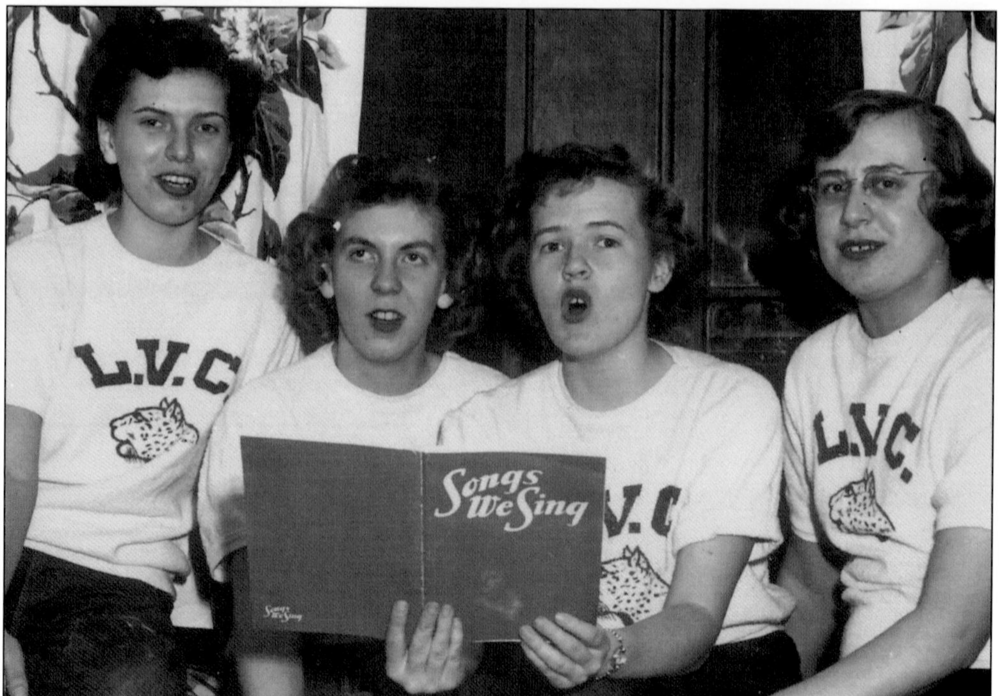

Women's Quartette, 1951. Shown above are Mary Ellenberger, Ruth Lininger, Vera Fern Vannoy, and Carol Shoemaker.

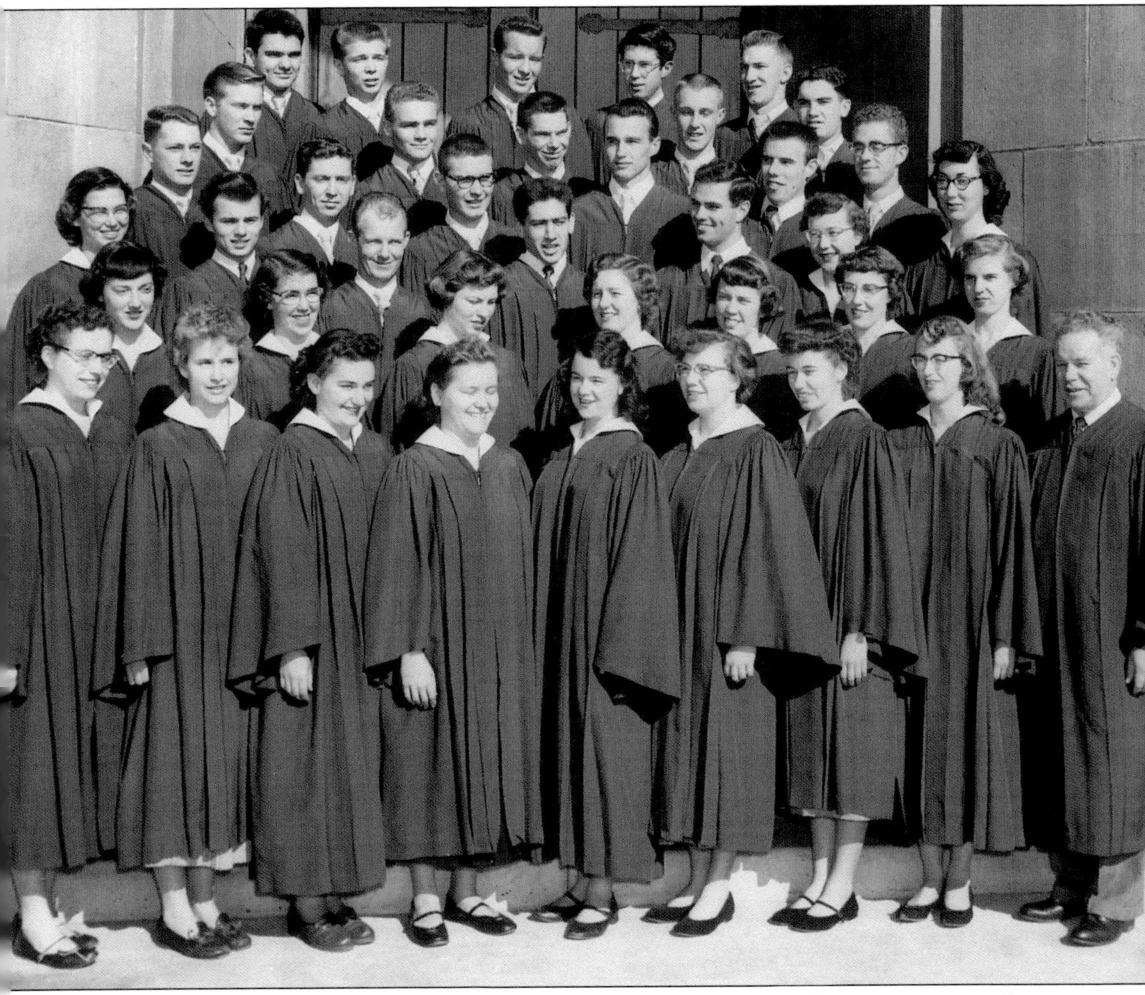

Chapel Choir, 1954–55. Pictured from left to right are: (first row front) Jeannine Christ, Carolyn Gilbert, Raylene Harmon, M. Brubaker, Edith Cosner, Esther Jordan, Frances Brubaker, Pat Meuli, director Elias Brightbill; (second row) Donna Hardy, Marilyn Dickerson, Marian Brandt, Shirley Ulrich, Jackie Clapp, Shirley Neher, Marilyn Waters; (third row) Evelyn Clifton, Tom Schultz, Tom Underwood, Don Bennett, Galen Snell, Doris Shoemaker, Esther Williams; (fourth row) Don Border, F. Knebel, George Camp. Roy Ott, Mark Coffman, Dick Coffman; (fifth row) Robert Dial, Dale Snell, Wayne Buck, Jack Brennecke, Mel Jackson; (sixth row) Ed Davis, Bob Heiny, Harold Butterbaugh, Alfred Adams, B. Hardenbrook.

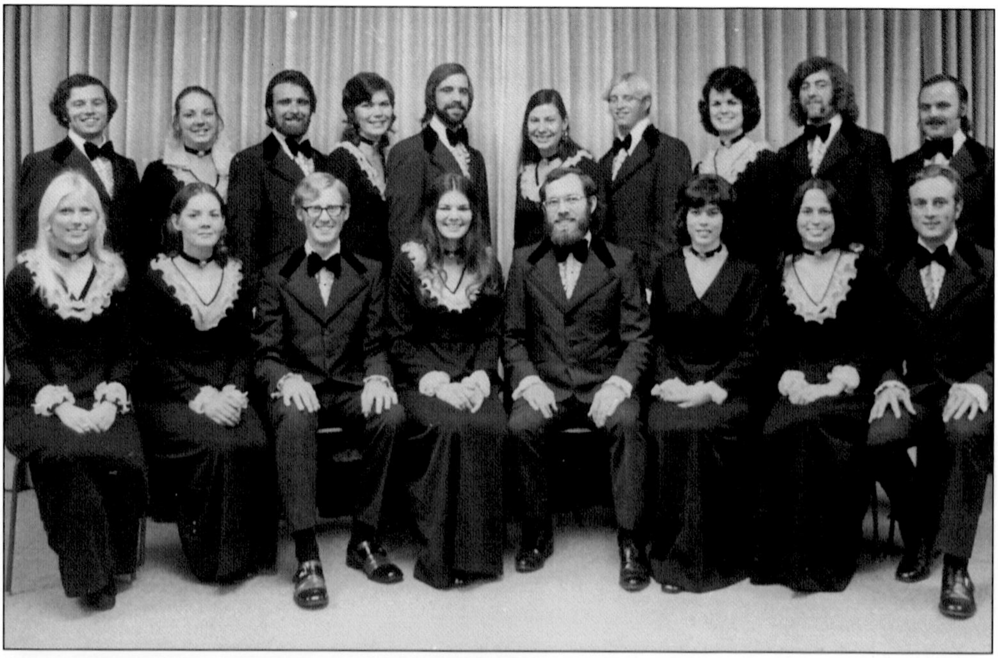

Early 1970s Choral Group. Tom Schultz was director.

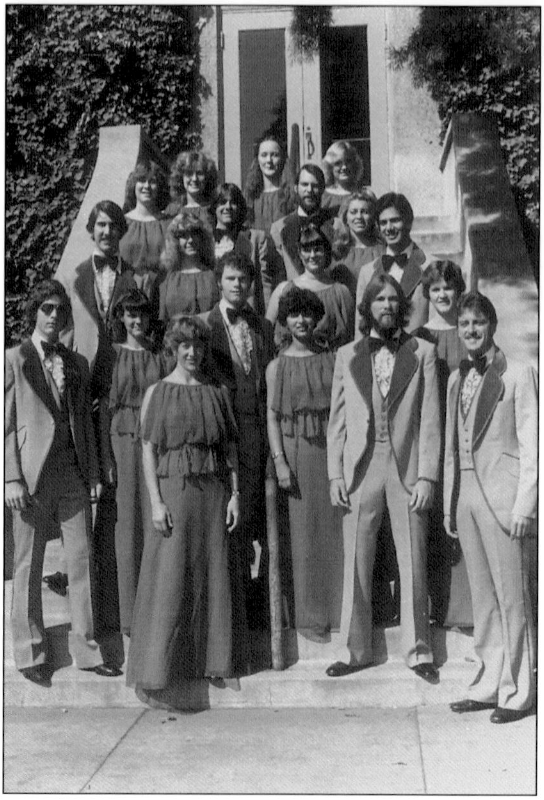

1980s Choral Group. Pictured from left to right are: (first row, front) director Janice Long, Melanie Pereira, Teddy Barber, Jane Faye, Paul Bishop; (second row) Rodney Leard, Rosana Eller, Dave Dever, Gail Heisel; (third row) Brian Lapp, Tracy Brown, Rick Wright, Sander Eller, Lynn Sterrenberg, Norman Pulido; (fourth row) Cheryl Crane, unidentified, Deborah DeRhoades, unidentified.

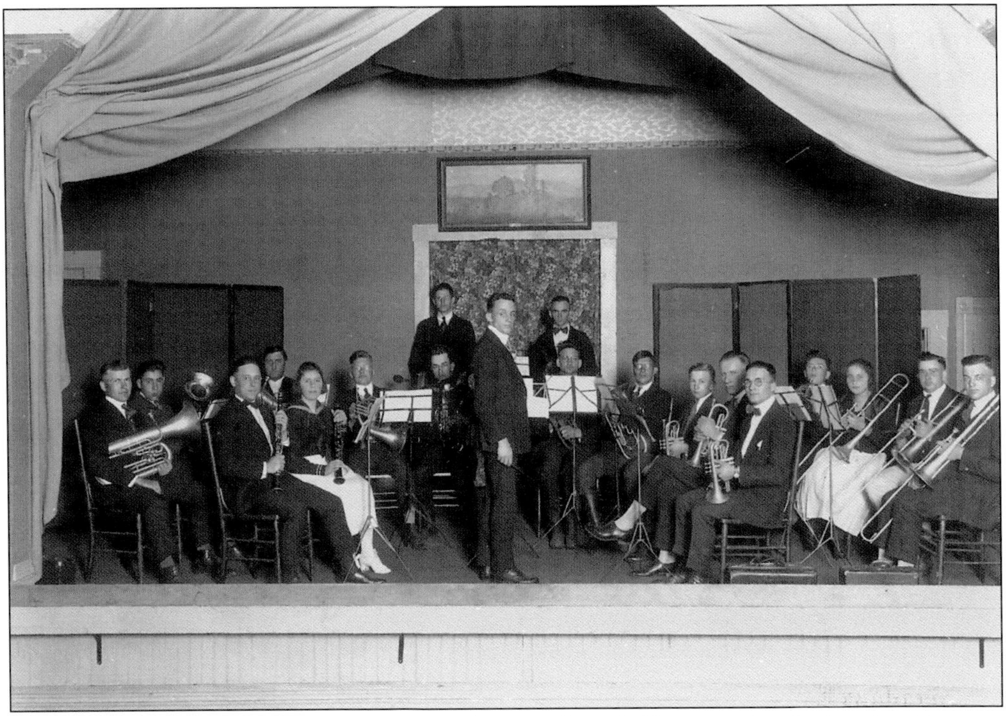

The La Verne College Band, 1921. Members included: Truman Funderburgh, director; coronets—Ralph Netzley, Ralph Shrock; clarinet—Cecil Brower; altos—Harvey Emley, Harvey Brubaker, Gorman Rensberger; baritone—Earl Shrock; trombone—Perry Shrock; drums—William Riddlebarger, Joe Davis. (*Orange Blossom* 1921 Annual, p. 19.)

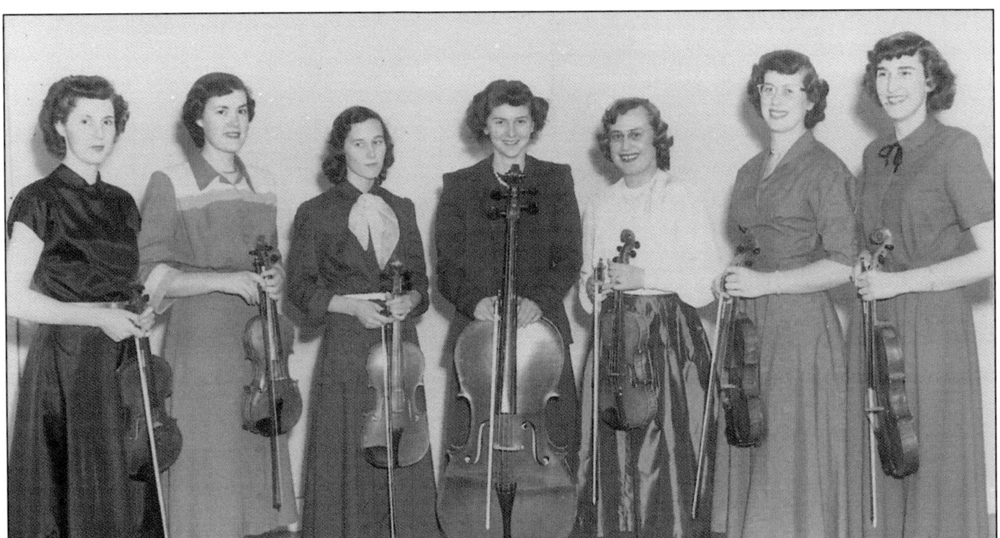

String Ensemble, 1951. Members pictured are Juanita Getchman, Mary Heiny, Joan Guyton, Marjorie Bolton, Carol Shoemaker, Pat Keim, and Marilyn Neher.

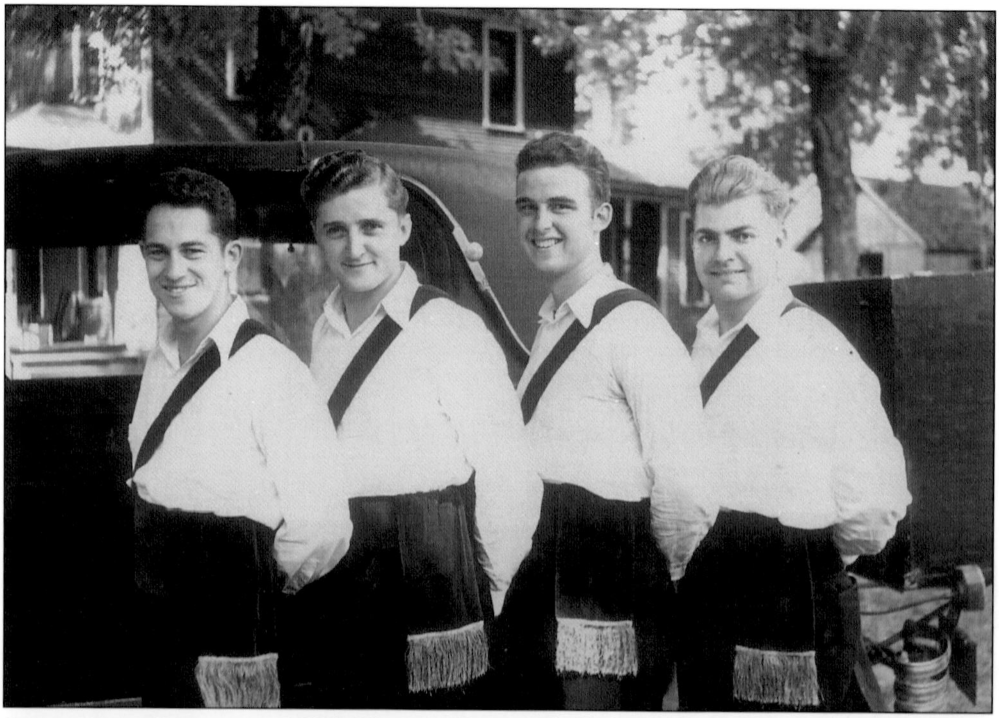

Apollo Four Quartette, 1929–33. Members included Albert Gnagy, Marvin Bollinger, Vernon Heckman, and Dan Stover.

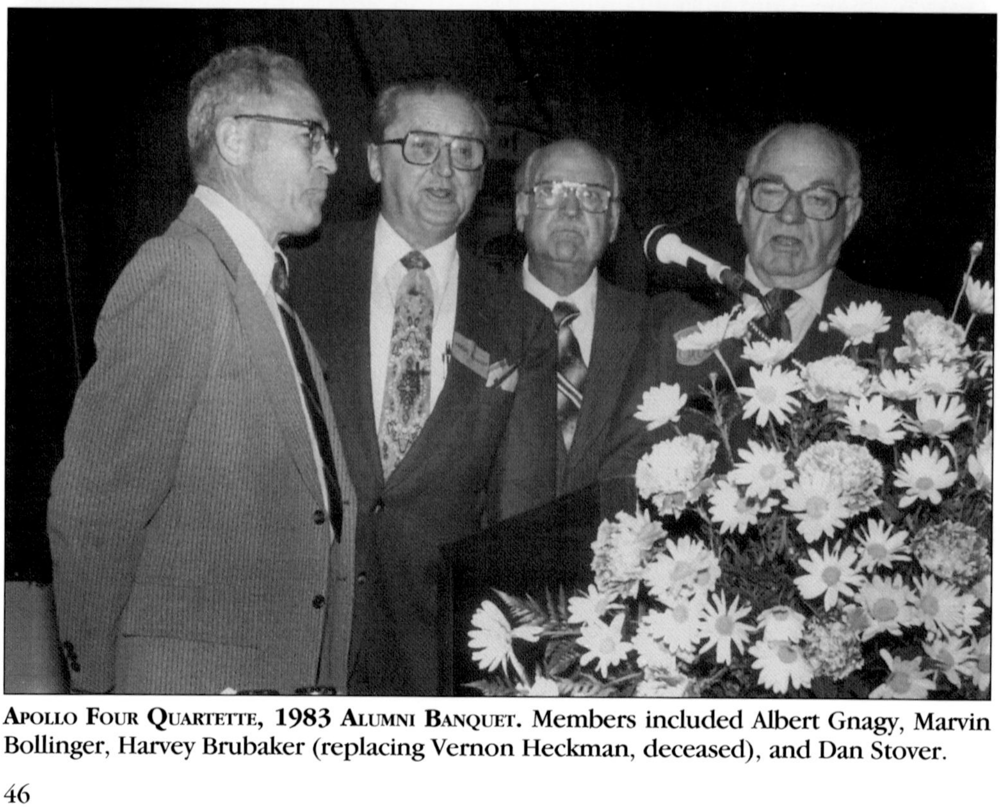

Apollo Four Quartette, 1983 Alumni Banquet. Members included Albert Gnagy, Marvin Bollinger, Harvey Brubaker (replacing Vernon Heckman, deceased), and Dan Stover.

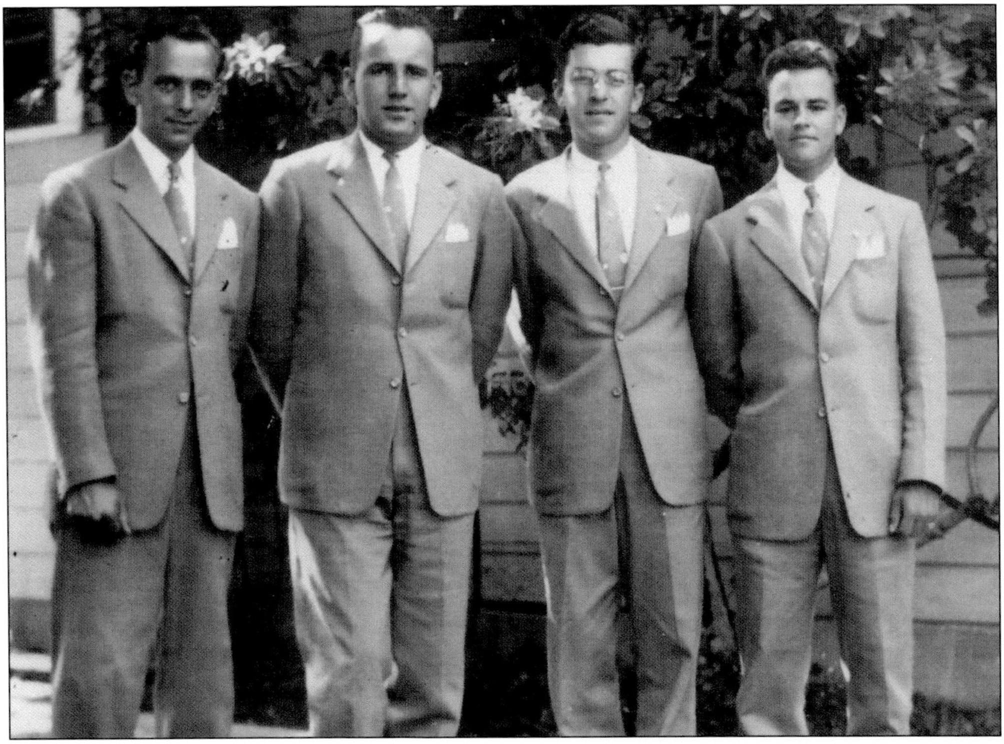

1940s Collegeairs Quartette. Members included Don Miller, Dick Landis, Chuck Butterfield, and Arthur Snell.

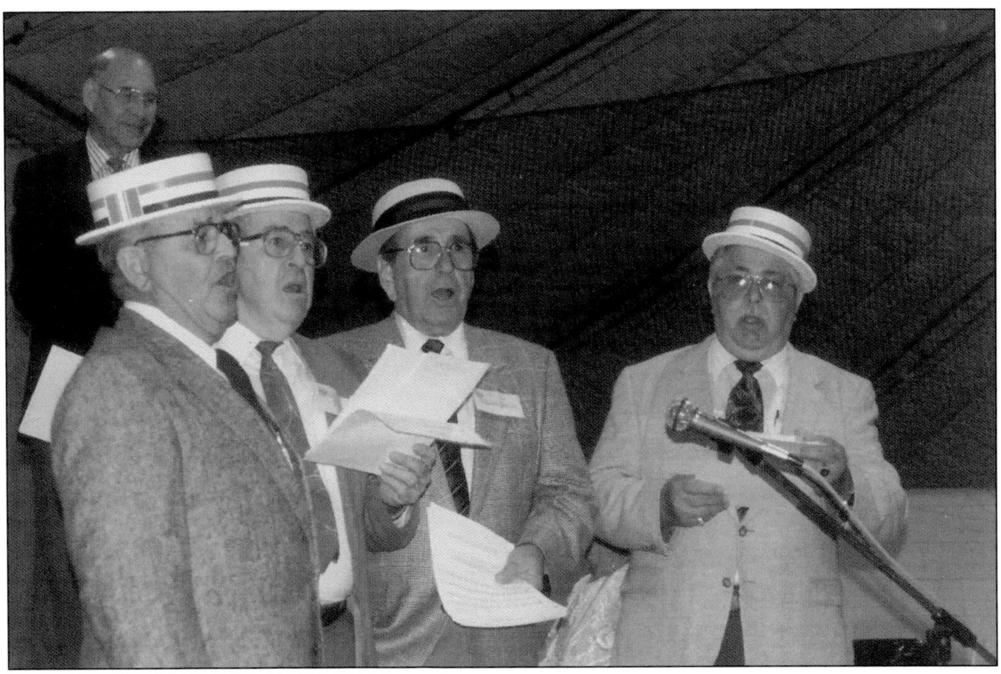

Collegeairs Quartette at 1992 Alumni Banquet. Members included Arthur Snell, Chuck Butterfield, Dick Landis, and Leonard Wolfe.

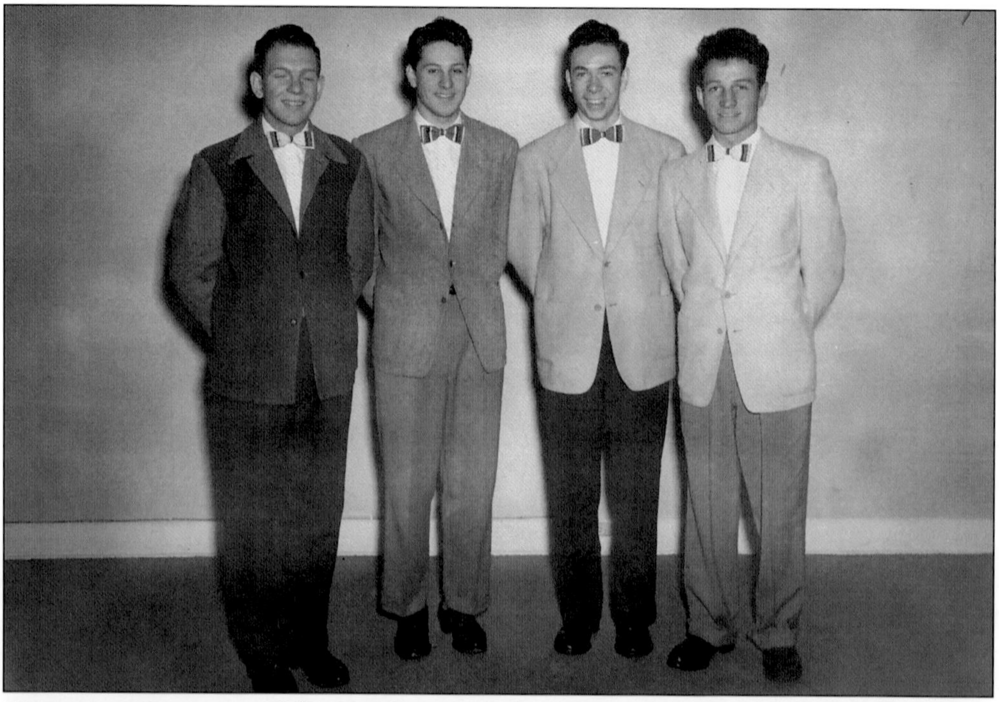

MELODIARES QUARTETTE, **1949**. Members included Sherlo Shively, Stanley Sutphin, Gerry Pence, and Dale Ott.

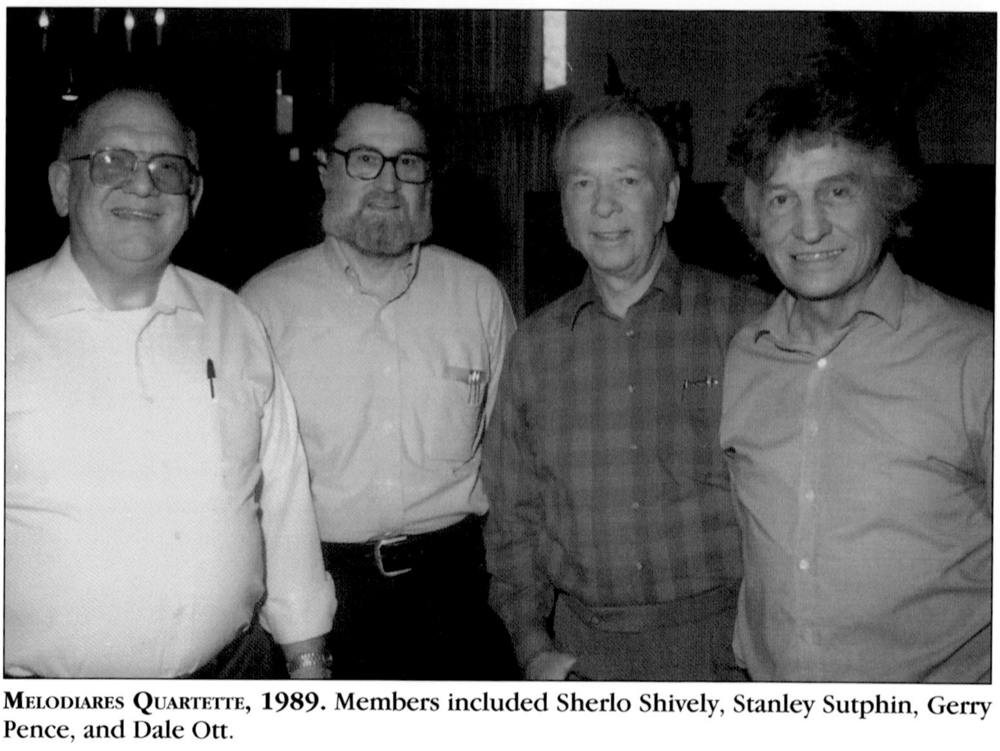

MELODIARES QUARTETTE, **1989**. Members included Sherlo Shively, Stanley Sutphin, Gerry Pence, and Dale Ott.

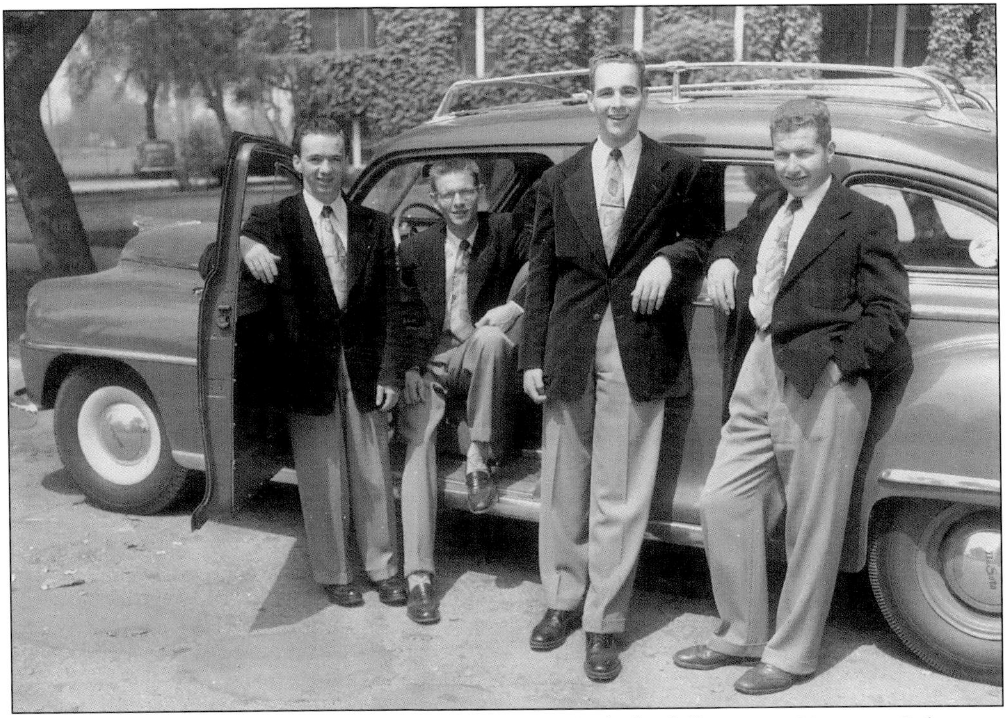

Khorman Quartette, Early 1950s. Members included Cliff Pence, Norman Johnson, Wayne Snell, and Ralph Click.

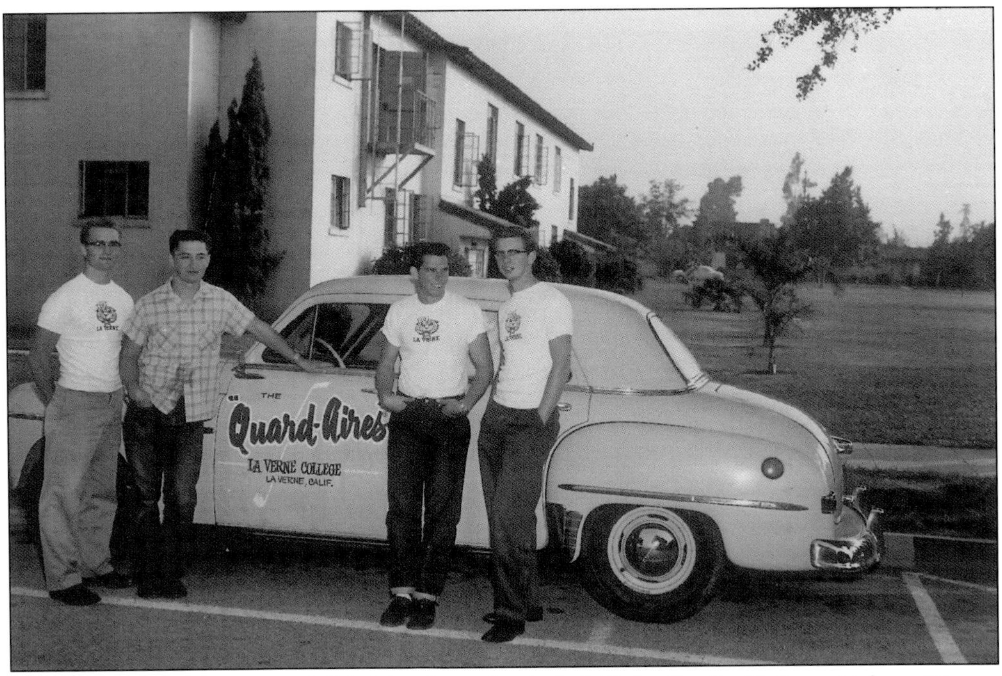

Quard-Aires Quartette, 1956. Members included Dale Snell, Nathan Liskey, Wayne Buck, and Bob Heiny.

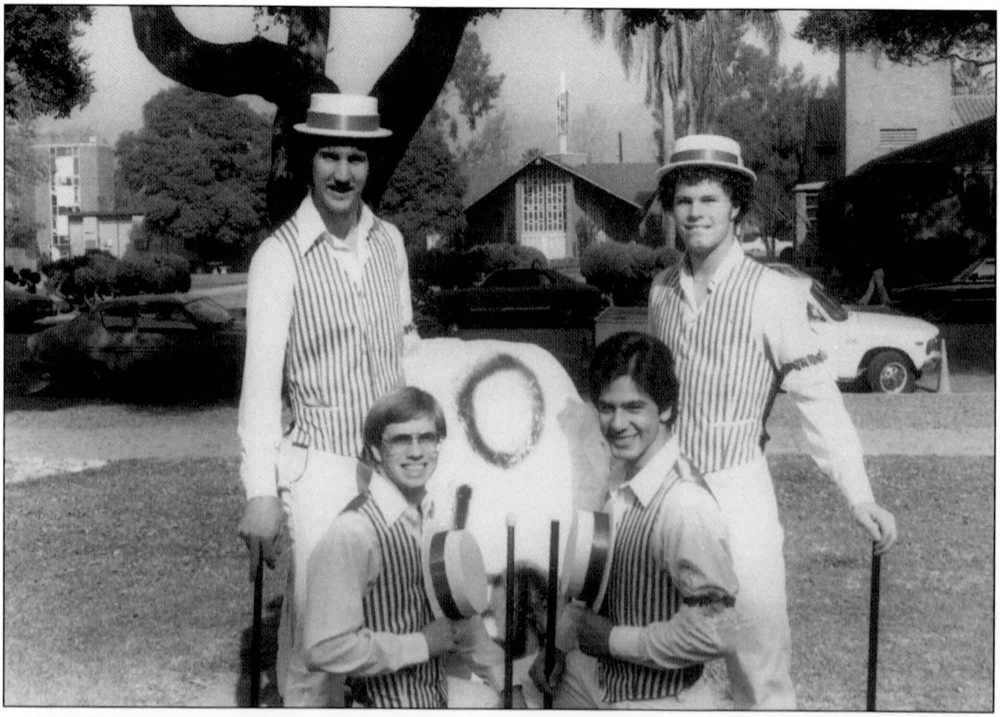

LA VERNE BARBERSHOP QUARTETTE, 1982. Members included Brian Lapp, Layne Heiny, Norman Pulido, and Dave Dever.

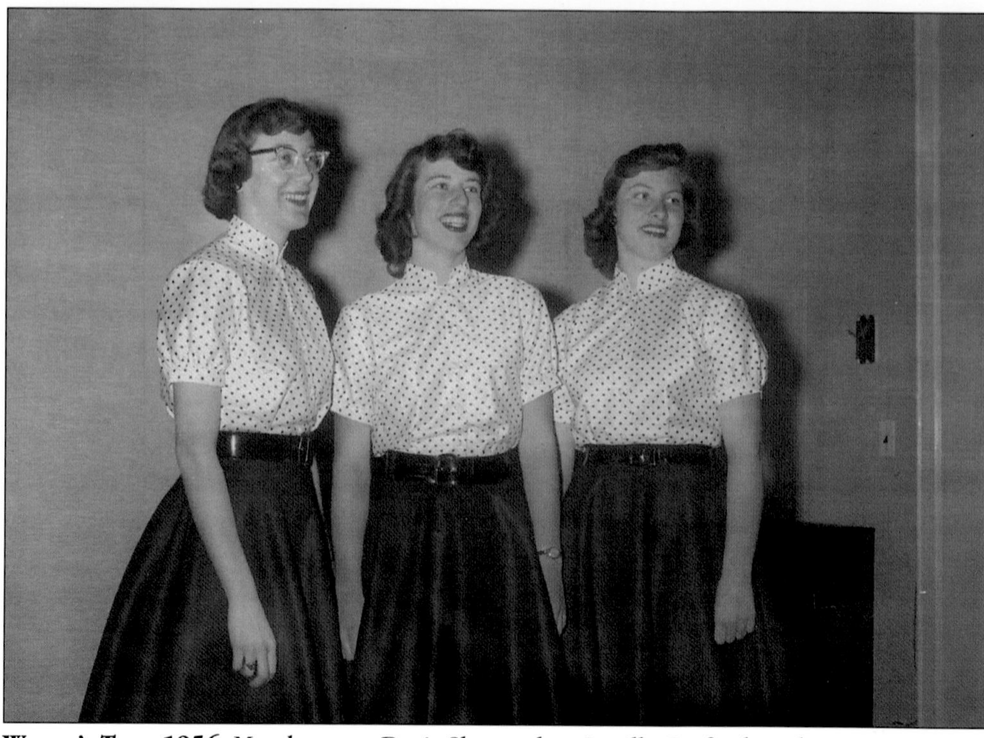

WOMEN'S TRIO, 1956. Members are Doris Shoemaker, Lucille Cayford, and Marian Brandt.

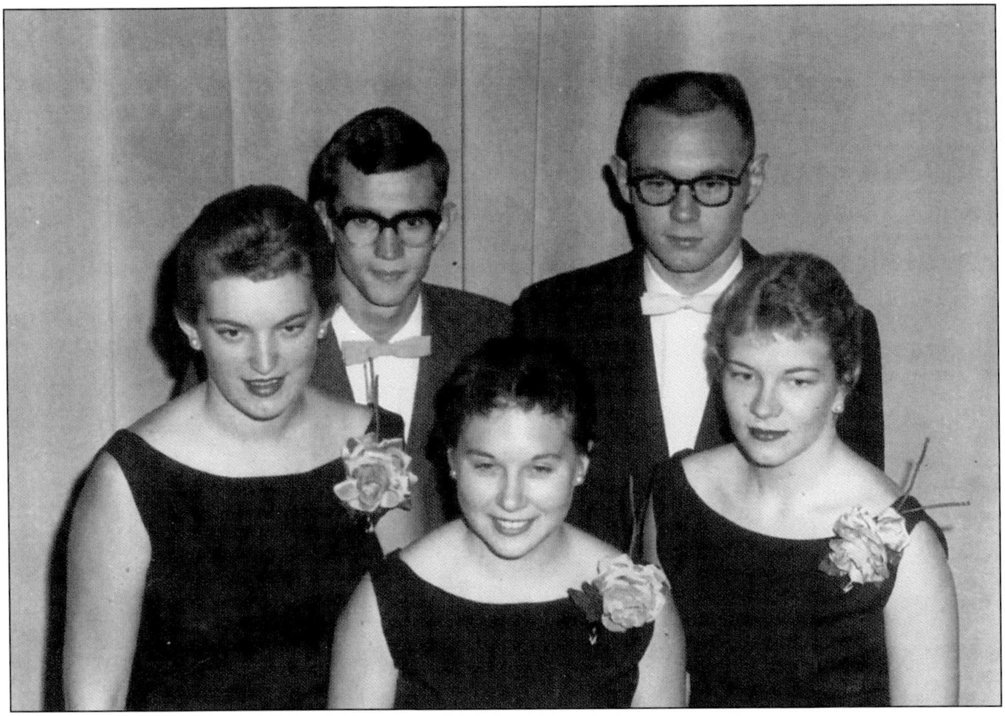

Mixed Quintette, Late 1950s. Members included Steve Kinzie, Fred Michael, Myrna Long, Nancy Bullard, and Donna Clark.

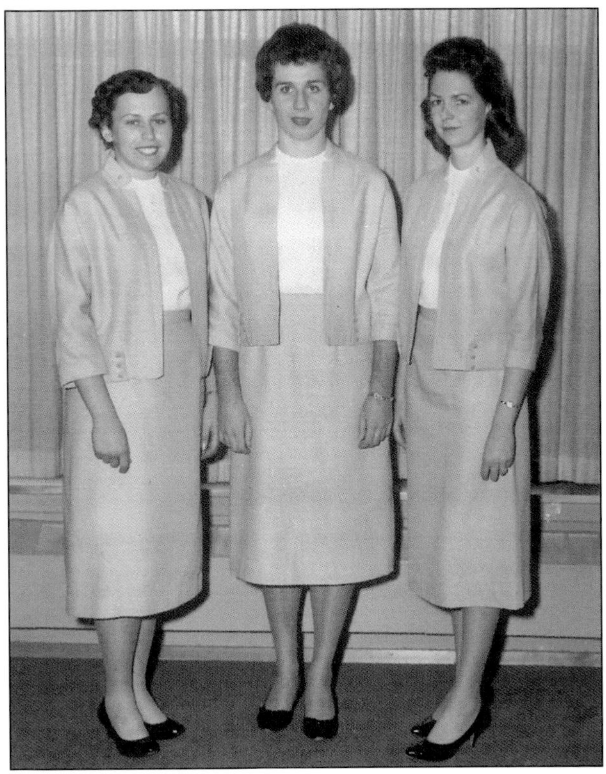

Women's Trio, 1959–60. Members included Cathy Crist, Karen Johnson, and Deanna Price.

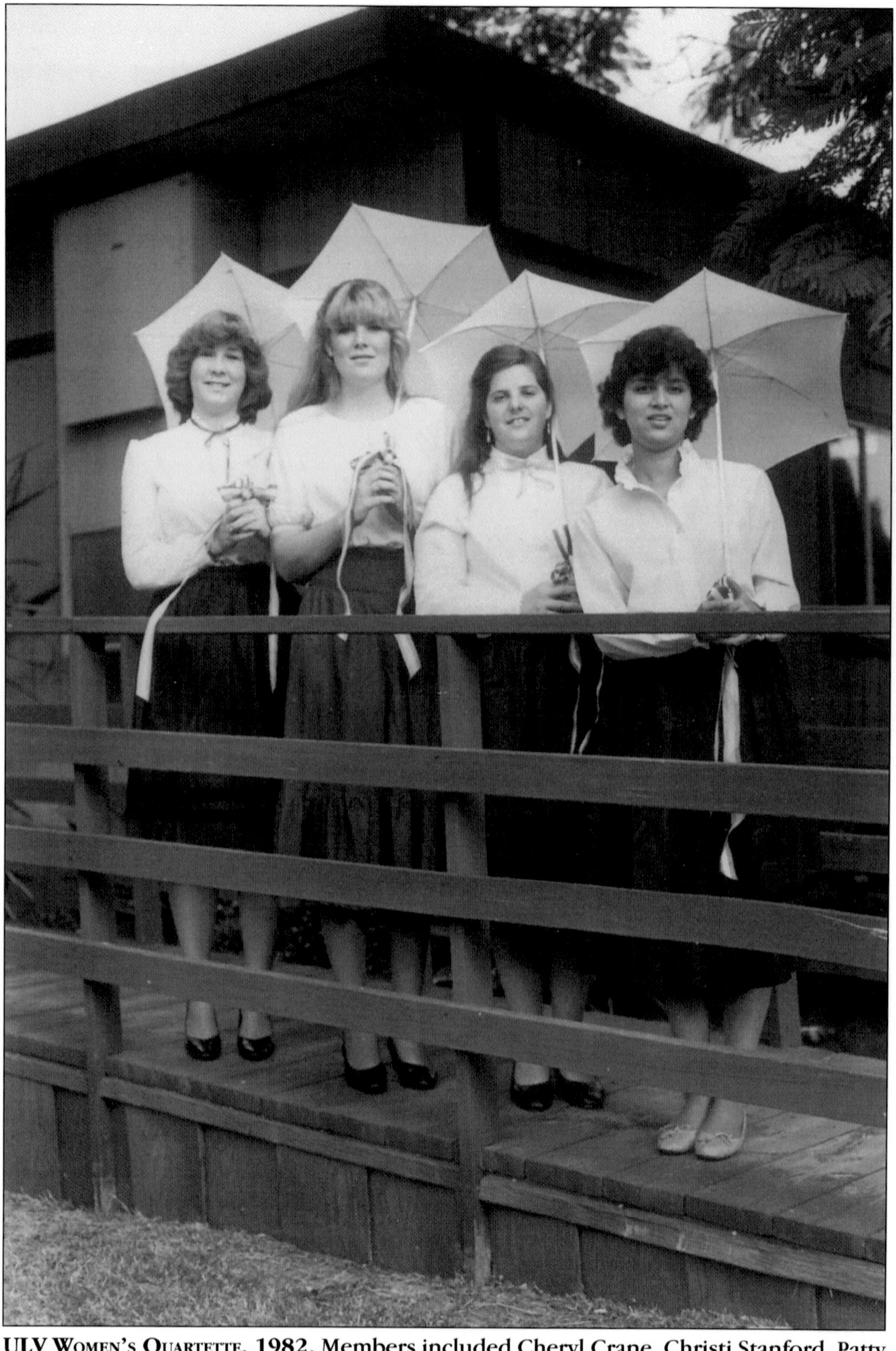

ULV Women's Quartette, 1982. Members included Cheryl Crane, Christi Stanford, Patty Thomas, and Melanie Pereira. (Photographer: Susan Chenea.)

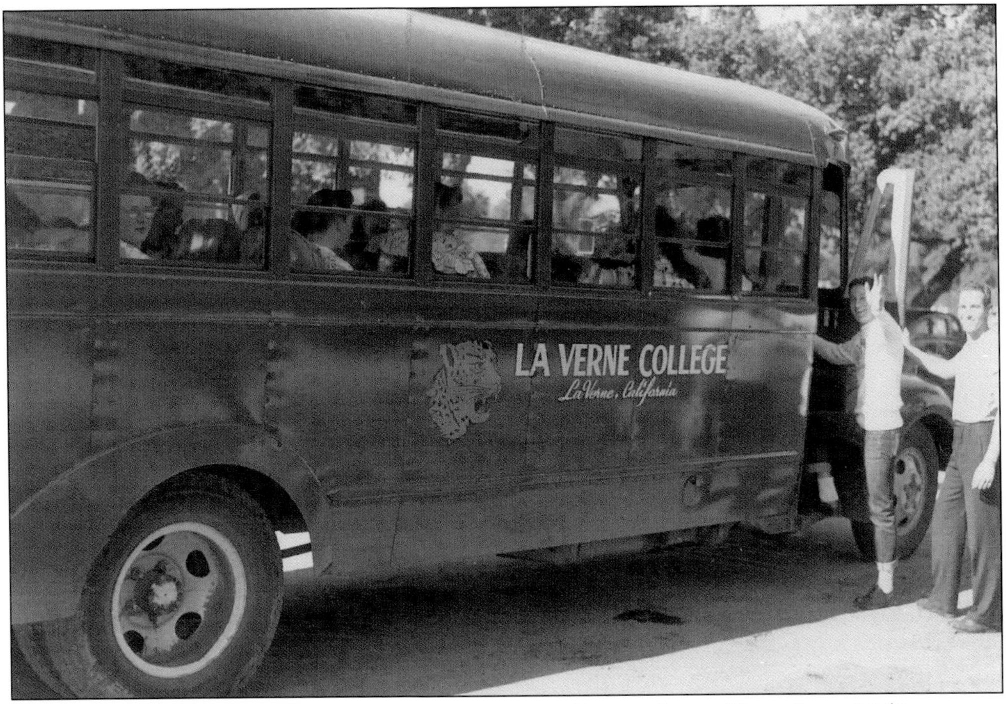

College Bus, "The Green Hornet," Loading for a Chapel Choir Tour, Late 1940s.

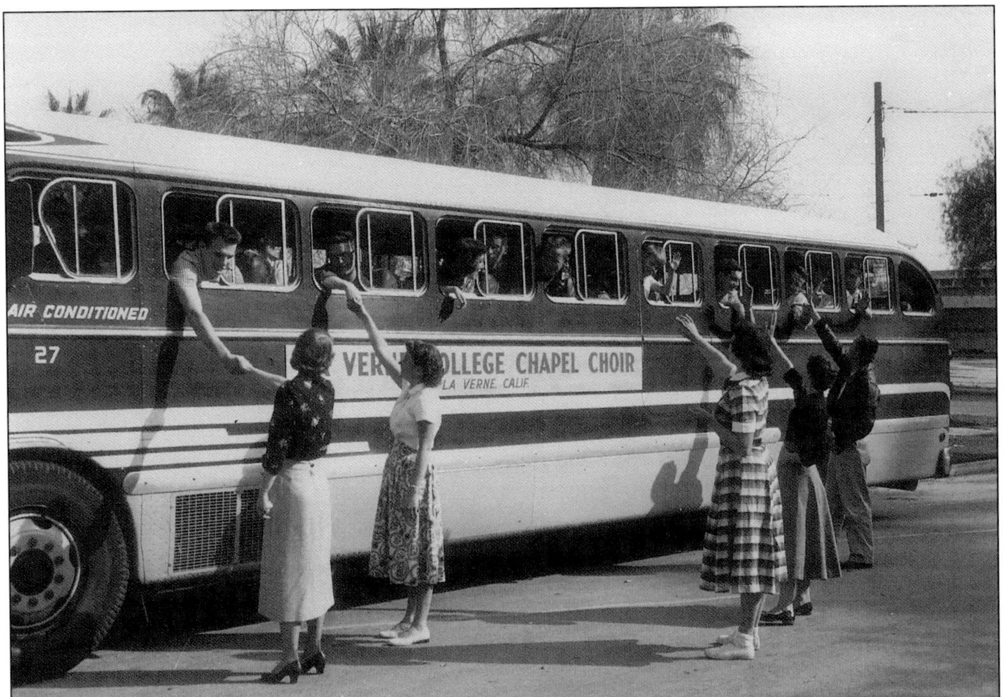

Chapel Choir Tour Bus, April 1956. This bus traveled 1,200 miles into northern California to sing at a dozen churches and the California State Capitol in Sacramento. (*Campus Times*, April 13, 1956.)

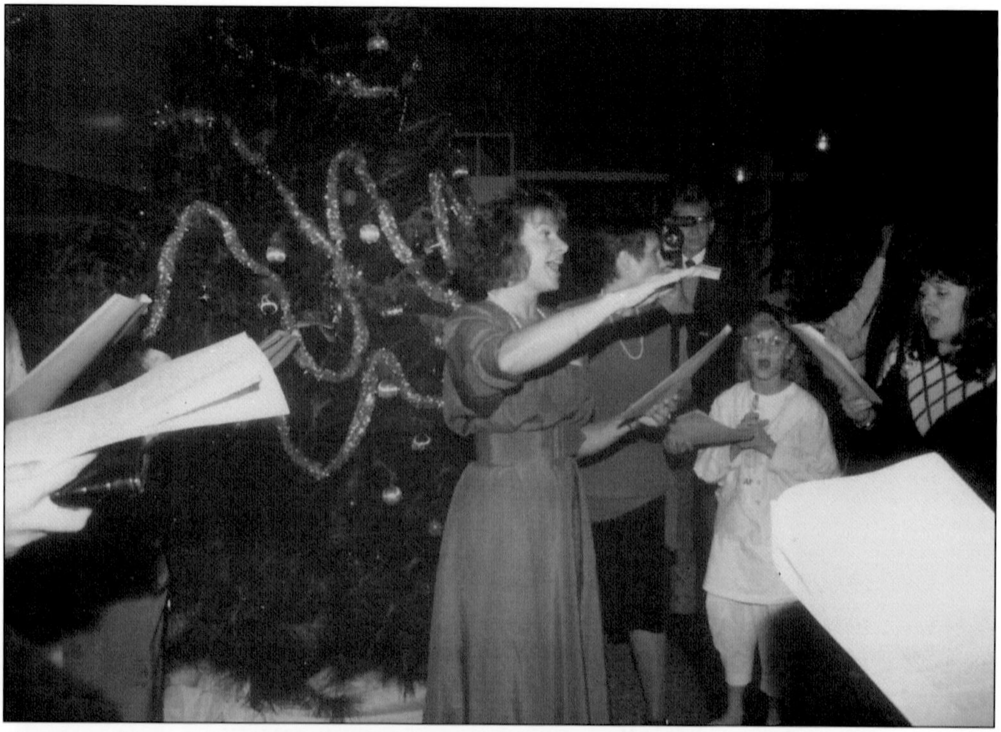

Christmas Dinner Caroling, 1988. Pictured leading is Deb Waas Gratz.

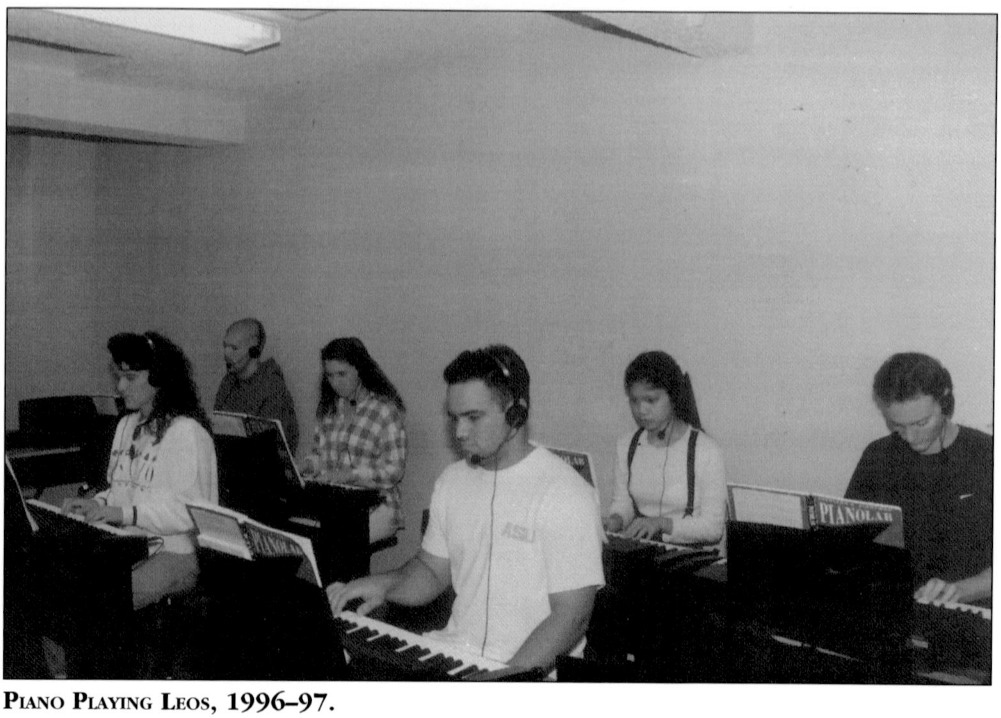

Piano Playing Leos, 1996–97.

Four

Sports

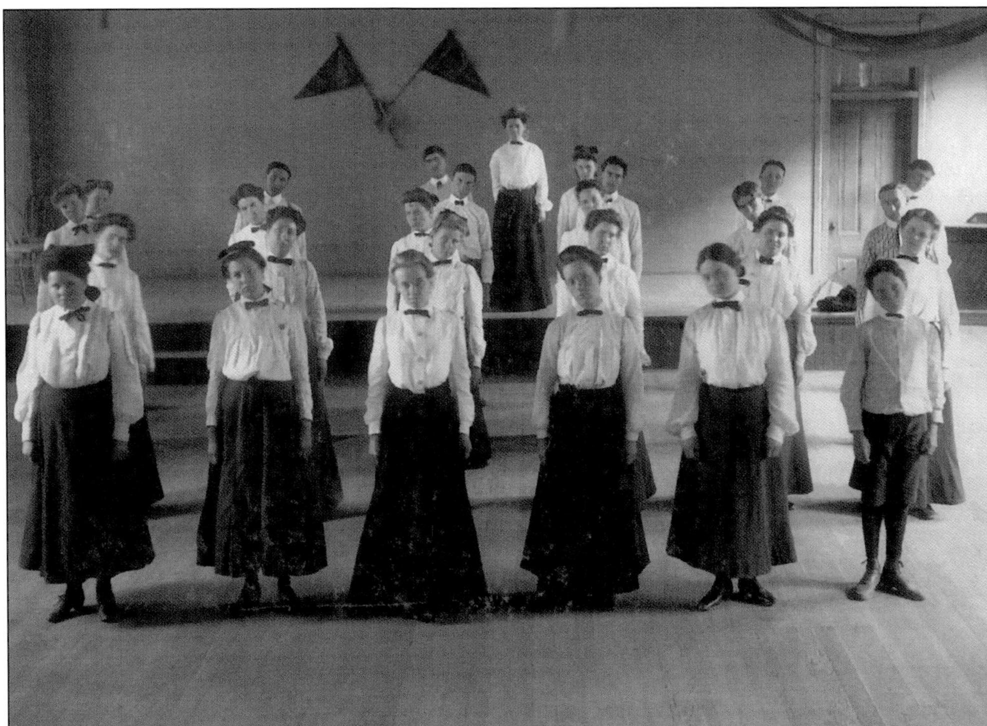

Physical Culture Class, *c.* 1907. The *Lordsburg College Catalog, 1906–07* lists Physical Culture under Courses in Elocution. "True education is that which uniformly develops body, mind, and soul. A sound mind can dwell only in a healthy body. It is the aim of physical culture to develop the pupils toward health and grace, to straighten the figure and lead each pupil to form such habits of life as will give the best physical foundation for intellectual and expressional development." (Photographer: Schwichtenberg, Pomona, Cal.)

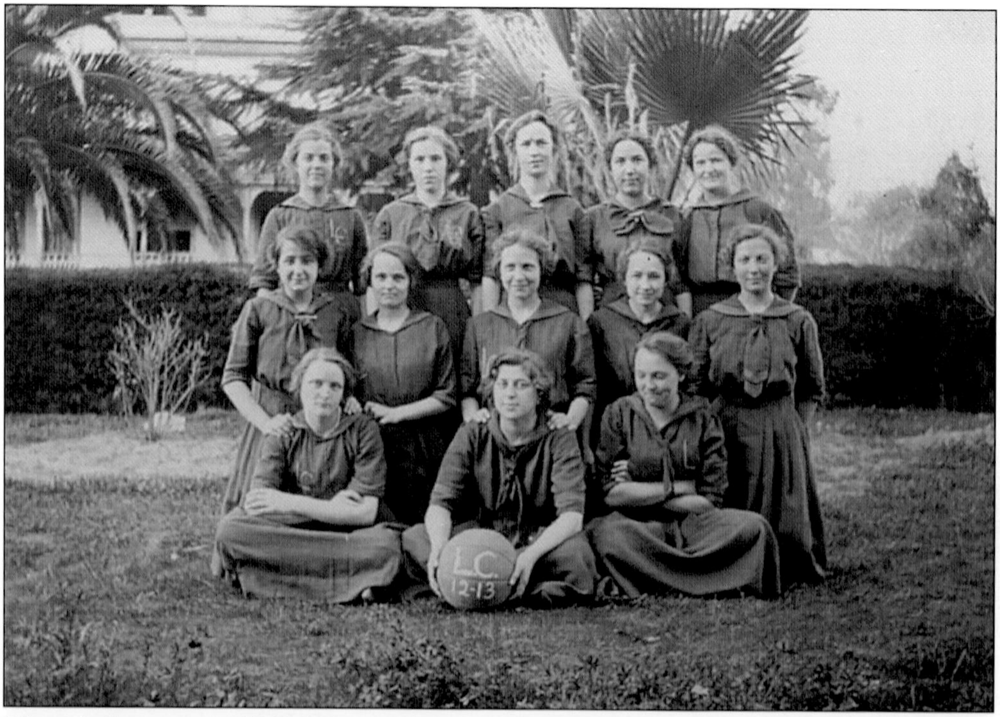

Women's Basketball, 1912–13.

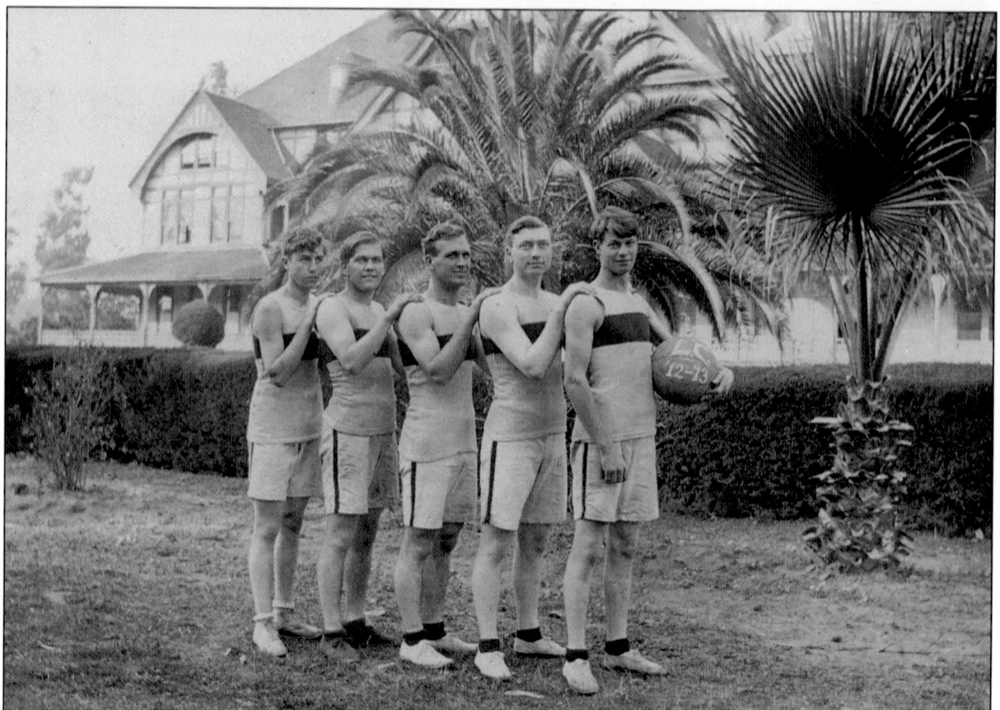

Men's Basketball, 1912–13. Pictured left to right, the last three are Raymond Evans, Paul Dresher, and Jesse Brandt.

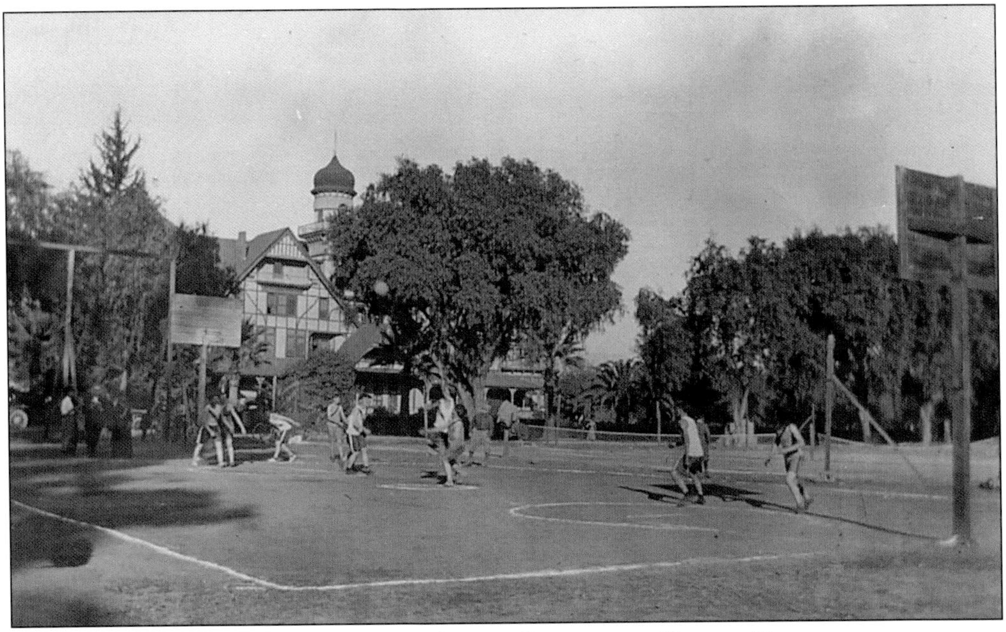

DIRT FLOOR BASKETBALL COURT, ACROSS SECOND STREET FROM COLLEGE BUILDING.

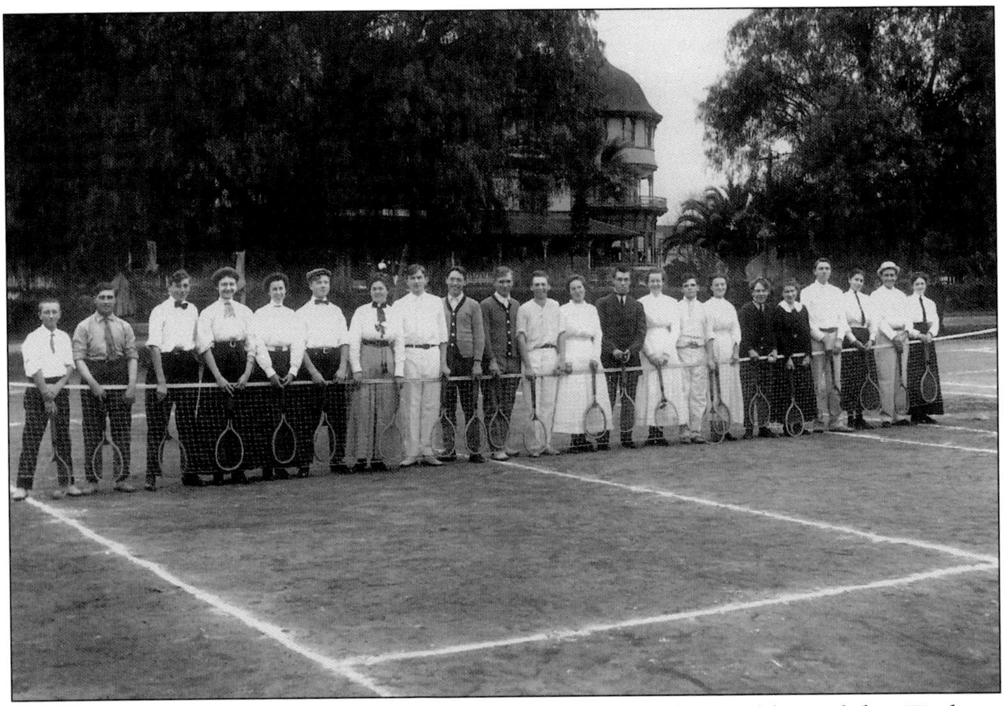

TENNIS CLUB. "Our tennis club is the most enthusiastic of the athletic clubs. We have about 30 wide–awake members. . . . As a rule the girls cannot play quite so well as the boys but they are learning to strike the ball better and it is believed that they will soon pass the gentlemen. Our courts. . . are well shaded by eucalyptus and pepper trees. California days are ideal for tennis players, and the weather does not often interfere." (1912 *Poinsettia* yearbook, p. 52.)

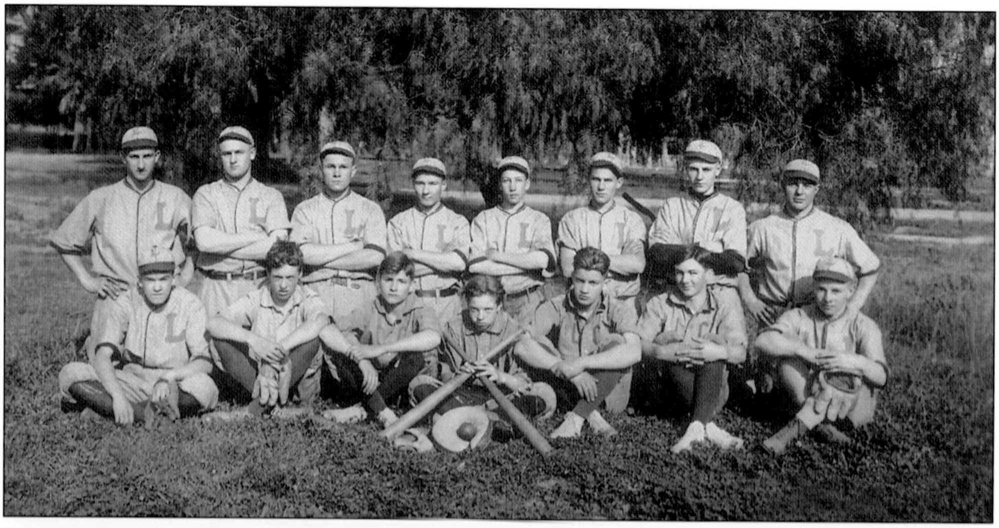

Academy Baseball Team, 1918. "Our boys are out every evening now practicing baseball. We have entered the league with the hope of success. . . . What La Verne needs is a good coach for all lines of athletics. When that is brought about La Verne will be in the first line." Pictured from left to right are: (first row) Dwight Welch, Byrl Harper, Guy Jordan, Chase Harper, Alvin Marshburn, Cecil Jordan, Marion Roynon; (back row) Jesse Whistler, Archie Brooks, Alva Lentz, Ralph Netzley, Howard Beckner, John Price, Russell Grossnickle, Leland Brubaker. (1918 *Orange Blossom* yearbook, p. 65.)

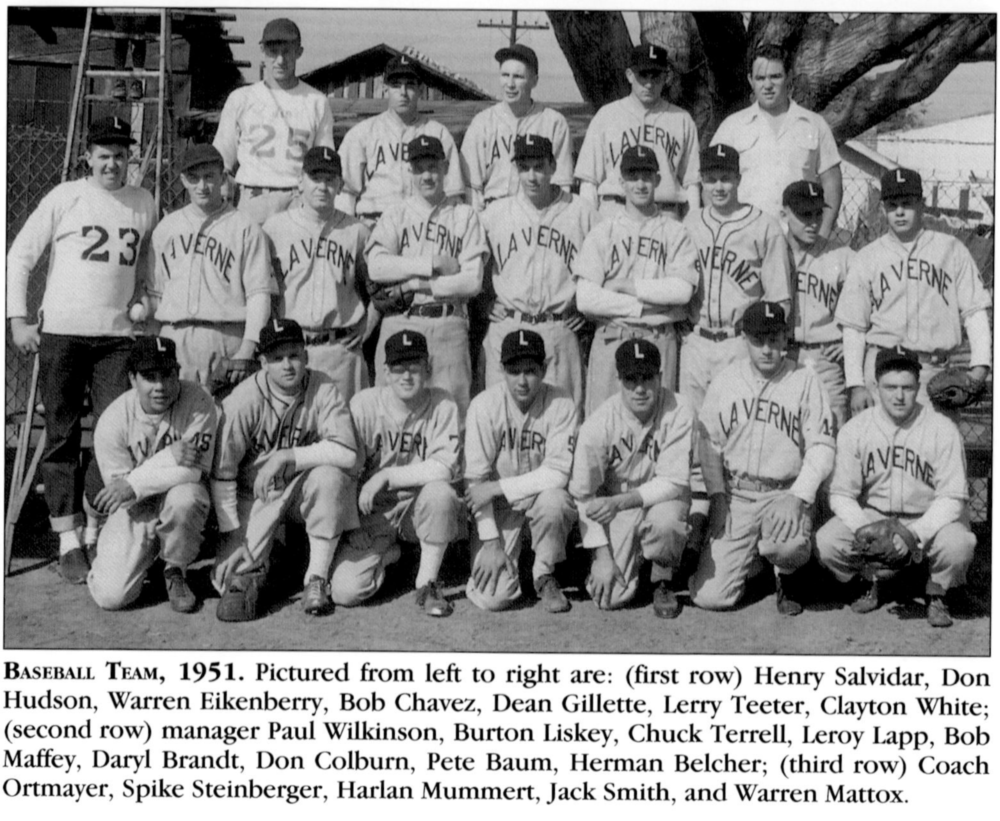

Baseball Team, 1951. Pictured from left to right are: (first row) Henry Salvidar, Don Hudson, Warren Eikenberry, Bob Chavez, Dean Gillette, Lerry Teeter, Clayton White; (second row) manager Paul Wilkinson, Burton Liskey, Chuck Terrell, Leroy Lapp, Bob Maffey, Daryl Brandt, Don Colburn, Pete Baum, Herman Belcher; (third row) Coach Ortmayer, Spike Steinberger, Harlan Mummert, Jack Smith, and Warren Mattox.

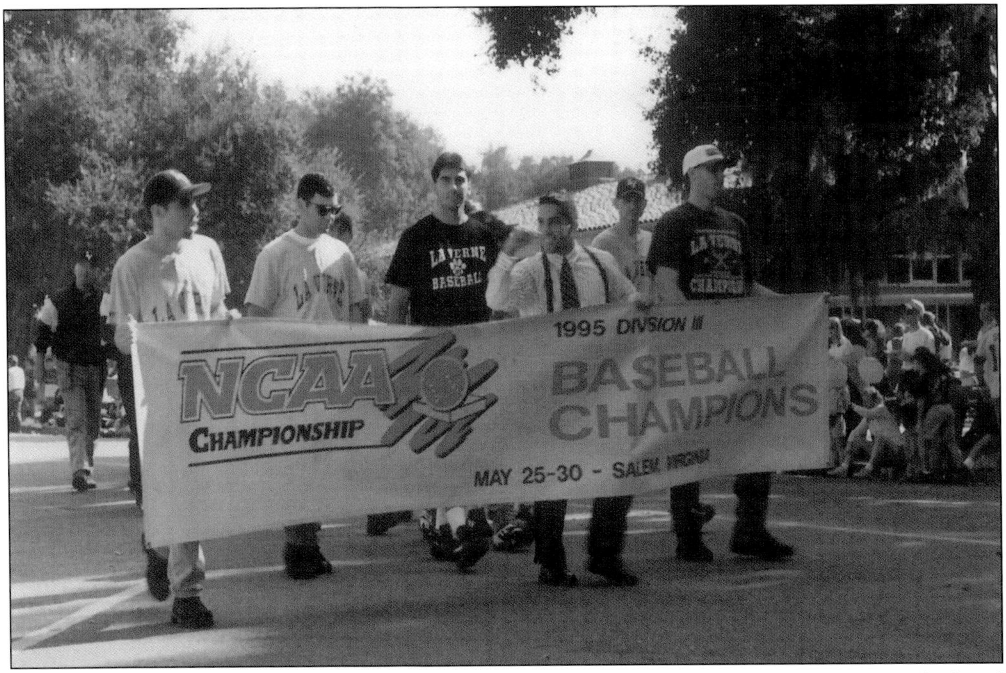

1995 Division III Baseball Champions in Homecoming Parade. Walking just behind the banner are Steve Reyes, Jake Ganajian, Pat Murphy, Eddie Bustamente, and J.T. Romero.

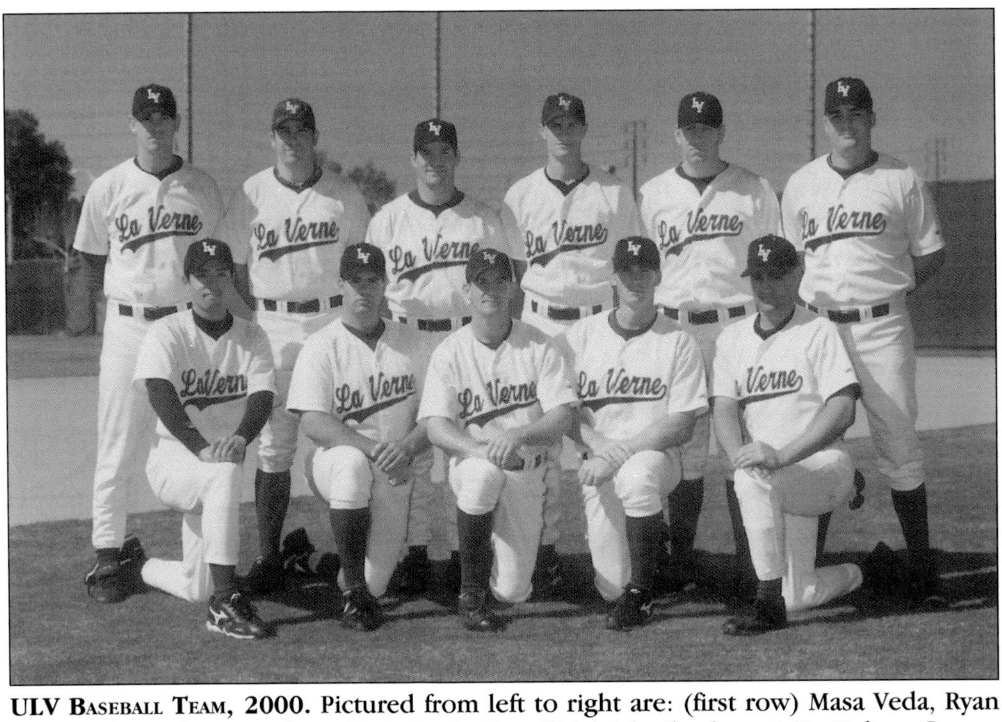

ULV Baseball Team, 2000. Pictured from left to right are: (first row) Masa Veda, Ryan Christoph, Andrew Woolsey, Trek Davis, Bret Kalcivich; (back row) Bo Balzar, Garren Inidian, Coach Bobby Lee, Cory Rooper, Kyle Spielbeiler, and Jay Nerenberg.

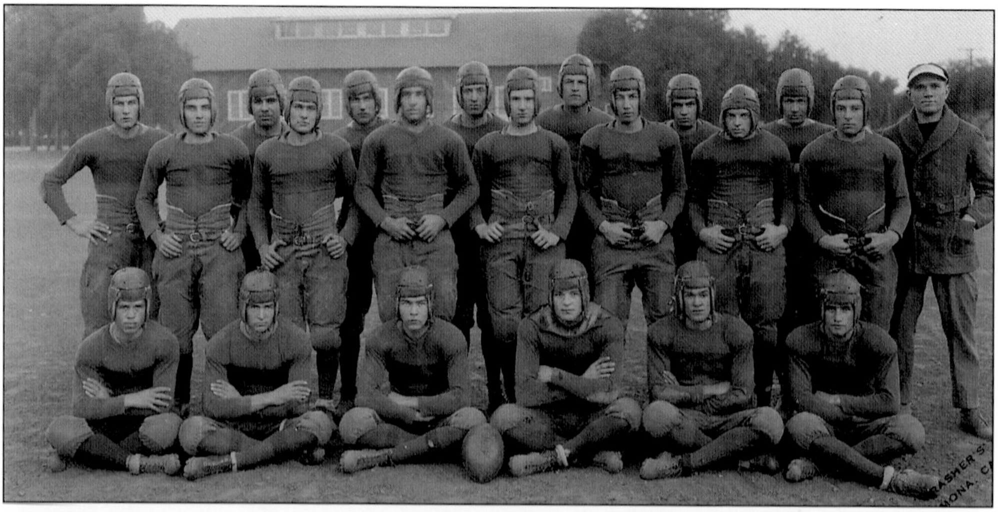

1922 Football Team. Pictured from left to right are: (front row) Raymond Root, Guy Jordan, Alva Brower, John Brooks, Dwight Welch, Ben Hepner; (back row) Bert Betts, Ernest Landis, Ivan Brooks, John Price, Levi Dickey, Jake Goeber, Byrl Harper, Phil Smith, Paul Throne, Howard Beckner, Alvin Marshburn, Chase Harper, Paul Harris Moore, Marion Roynon, and Coach Claude Arnett. (Photographer: Frasher's, Pomona, Cal.)

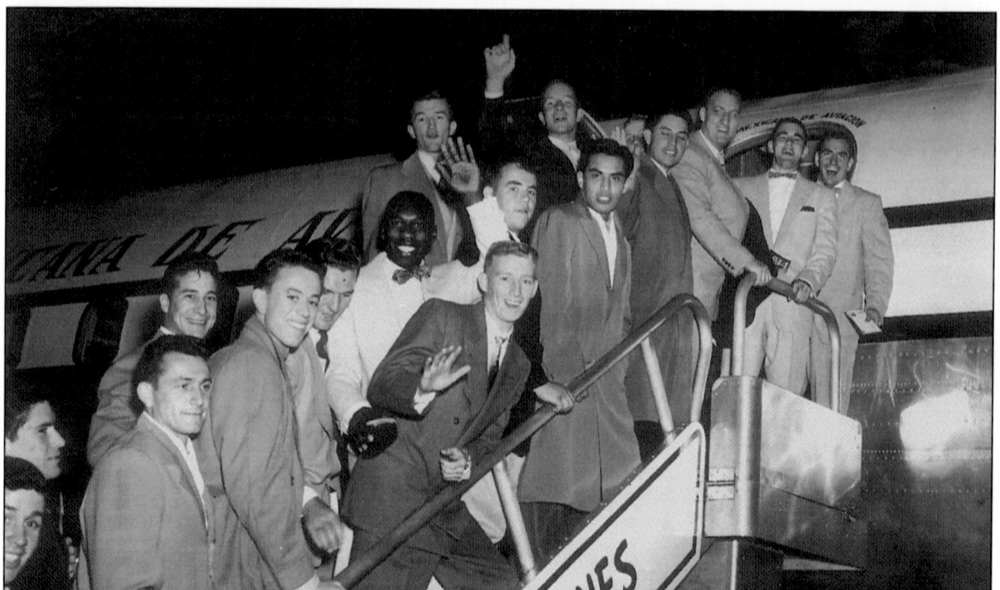

1953 Football Team Traveling to Mexico City to Play Mexico City College. "It was a 5 hour 14 minute flight from Los Angeles to Mexico City. . . . While in Mexico City the team used bottled water and oxygen was furnished at the game because of the high elevation of 7,800 feet." Picture includes half of the traveling group: Dave Diaz, Jack Bridenstein, Jack Smith, Reuben Gonzales, Bob O'Neill, Elvis Cayford, Fred Wilson, Gene Moore, Burton Liskey, Warren Maddox, Fabio Clett, Ron Butterbaugh, Ramon Morales, Emmet Monasco, [Don Bennett], and Bill Swet. (*Campus Times*, November 11, 1953, p. 8.)

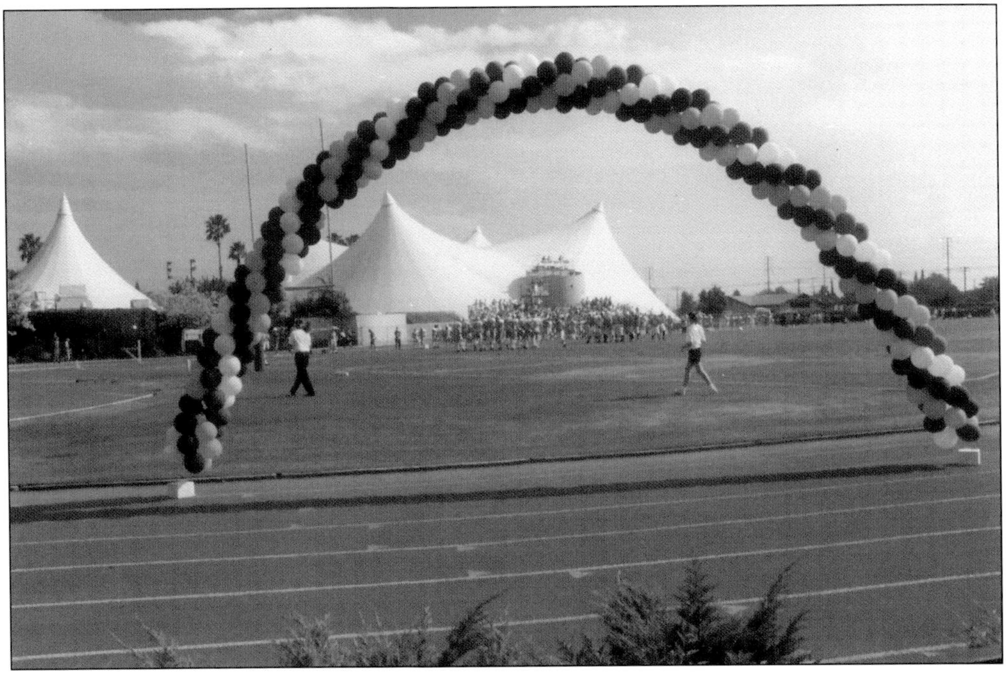

HOMECOMING FOOTBALL GAME, 1990S.

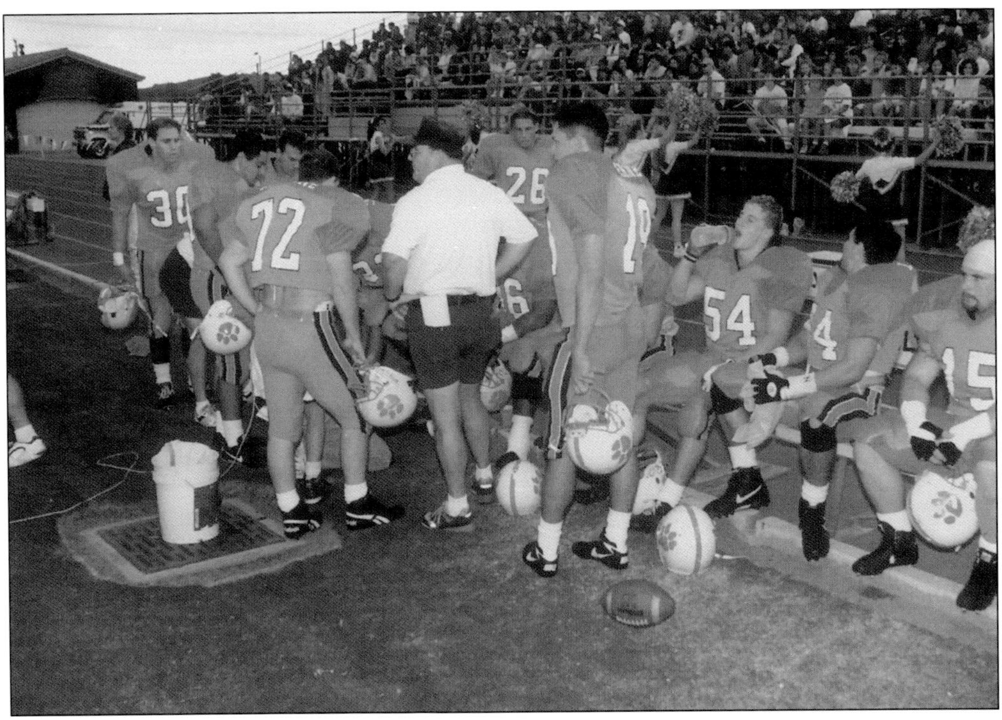

FOOTBALL SIDELINES, 1990S.

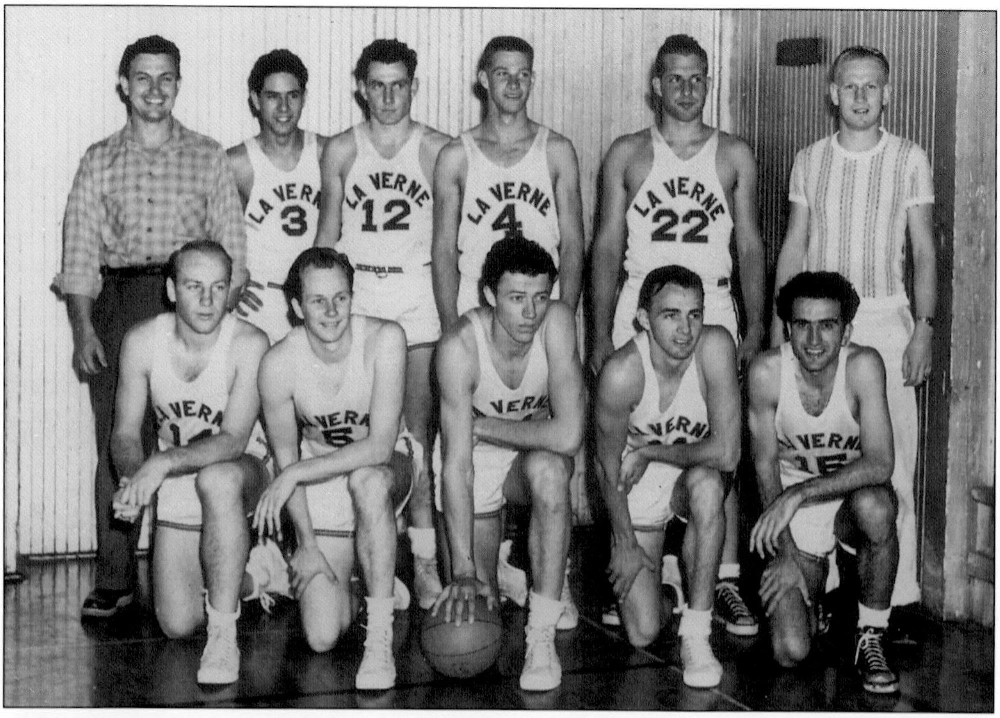

1951 Basketball Team. Pictured from left to right are: (front row) Lerry Teeter, Don Colburn, Bill O'Neill, Bill Landis, Nate Cisneros; (back row) Coach Dwight Hanawalt, Bobby Chavez, Jack Smith, Daryl Brandt, Dick Hepner, and Manager Mel Baughman.

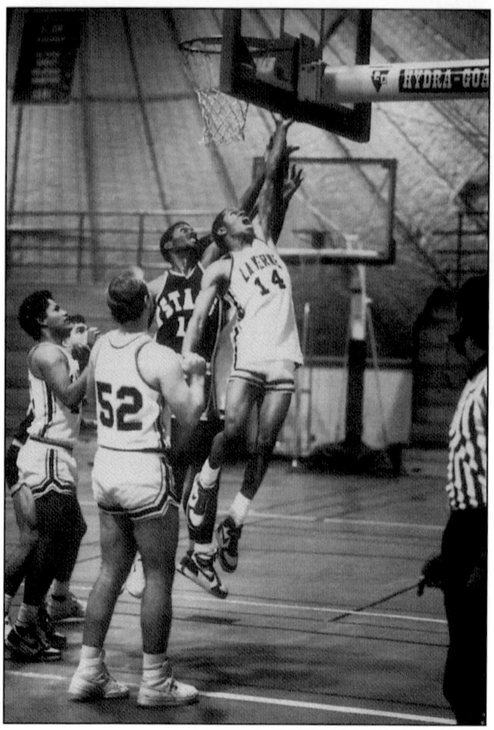

1987 JV Basketball Players. La Verne is in white, playing against Claremont. Players are Rob Hernandez, Dan Nazarek, and David Lawrence. (Photographer: Cindy Darby.)

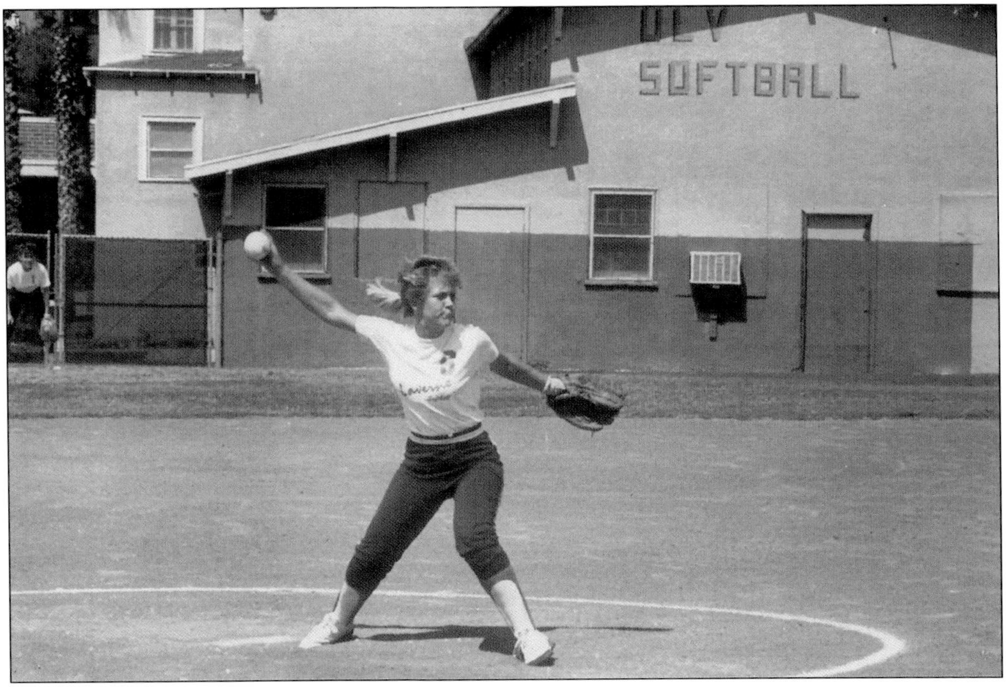

Women's Softball Player, Wendy Snyder, 1987. (Photographer: Albert L.)

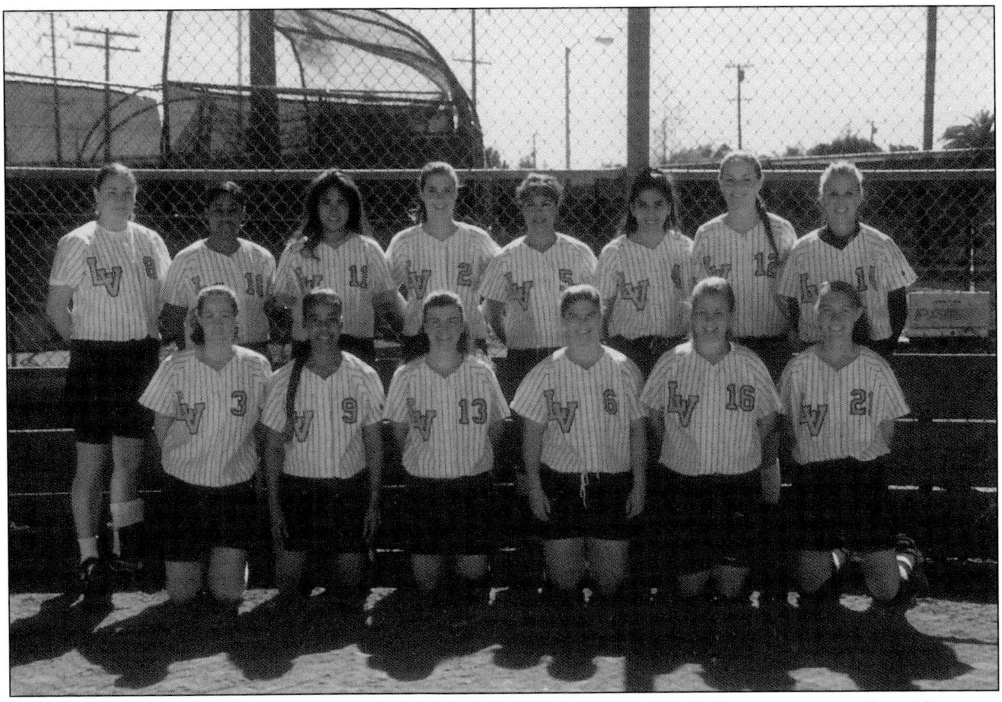

Women's Softball Team, 1997. Pictured left to right are: Katie Minor, Latika Clayton, Teresa Garcia, Jamie Anderson, Lil Lomeli, Jennifer Thompson, Lindsey Weber, Lori Grey, Michelle Geiger, Angel Mejico, Kelly Perkins, Jamie Pool, Teresa DaValle, and Jenna Bowman.

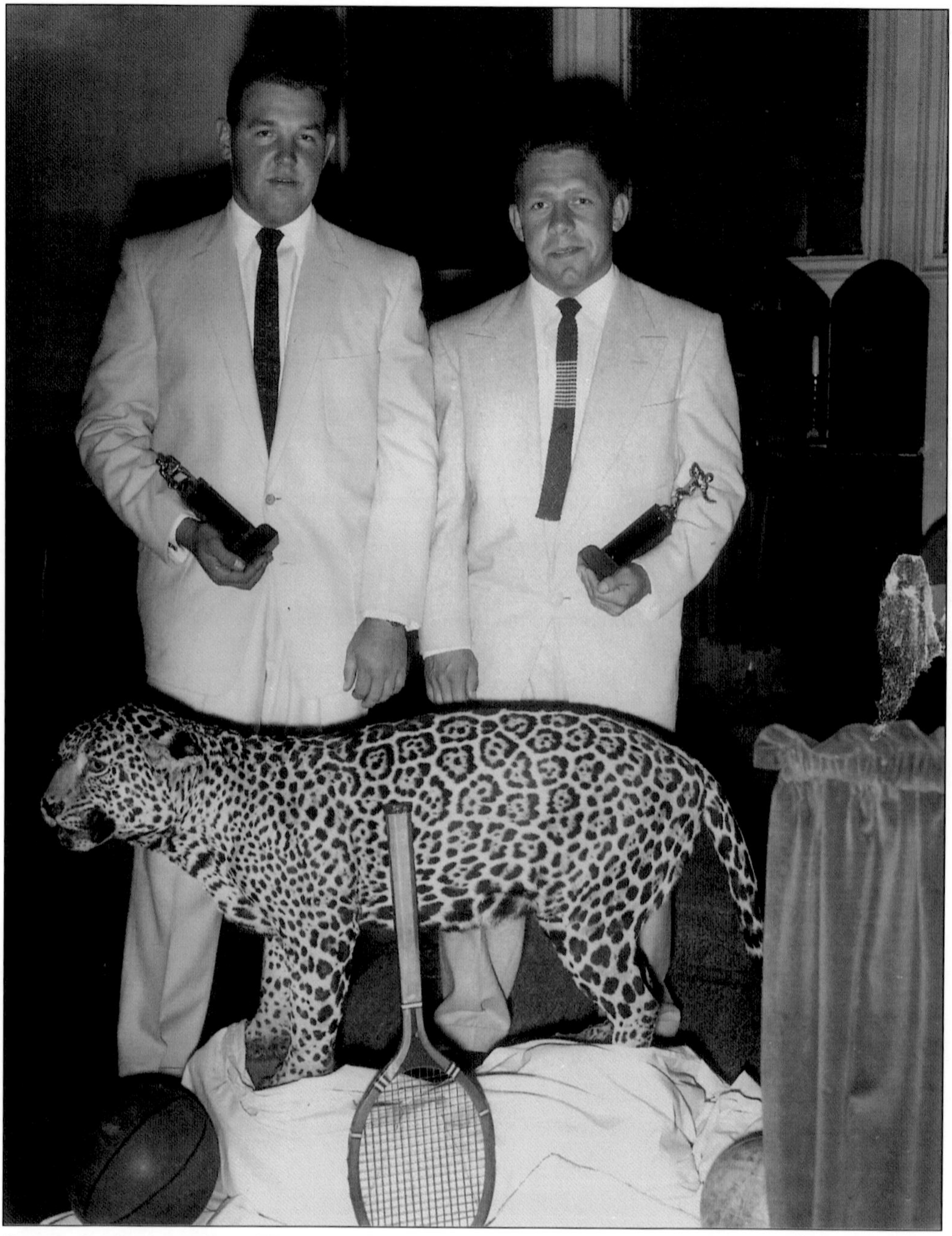

Sports Awards for Dick Hart and Jim Milhon, Posing with Leo, 1958.

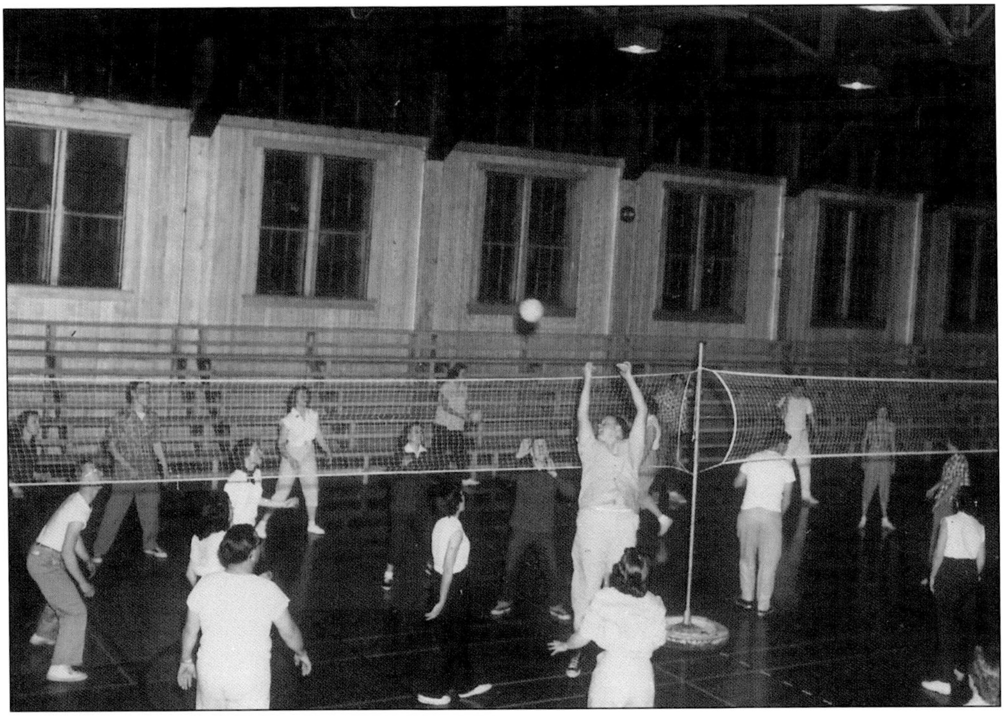

Intramural Volleyball Game, 1950s.

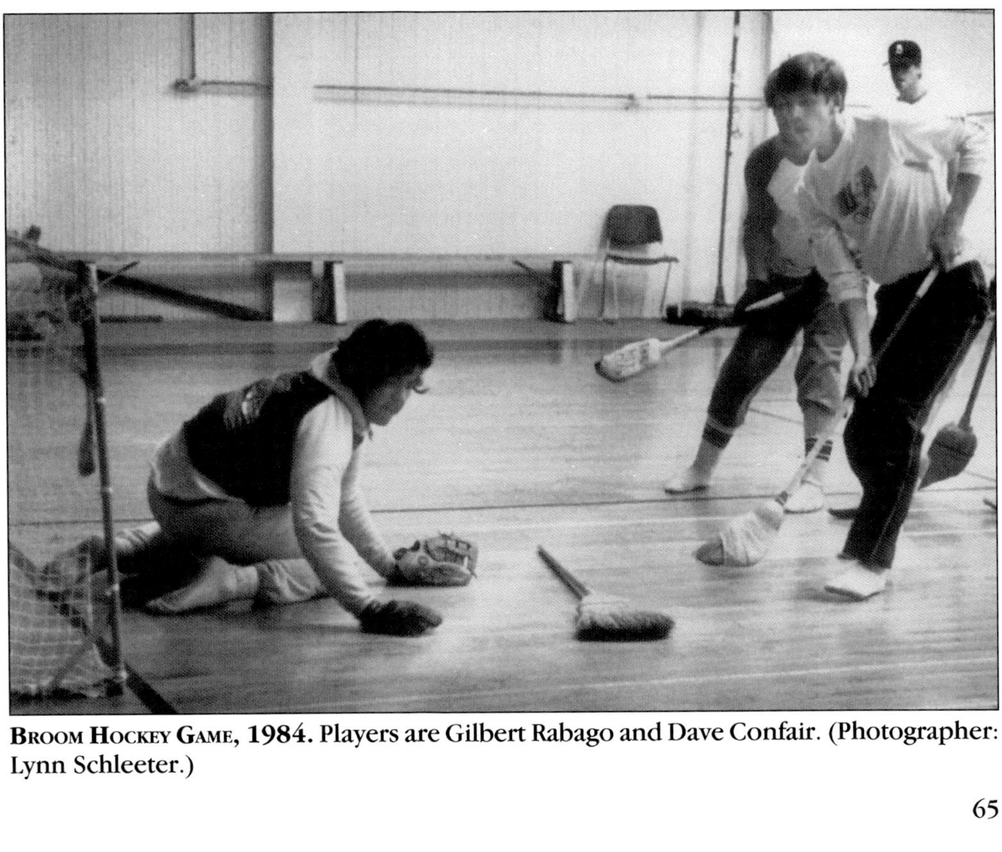

Broom Hockey Game, 1984. Players are Gilbert Rabago and Dave Confair. (Photographer: Lynn Schleeter.)

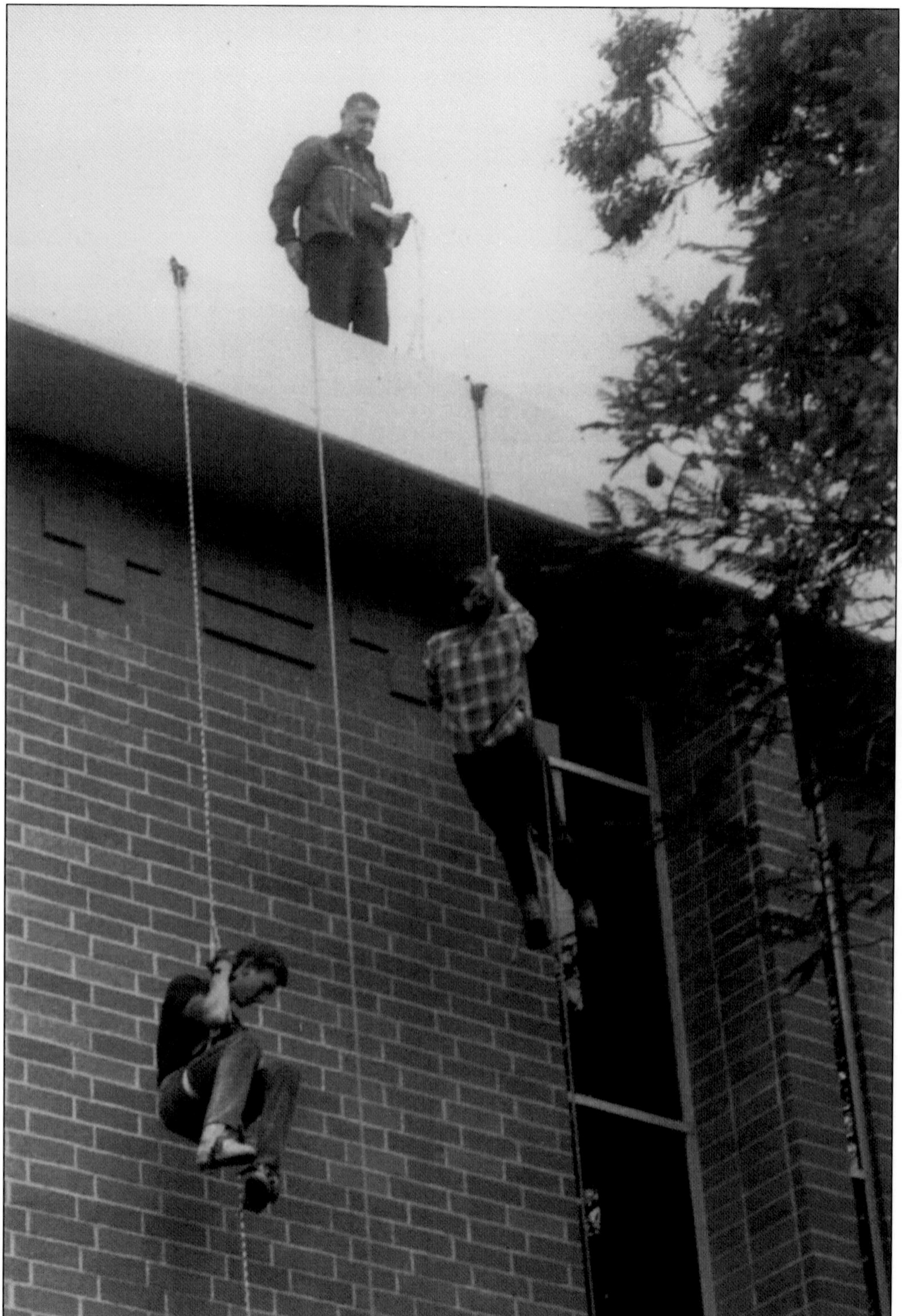

COACH ROLAND ORTMAYER INSTRUCTING HIS CLIMBING CLASS FROM THE ROOF OF THE SCIENCE AND EDUCATION BUILDING, 1988–89.

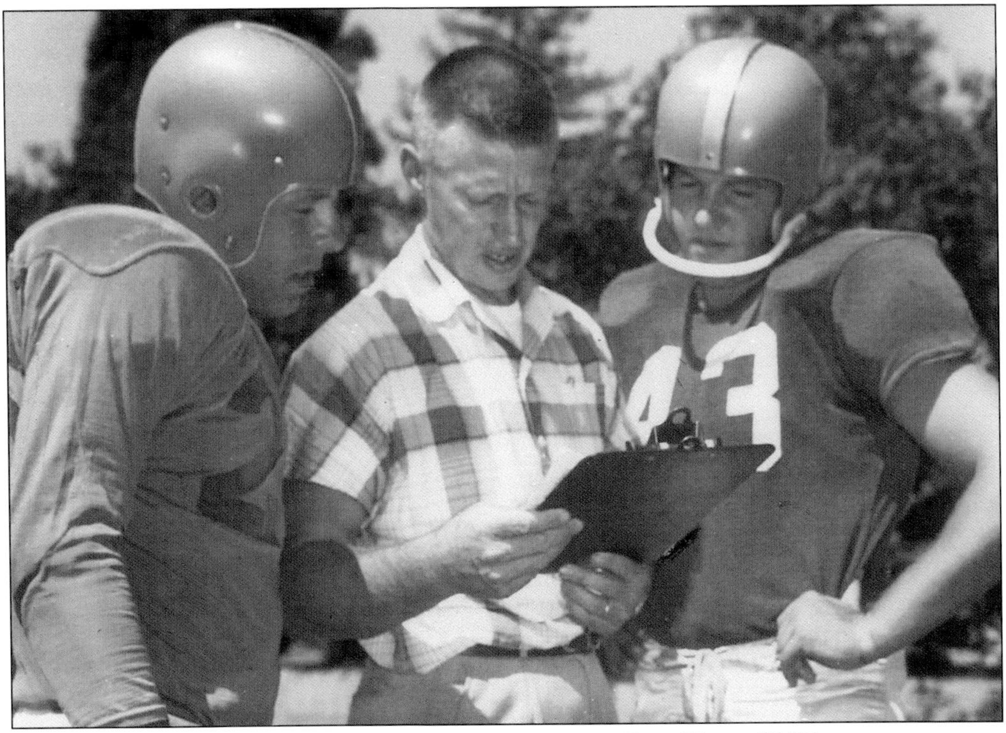

Coach Roland Ortmayer, Center, with Jim Milhon and Dick Hart, 1957.

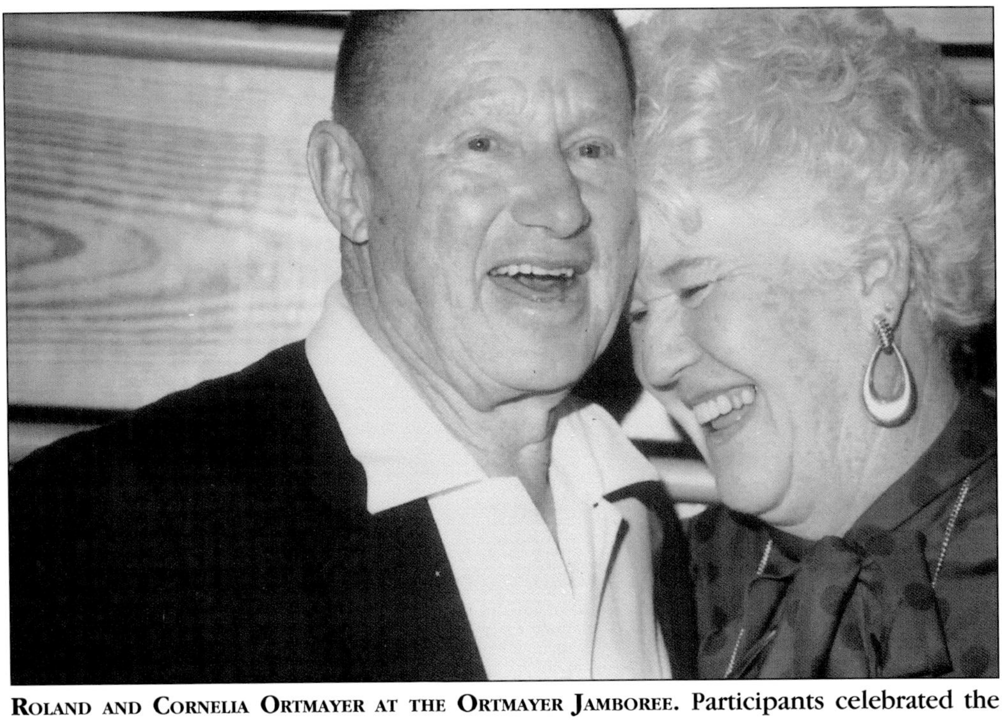

Roland and Cornelia Ortmayer at the Ortmayer Jamboree. Participants celebrated the Ortmayers' years of service to La Verne.

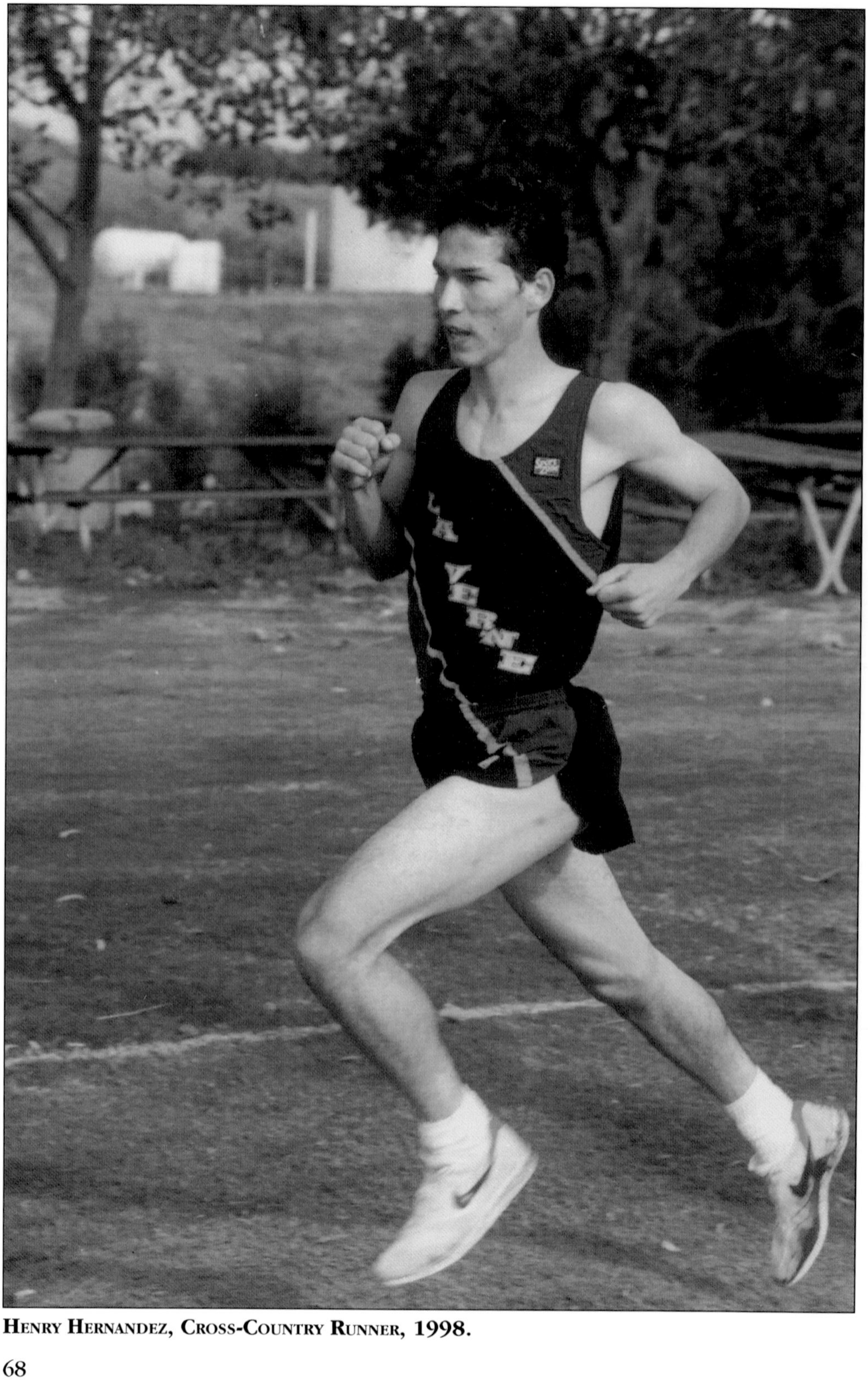

HENRY HERNANDEZ, CROSS-COUNTRY RUNNER, 1998.

Five

Campus Living and Eating Experiences

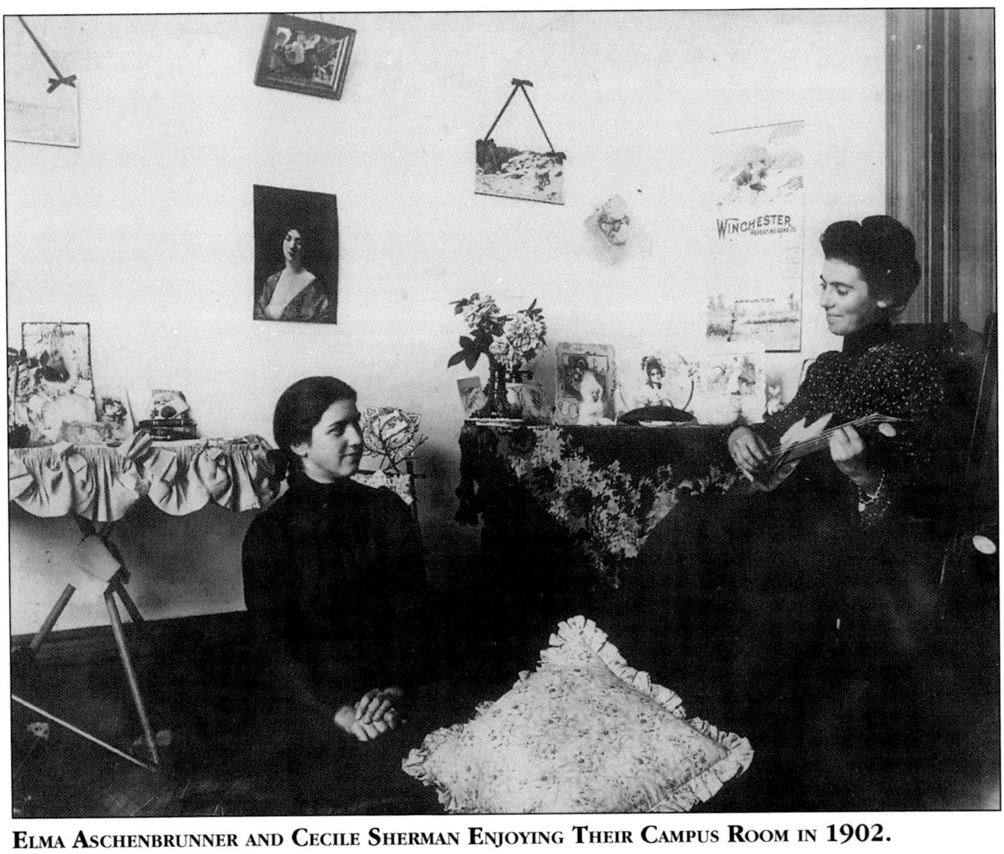

Elma Aschenbrunner and Cecile Sherman Enjoying Their Campus Room in 1902.

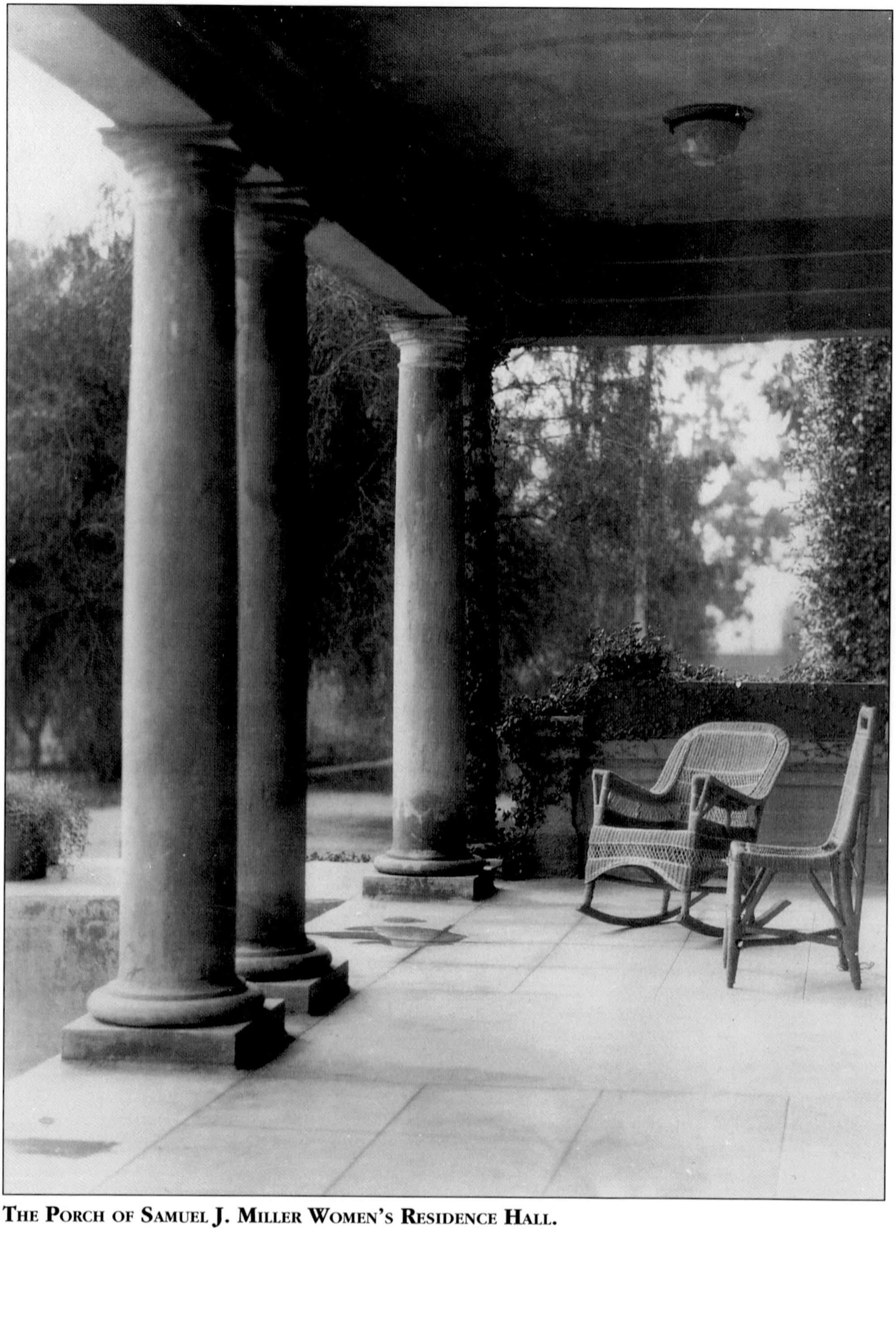

THE PORCH OF SAMUEL J. MILLER WOMEN'S RESIDENCE HALL.

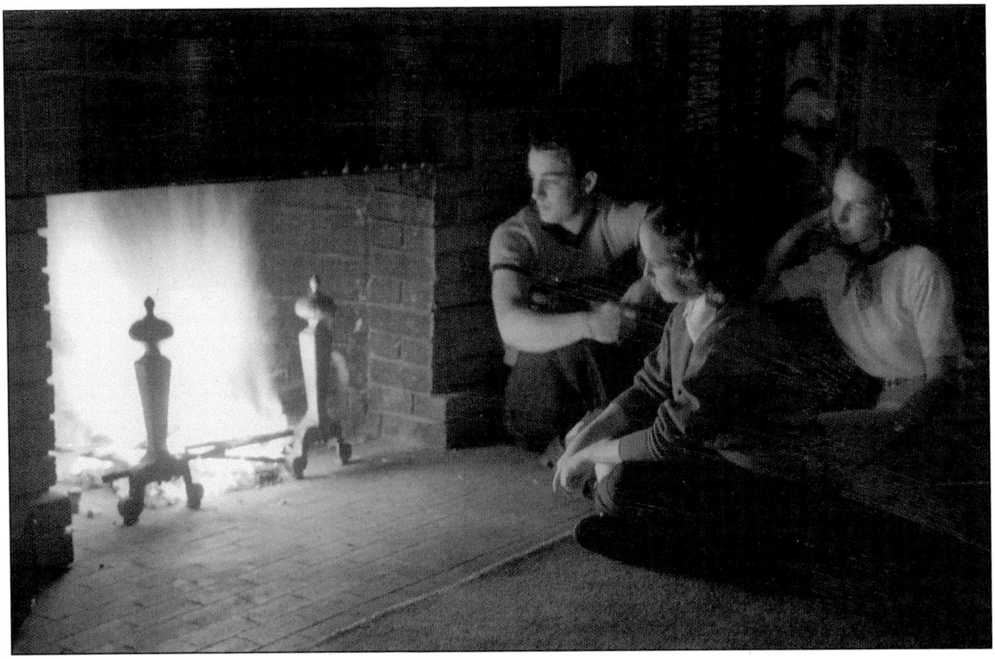

ENJOYING THE FIREPLACE IN MILLER HALL LOUNGE, 1951.

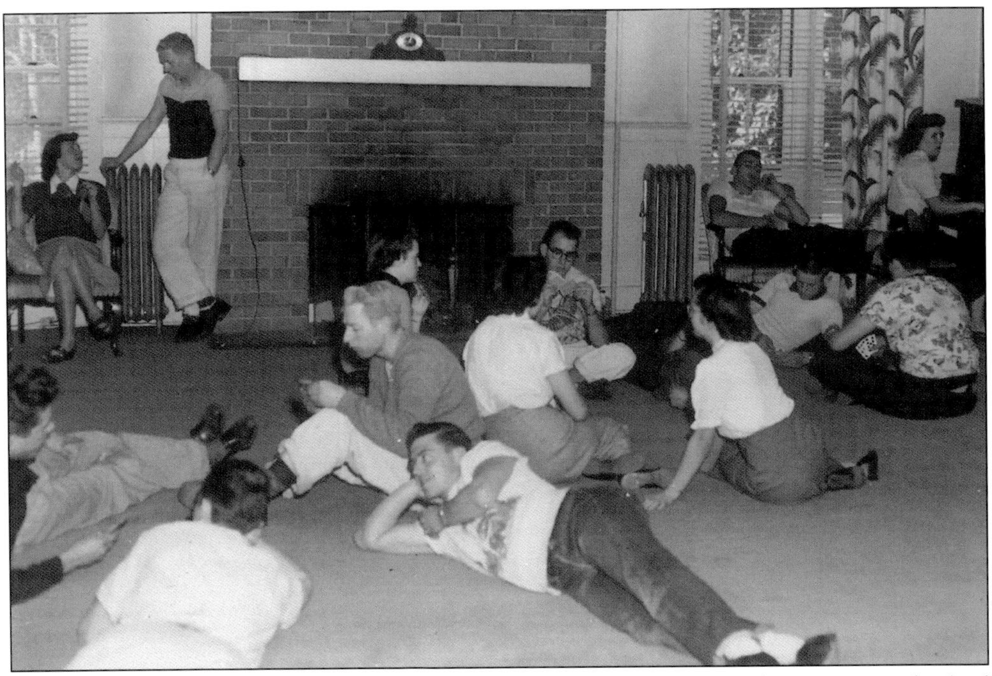

AFTER DINNER RELAXATION IN MILLER HALL LOUNGE, 1950s. "Many good times are to be had in Miller Hall. Everything from breakfast at 7:00 a.m. to the spreads in the wee hours of the night-life centers in the dorm. The lobby is the place for just plain fun after lunch and dinner. A toy box is chuck full of checkers, dominoes, chess, and Chinese checkers—just everything to occupy little minds at rest. Miller Hall is the center of many happy memories for L.V.C.ers." (*Campus Times*, October 21, 1953, p. 3.)

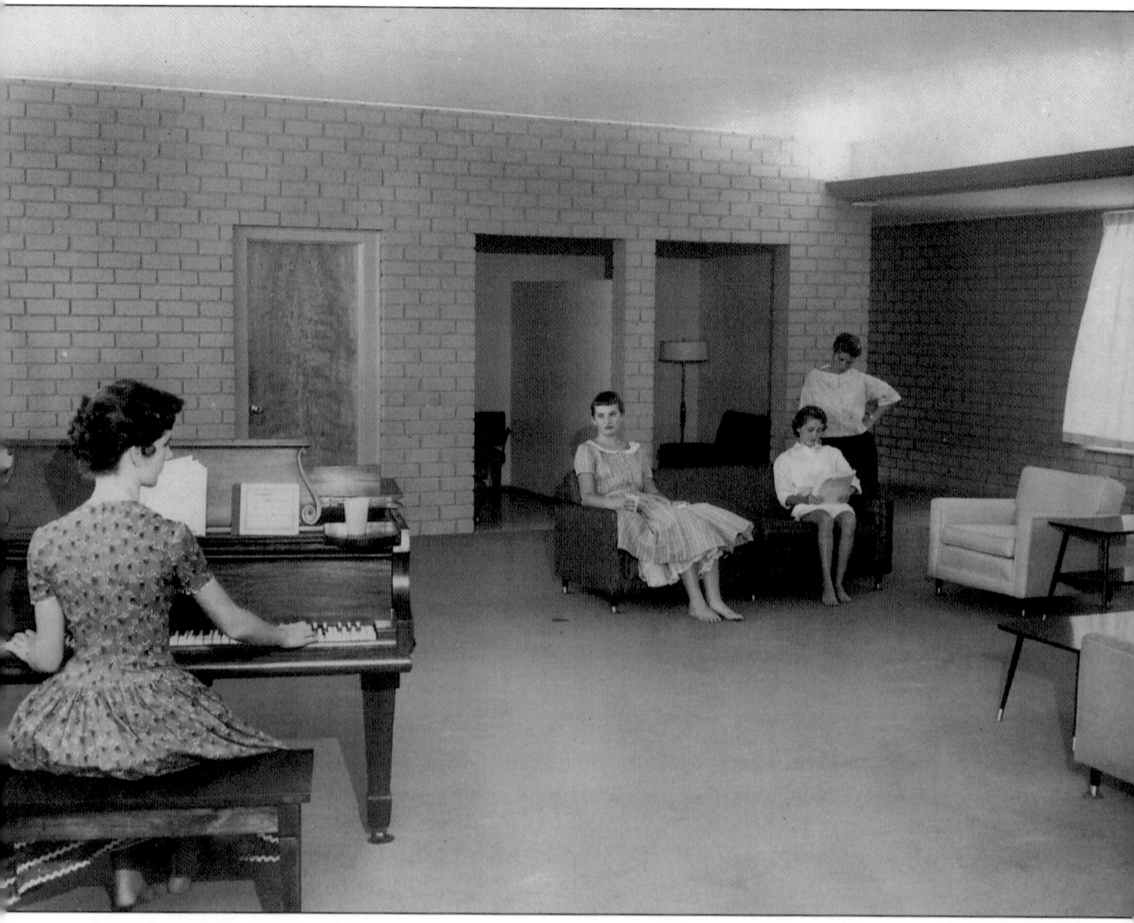

Studebaker-Hanawalt Women's Residence Lounge, 1957. Pictured are Deanne Buckendorff, Myrna Long, Nancy Ingram, and an unidentified person.

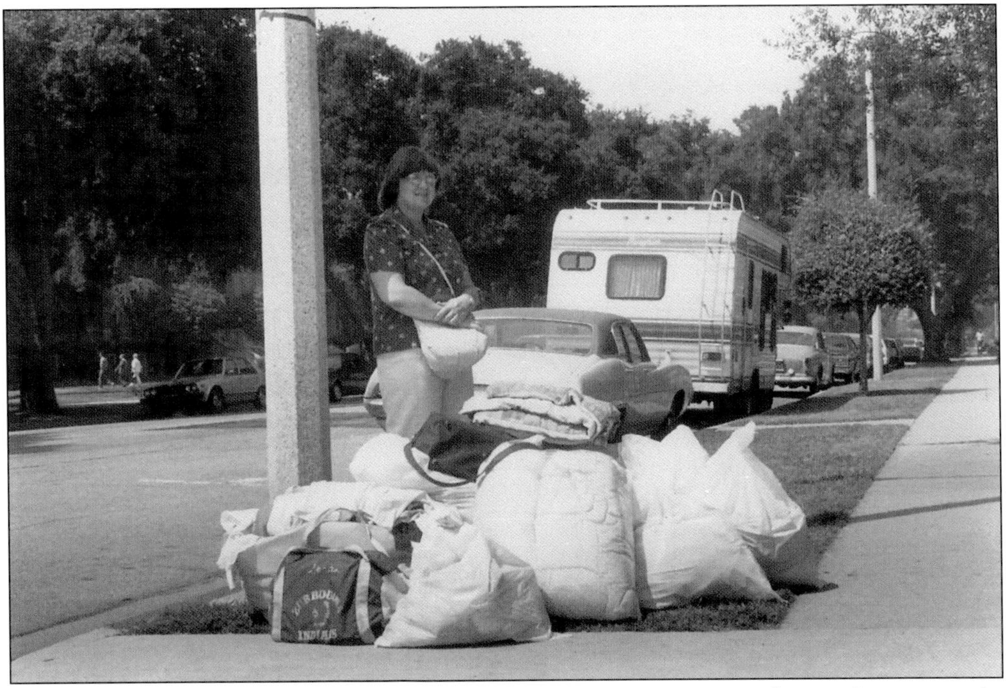

Mrs. Penny Tinnell Stands Guard. Her daughter, Terry, moved into her room in Studebaker-Hanawalt Residence Hall in 1983. (Photographer: Susan Chenea.)

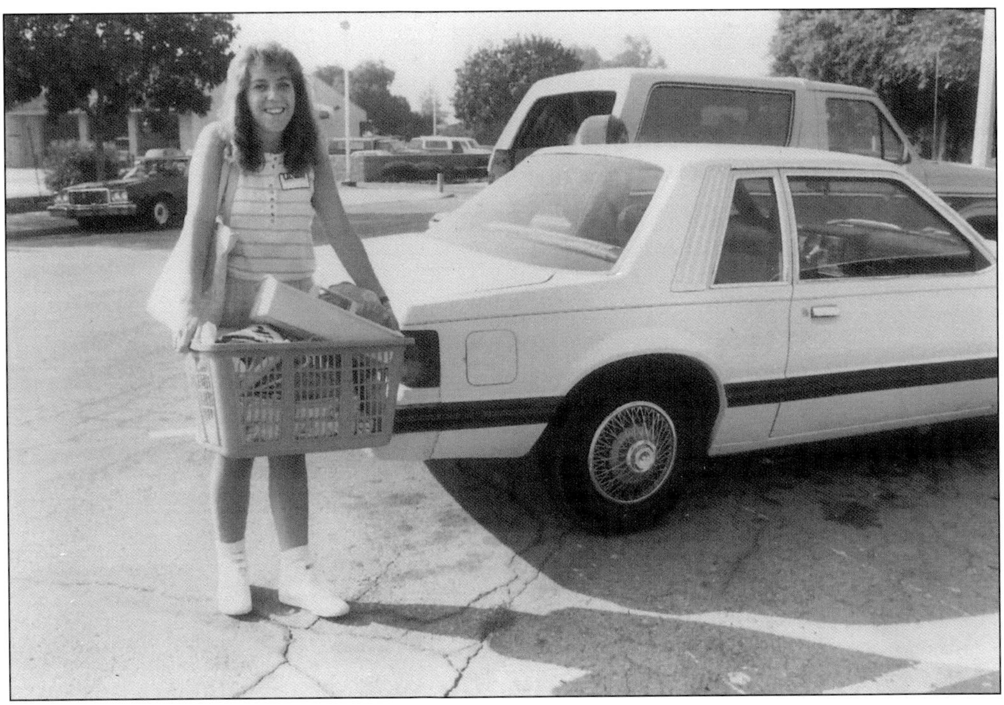

Keri Rock On Move-In Day, 1988.

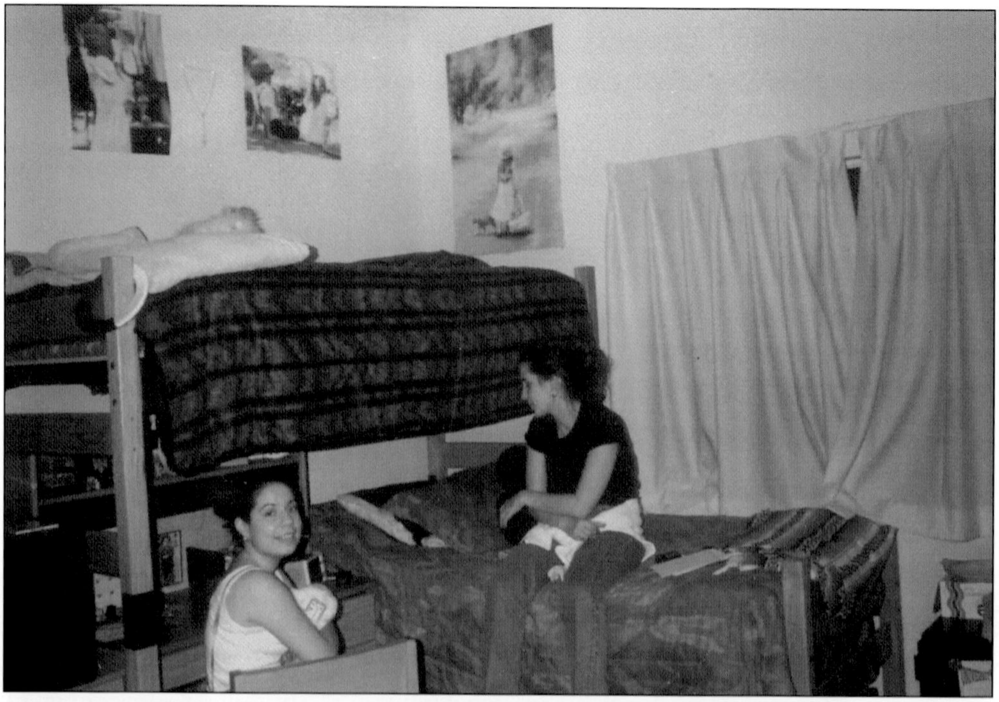

1990s Dorm Room. Residents pictured are Aurora Montiel and Julie Mayer.

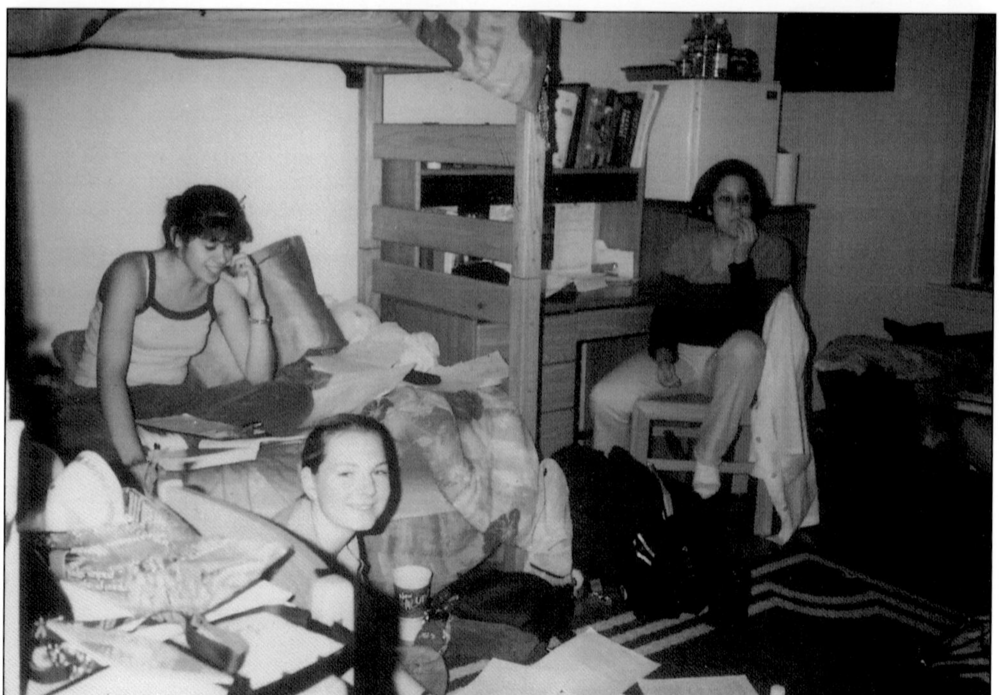

1990s Dorm Room. Residents pictured are Gloria Ramirez, Alena Vlna, and Mindy Salazar.

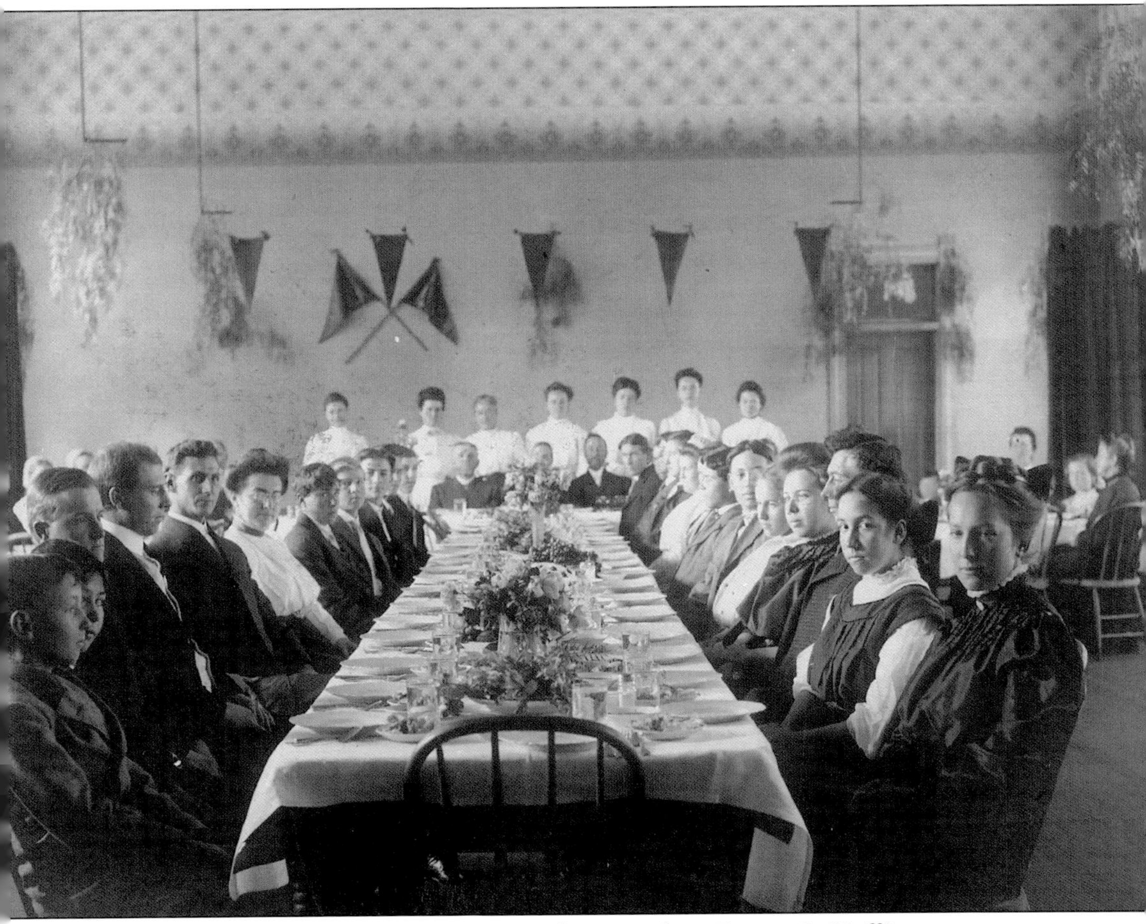

THANKSGIVING DINNER ON CAMPUS IN 1908. (Photographer: Ernest G. Hoff.)

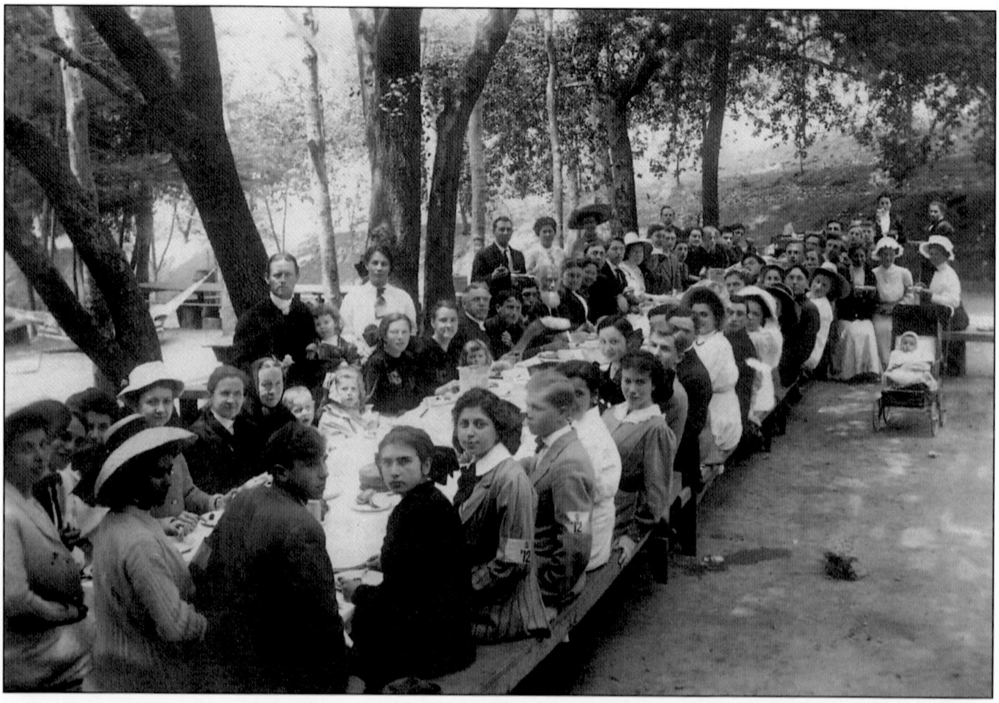

Students and Friends at Lordsburg College May Day Picnic at Stoddard's Canyon, 1910.

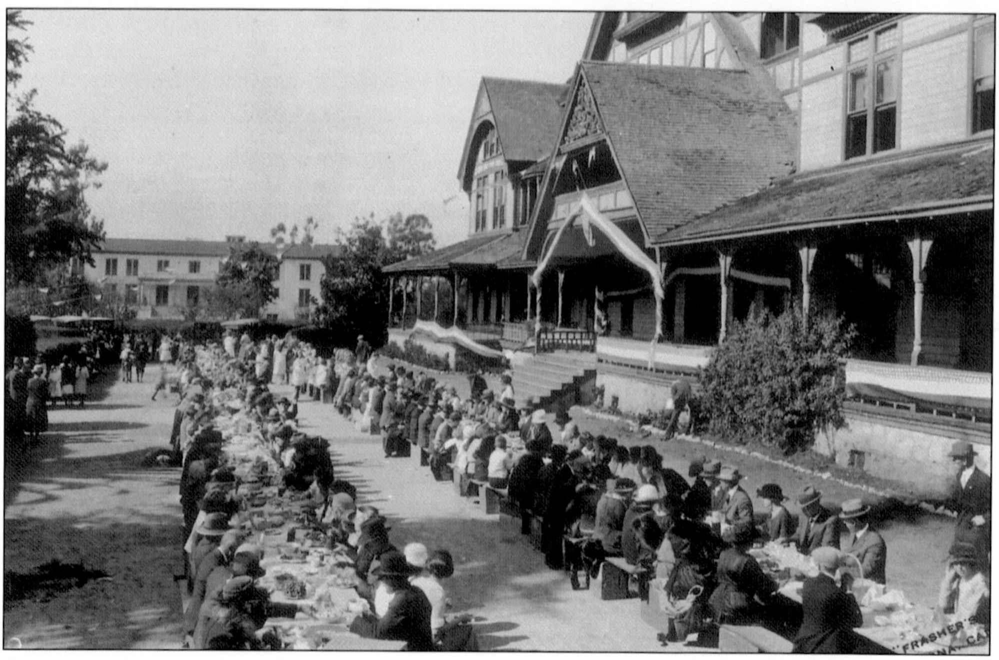

Armistice Day Picnic, 1919, in Front of College Building With the Newly Completed Miller Hall in the Distance. The two oak trees on the lawn west of the present Wilson Library were planted on this day with rocks and plaques honoring students who had died in World War I. (Photographer: Frasher Photo.)

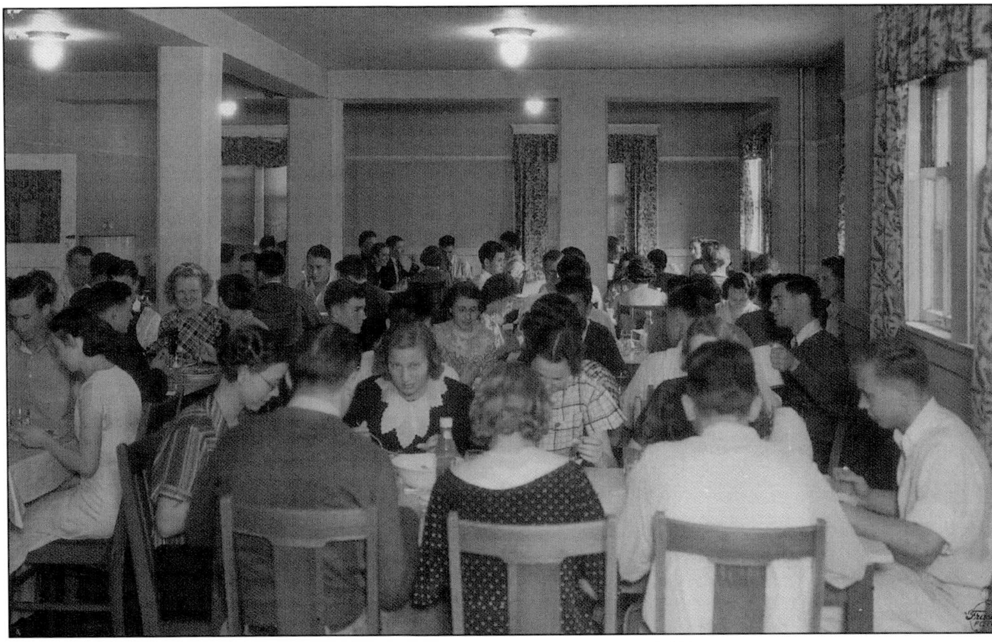

A Crowded Dining Hall in Miller Hall Basement, Early 1950s.

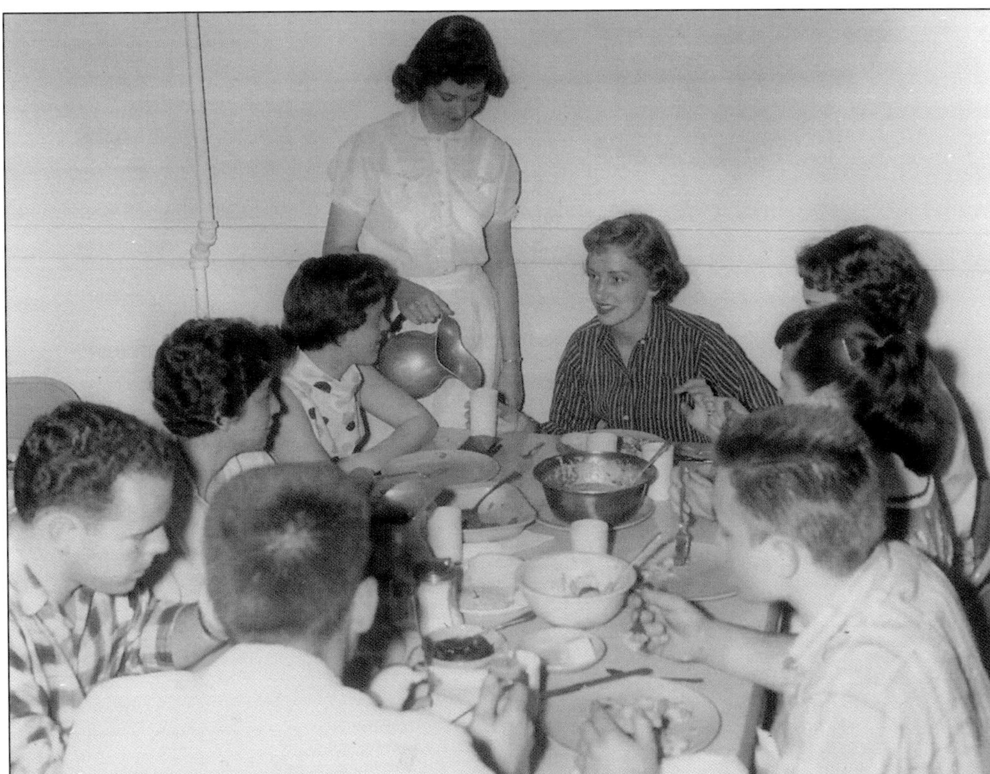

Miller Dining Hall Even More Crowded By 1959. Diners include Don Kindell, Angel Azar, Roberta Garman, Lenore Wilkinson, and Sharon Burton.

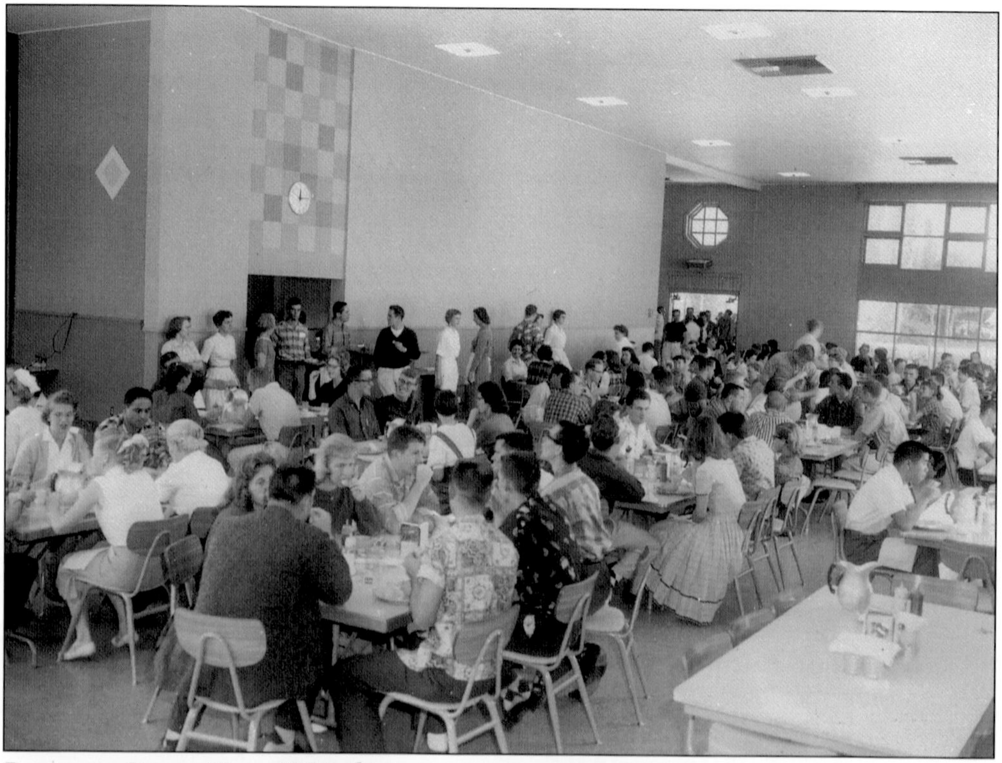

Davenport Dining Hall, 1959–60.

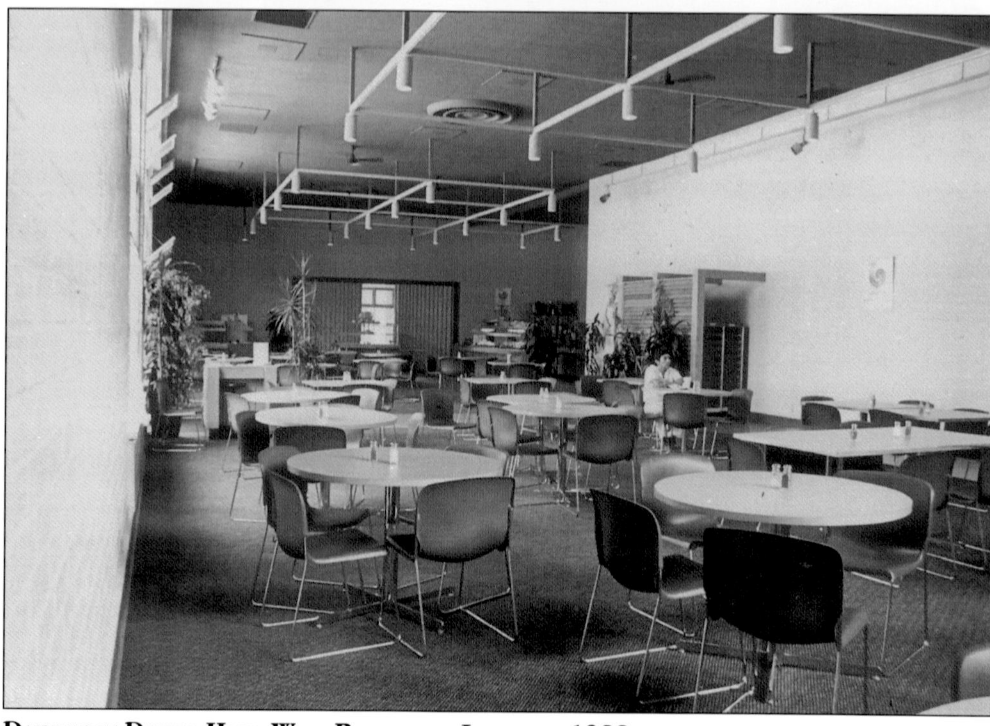

Davenport Dining Hall, With Remodeled Interior, 1988.

LUNCH IN THE QUAD BETWEEN FOUNDERS AND MILLER HALLS. Pictured are Mascot Leo and religion professor Jonathan Reed.

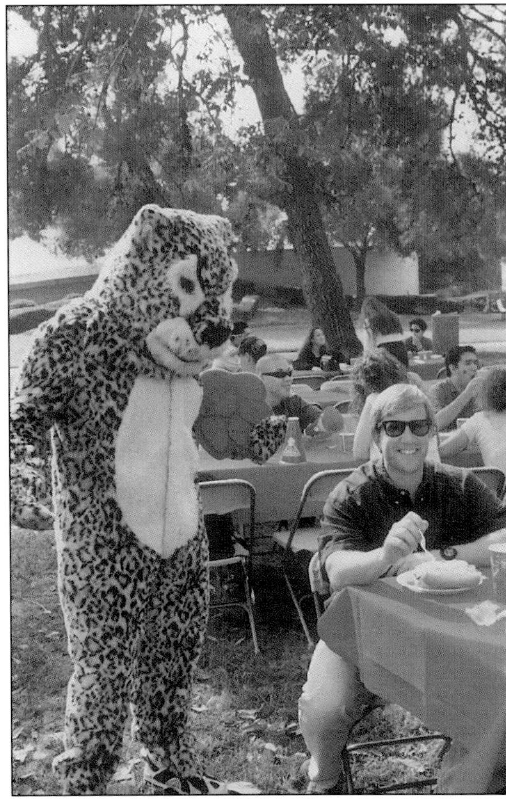

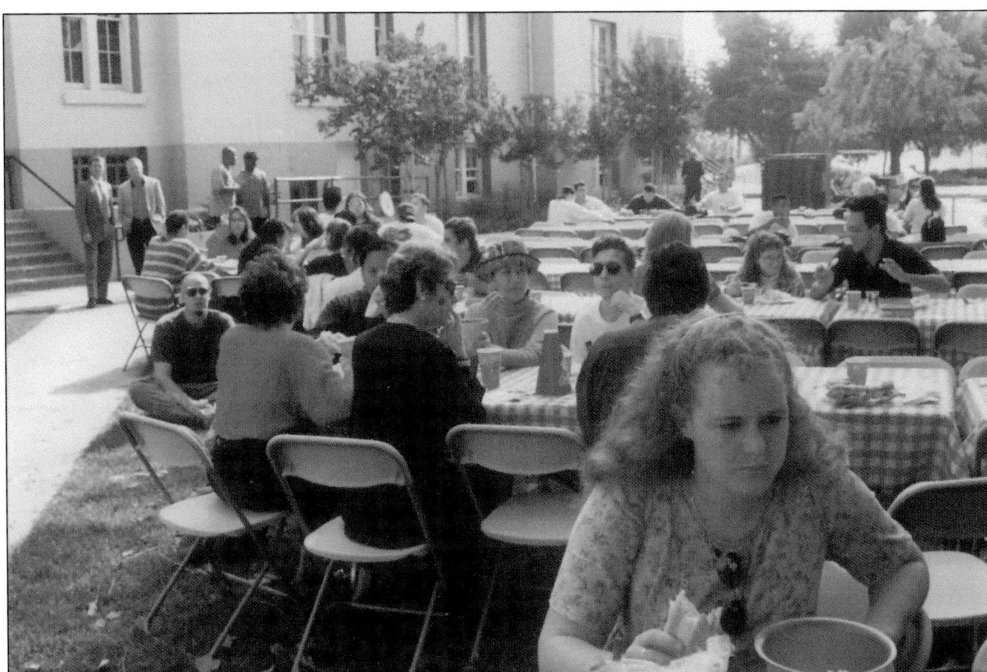

LUNCH IN THE QUAD WITH PROSPECTIVE STUDENTS.

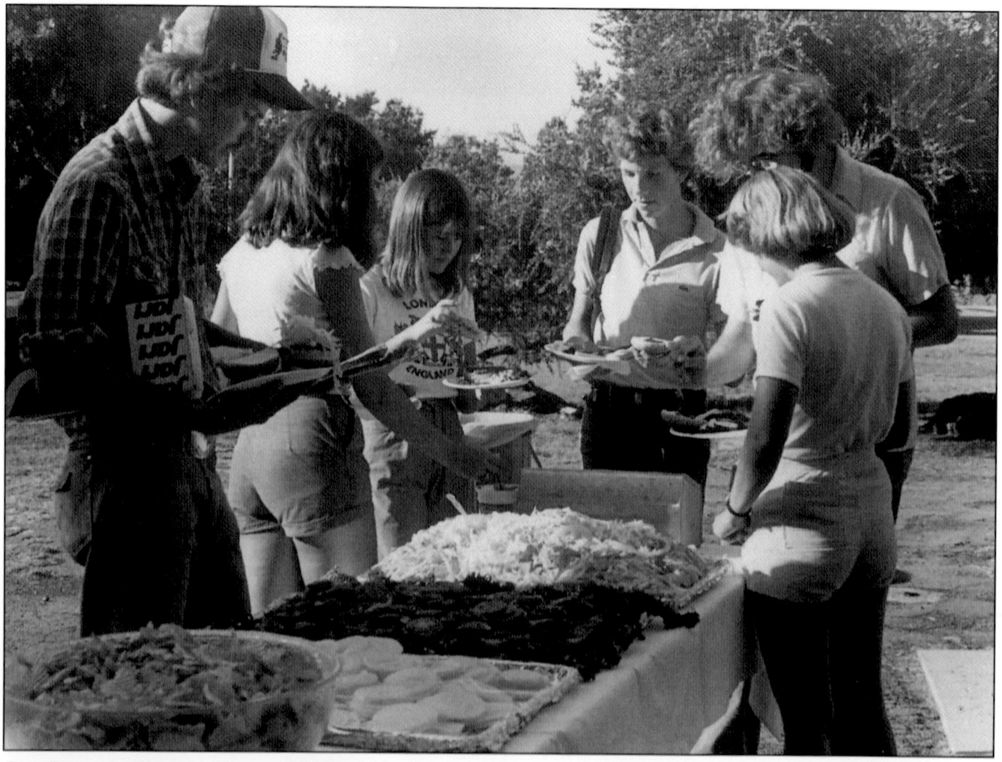

ALL SCHOOL PICNIC, EARLY 1980S.

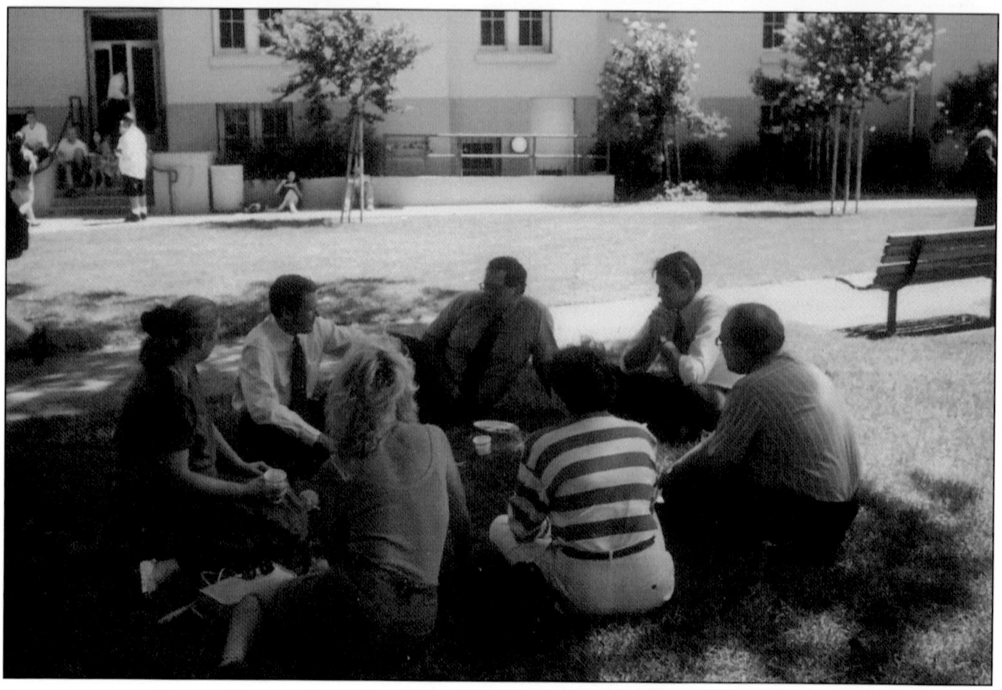

LUNCH ON THE LAWN. Pictured are President Steve Morgan, Dean John Gingrich, Dean Bill Relf, and Professors Aghop Der Kerabetian, Kathy Lamkin, Sharon Davis, and Kim Martin.

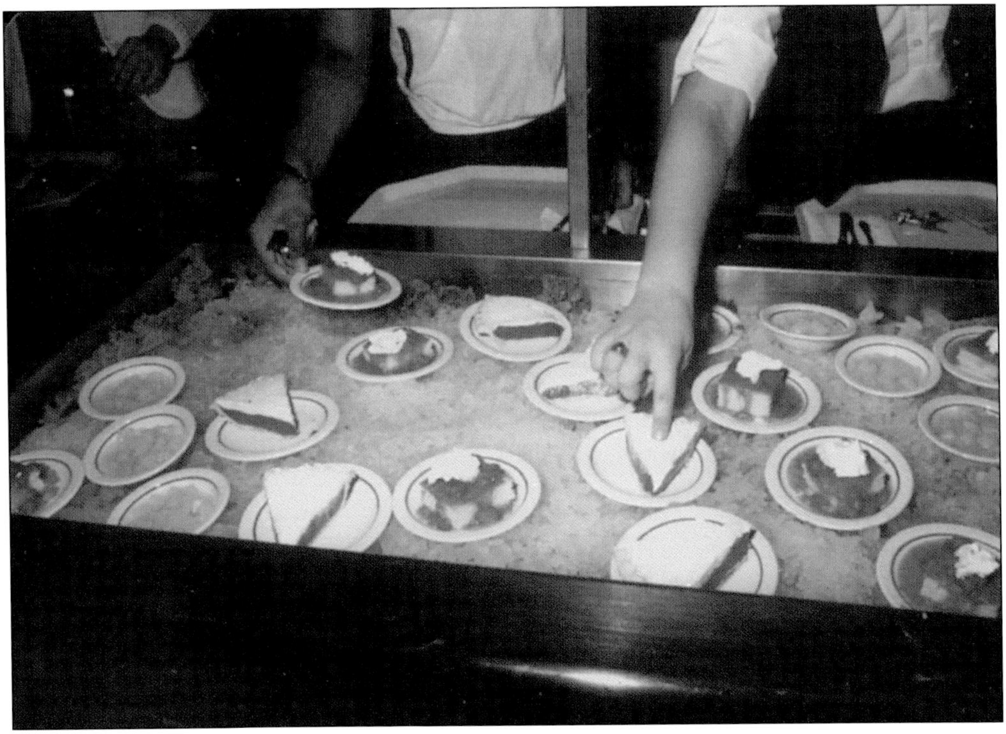

THIS PIECE OF PIE IS MINE!

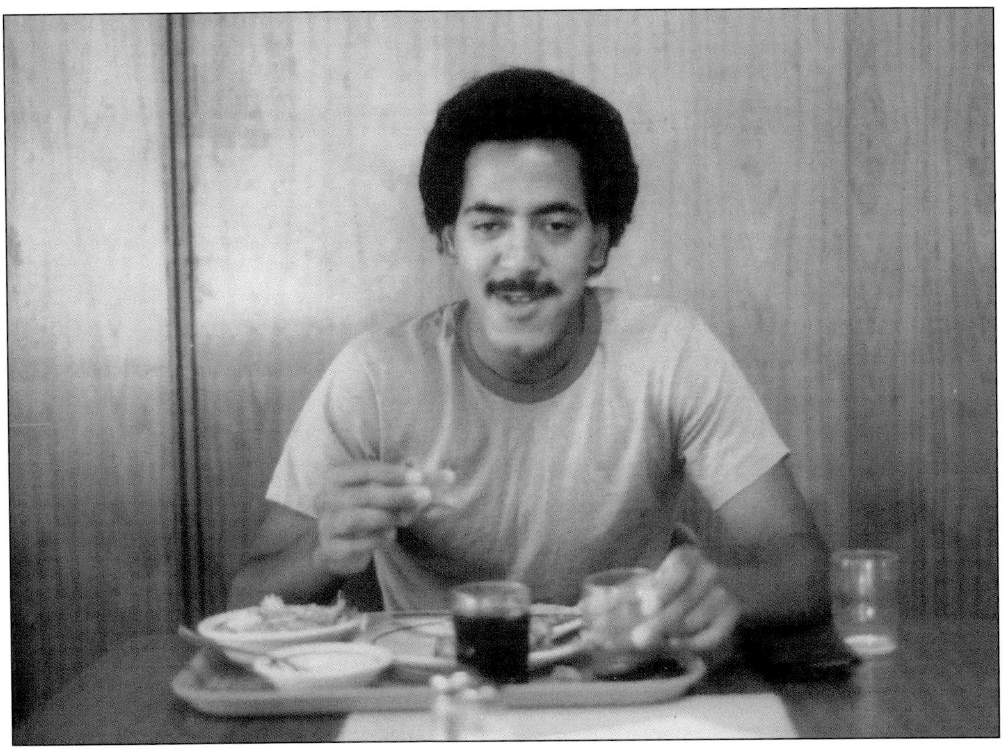

ROBERT ROSA ENJOYING LUNCH, 1980S.

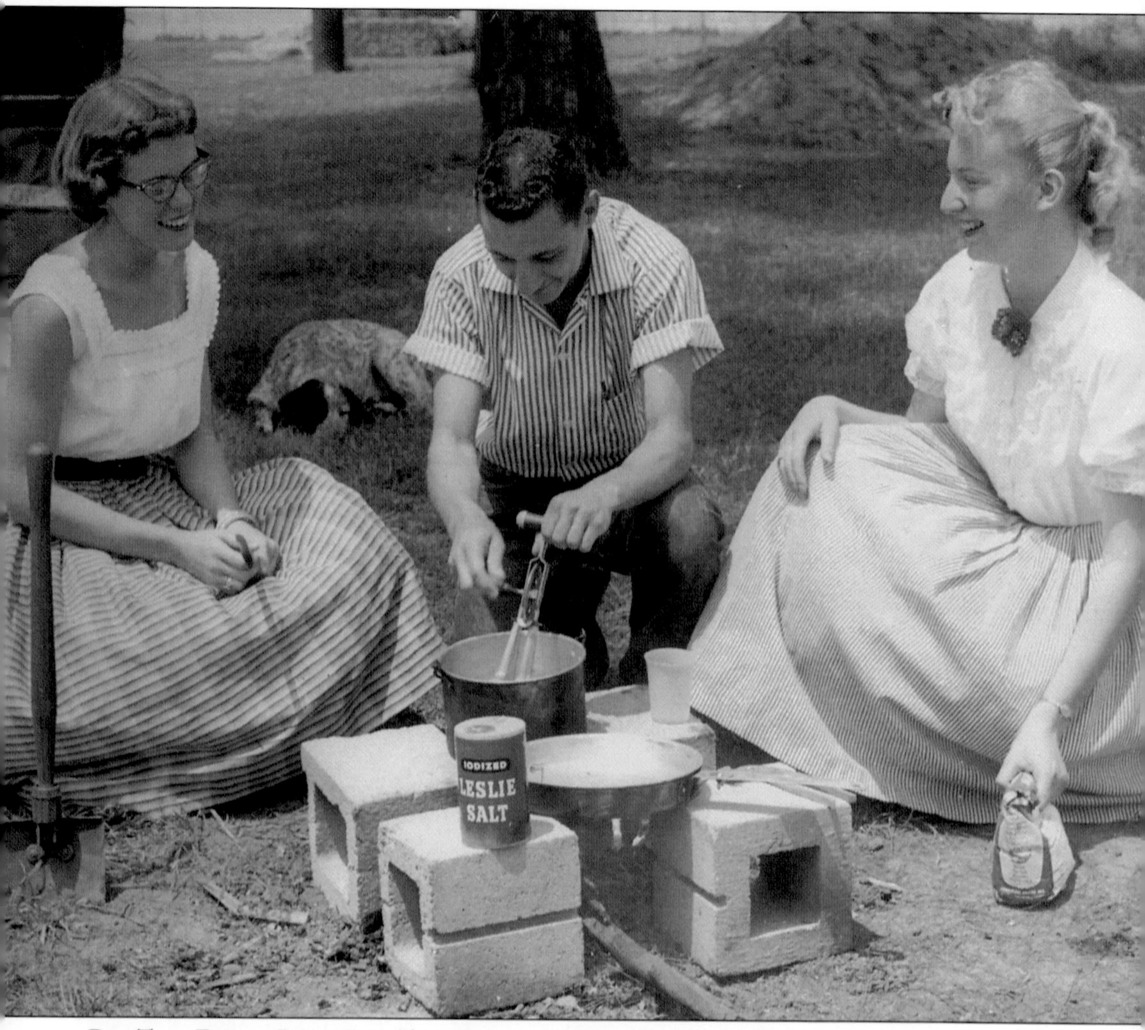

Did They Really Dress Like This When the "Real" Camping Meal was Prepared? Campers shown are Pat Tennyson, Bob Pucci, and Phyllis Long, 1958.

Six

Campus Scenes, Traditions, Signs, and Centennial

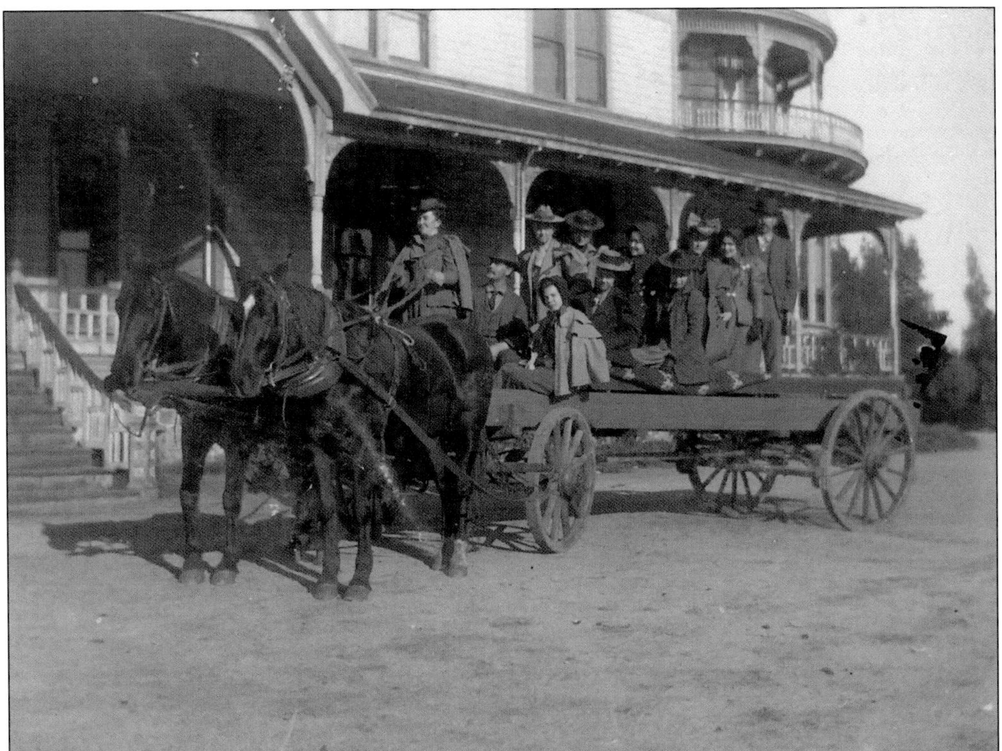

A Wagon Load in Front of Lordsburg College, 1890s. (Gift of Henry Kuns' Descendants, 1999.)

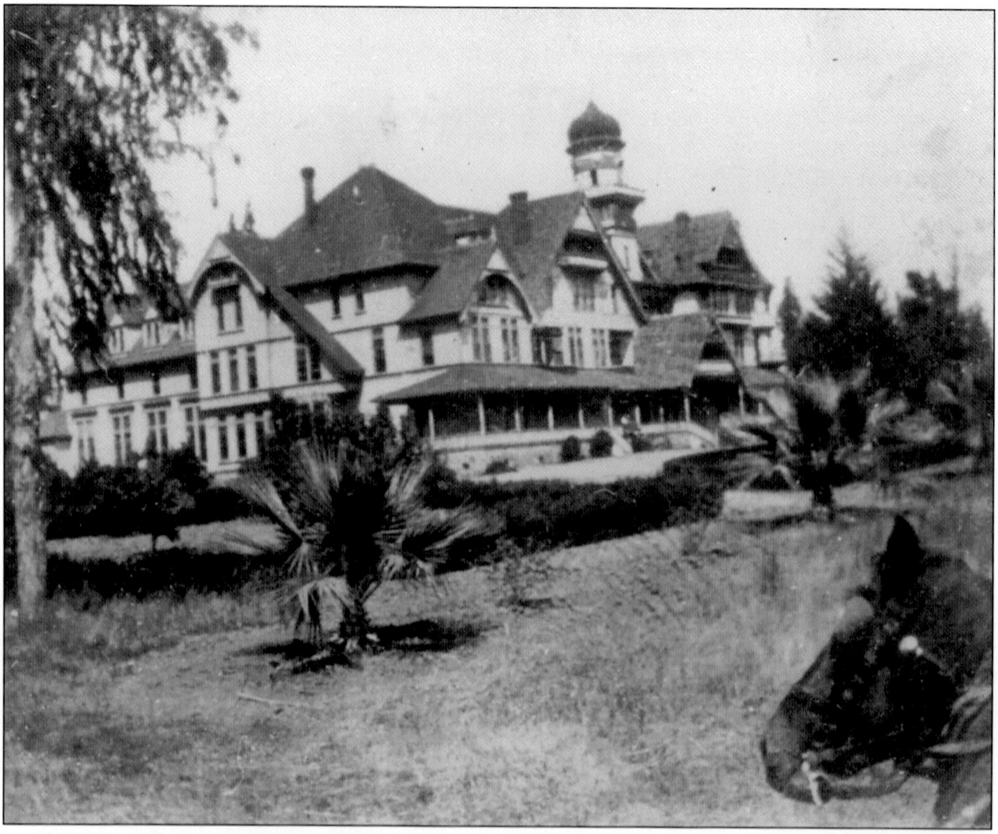

Lordsburg College, May 21, 1891. This picture is taken from the corner of Second and C Streets. Palms still stand on Second Street 109 years later.

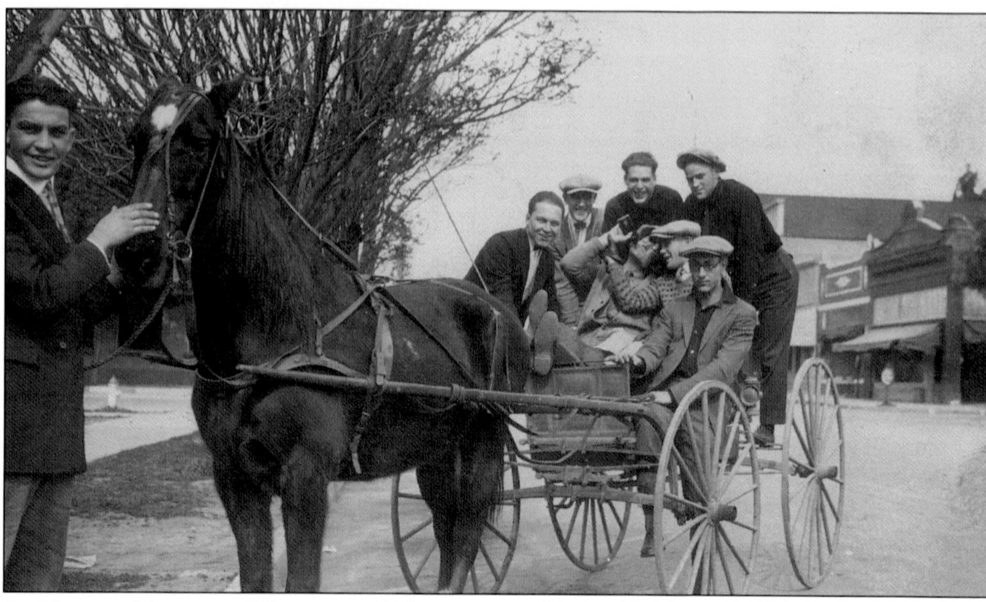

An Undated Photo of "Horseplay." The corner of D and Third Streets is in background.

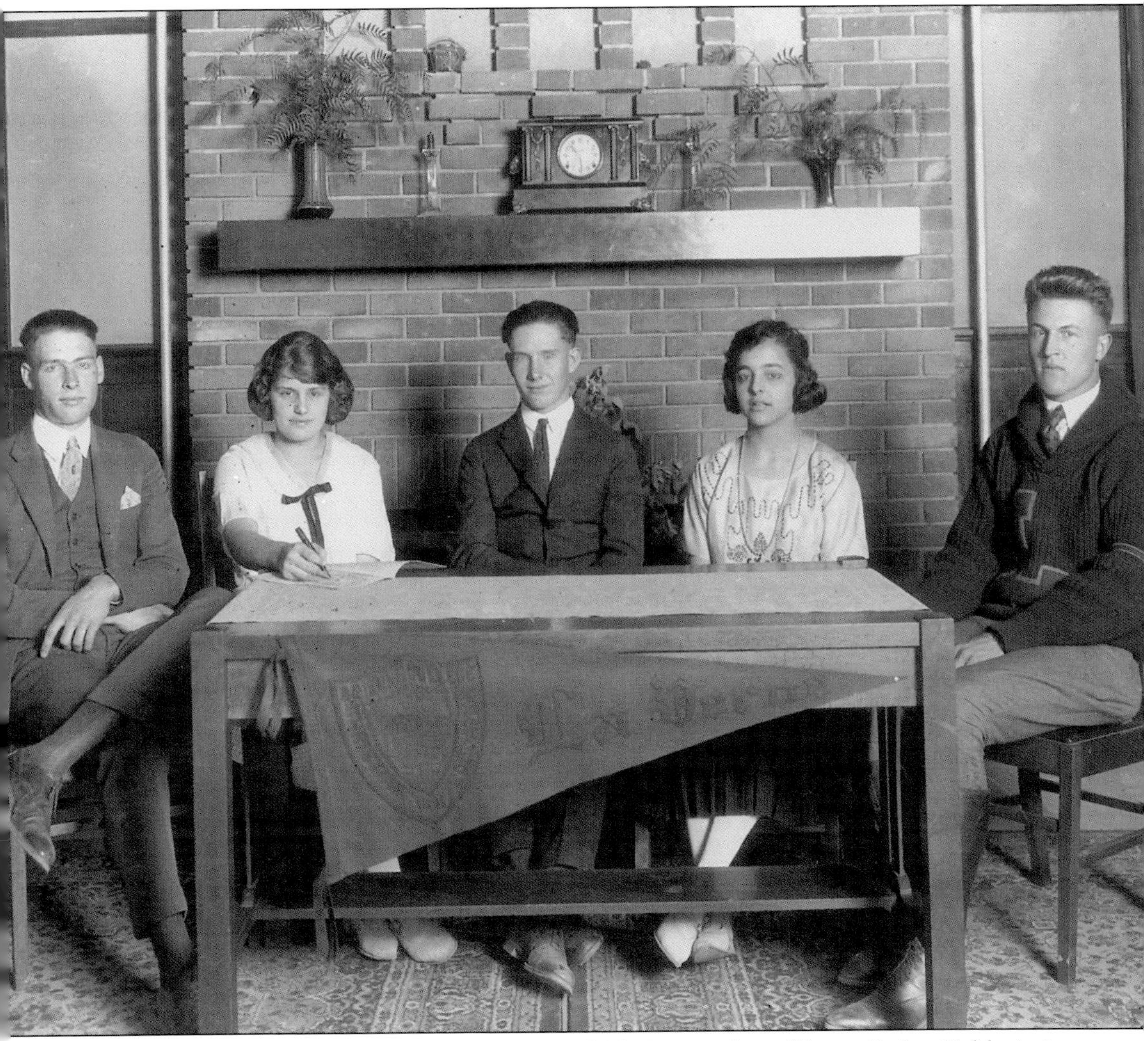

LA VERNE COLLEGE STUDENT BODY COMMISSION, 1923. Pictured are Wayne Bohn (Athletics), Martha Brubaker (Publications), Phil Smith (Finance), Viola Neher (Student Welfare), and Paul Throne (Debate). By the time the yearbook was published at the end of the school year, Levi Dickey and Walter Gilbert had replaced Smith and Throne.

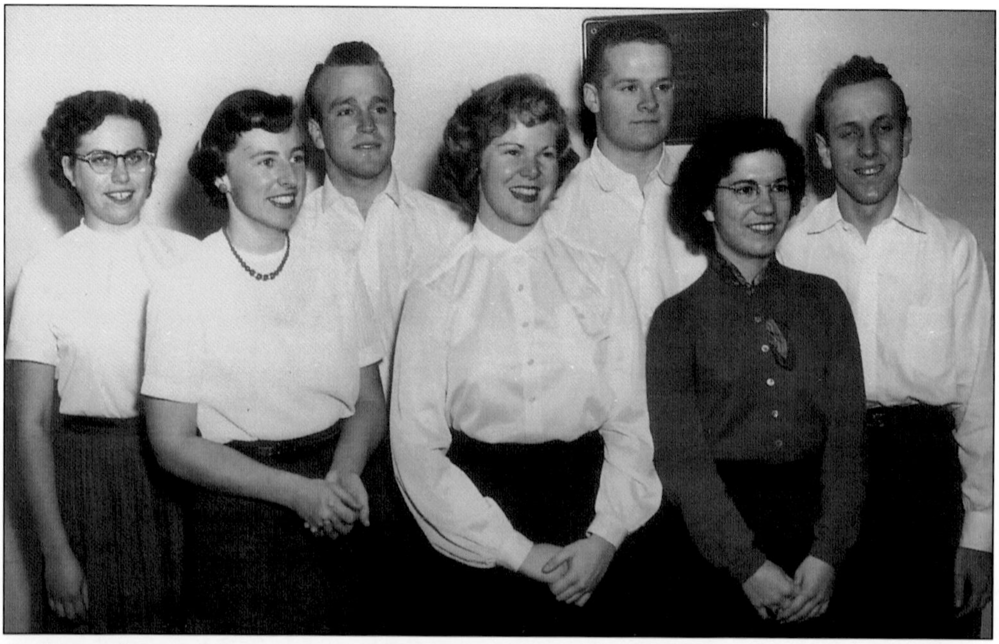

La Verne College Associated Student Body Officers, 1954–55. Pictured are Jeannine Crist, Carolyn Roberson, Stan Brooks, Evelyn Reid, Bertha Thomas, Don Boots, and Gorman Miller.

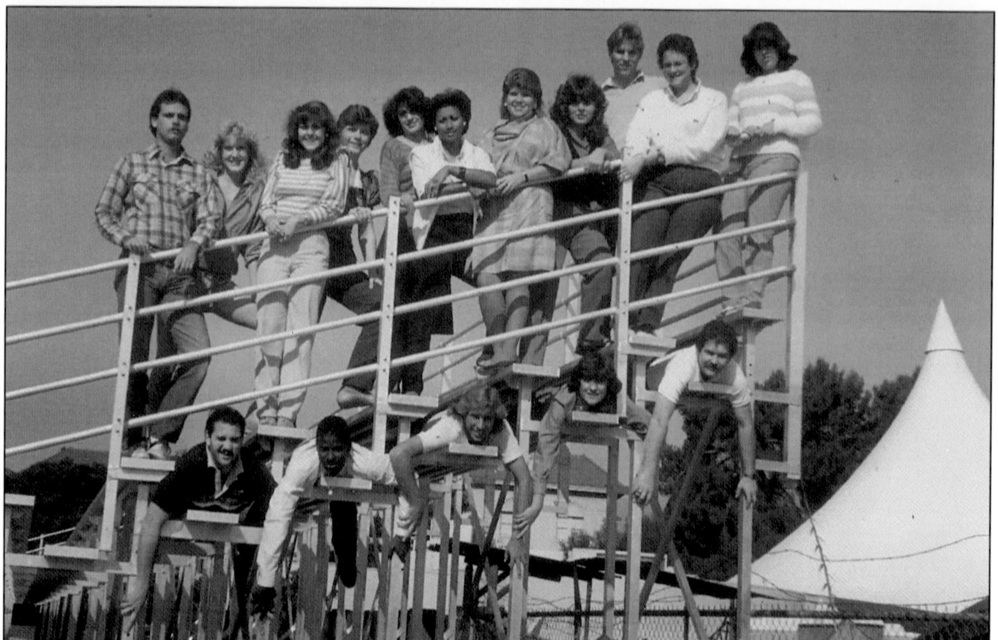

University of La Verne Associated Student Forum Officers, 1983–84. Pictured left to right are: (front row) Doug Werner, Rupert Grant, Todd Harper, Debie Cadena, Ken Mosley; (back row) Jeff Row, Julie Wheeler, Michelle Tancredi, chair Kris Way, Jackie Janbazian, Kesia Clark, Cyndi Casillas, adviser Ruby Montano, Daryl Williams, Maria Paiz, and Rosa Marez. (Photographer: Frank Johnston.)

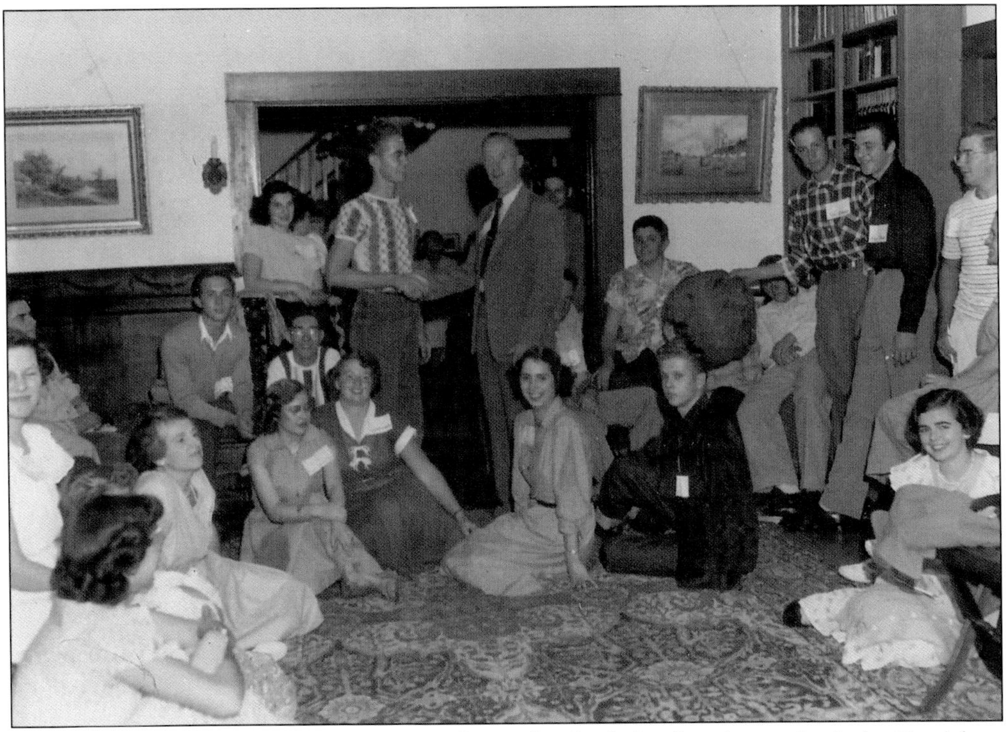

President's Reception for Freshmen, 1951. Individuals in the picture include: President Harold Fasnacht, Kenneth Sink, Dick Coffman, Carol Shoemaker, Paul Wilkinson, Victoria Wilhelm, Mary Mummert, Tom Davis, Larry Holland, Vera Fern Vannoy, Vivian Baldwin, Lois Butterbaugh, Ron Brooks, Wayne Call, and Particia Simmons.

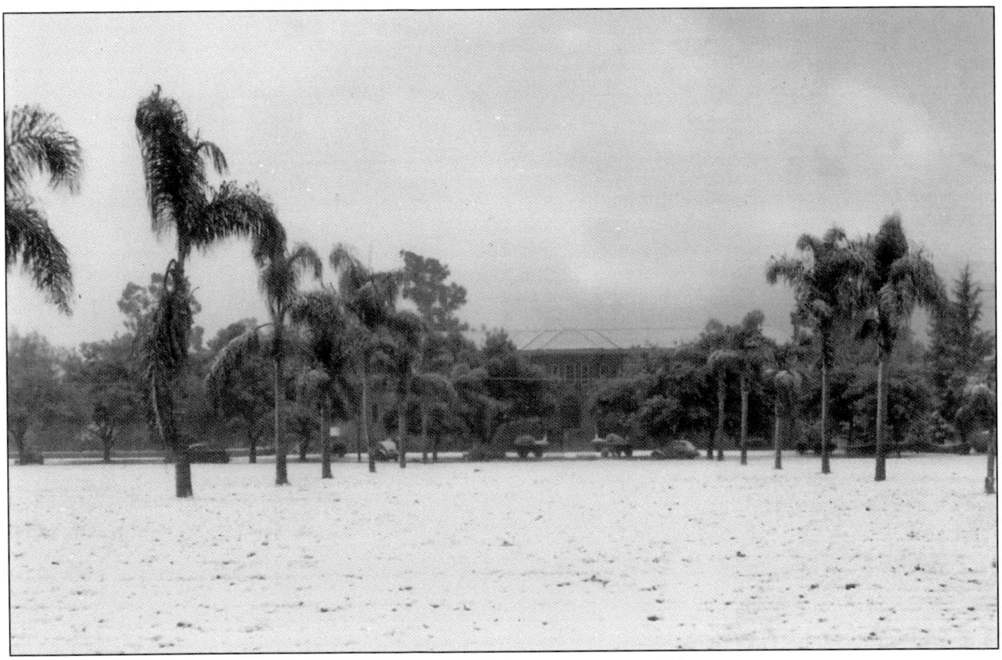

Founders Hall Viewed Across a SNOW–Covered Field, 1949.

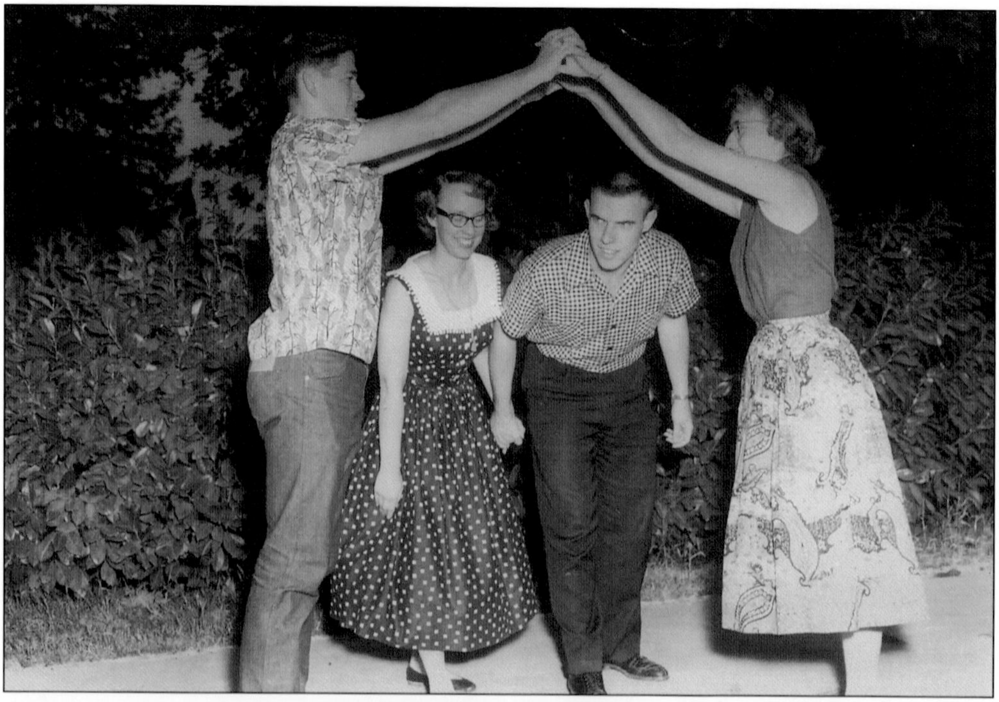

PRACTICING FOR A SQUARE DANCE TO BE HELD ON THE CONCRETE SLAB IN COLLEGE PARK, APRIL 13, 1956. Dancers are Howard Wolf, Irene Freeman, Mark Coffman, and Dorothy Campbell. "Men are expected to wear plaid or checkered shirts while women should be attired in full skirts." (*Campus Times*, April 13, 1956.)

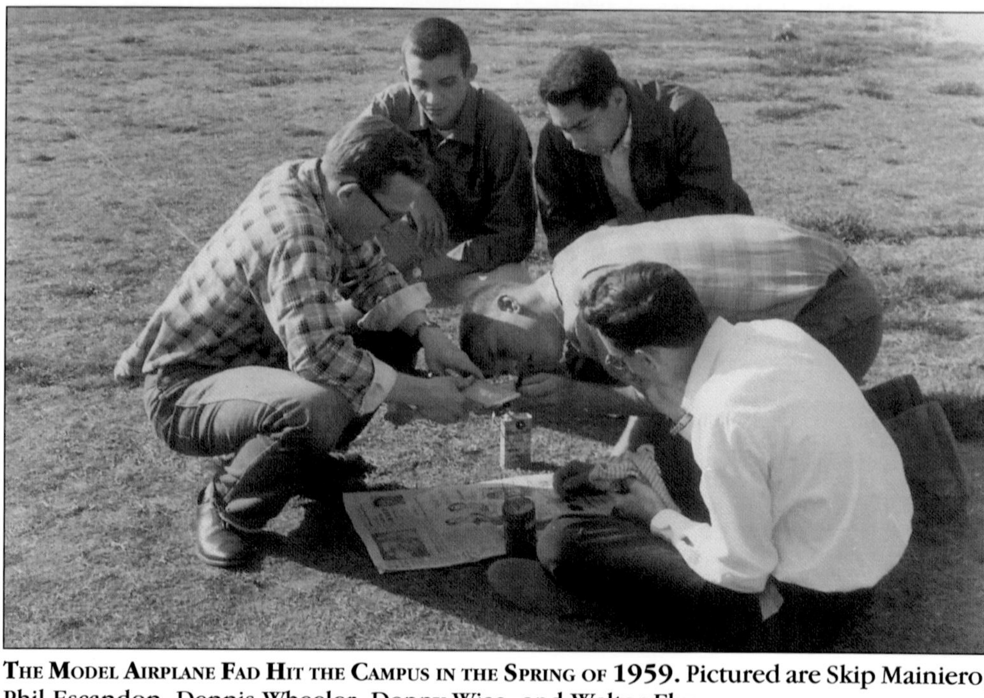

THE MODEL AIRPLANE FAD HIT THE CAMPUS IN THE SPRING OF 1959. Pictured are Skip Mainiero, Phil Escandon, Dennis Wheeler, Denny Wise, and Walter Eby.

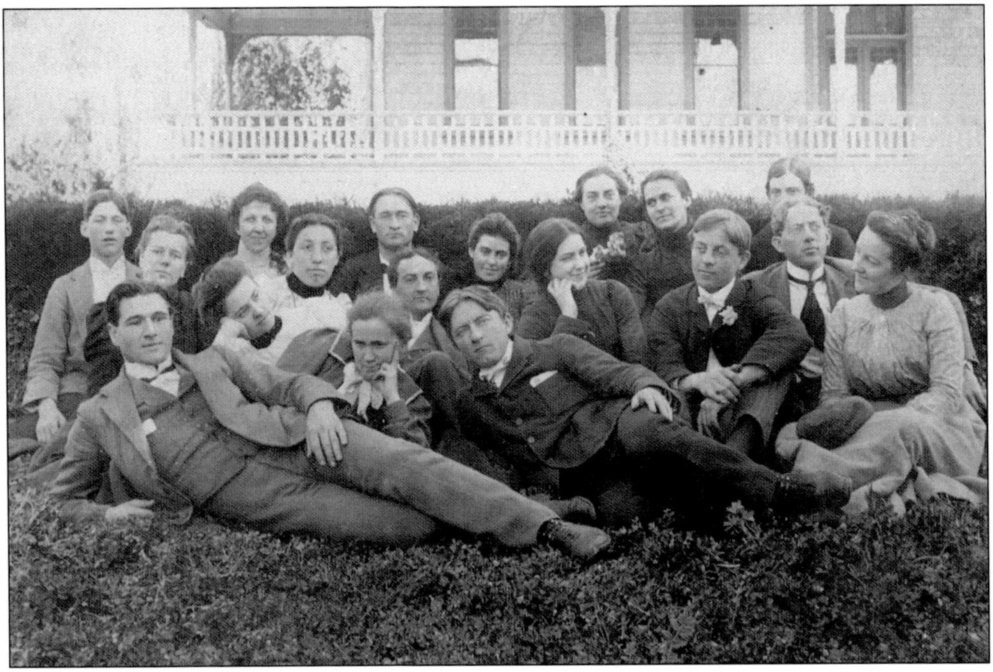

PROFESSORS AND STUDENTS ON THE LAWN, 1902. Pictured left to right are: (front row) Professor Metzger, teacher Miss Ames, Miss Gibson, Justus H. Cline, teacher Elma Aschenbrenner, Charlie Cline, Bud Cline, Laura Barklow; (back row) Enoch Overholtzer, Miss Studebaker, Stella South, Charlie Larimer, W.H. Wertenbaker, Cecile Sherman, Katherine Nusom, and Charles Fessler.

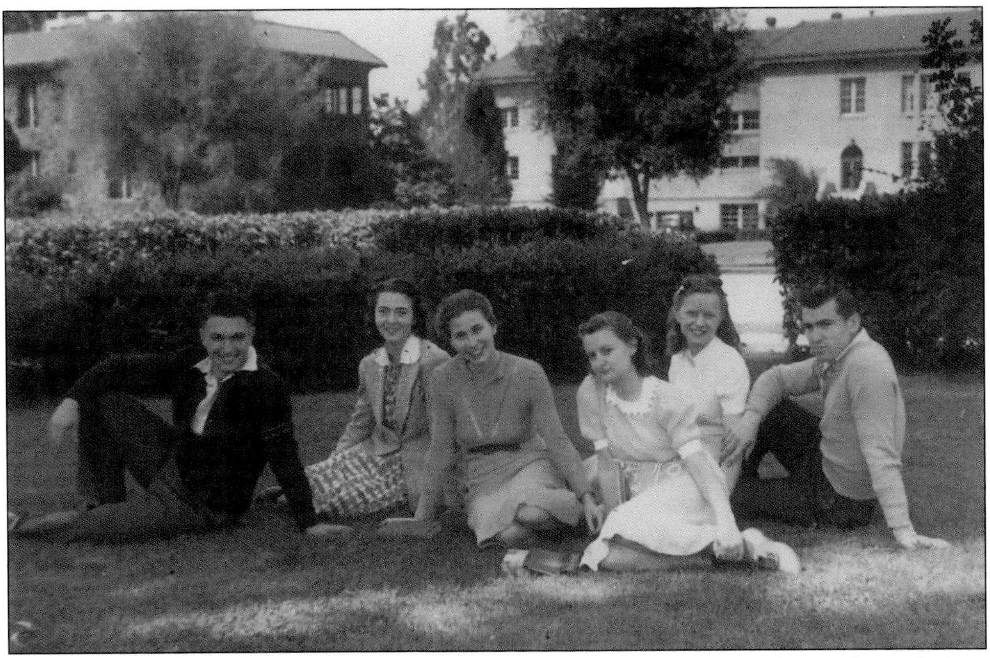

STUDENTS IN COLLEGE PARK, EARLY 1940s. Pictured are Dwight Hanawalt, Linda Brubaker, Barbara Davis, Hildegarde Weiss, Mary Esbensen, and David Studebaker.

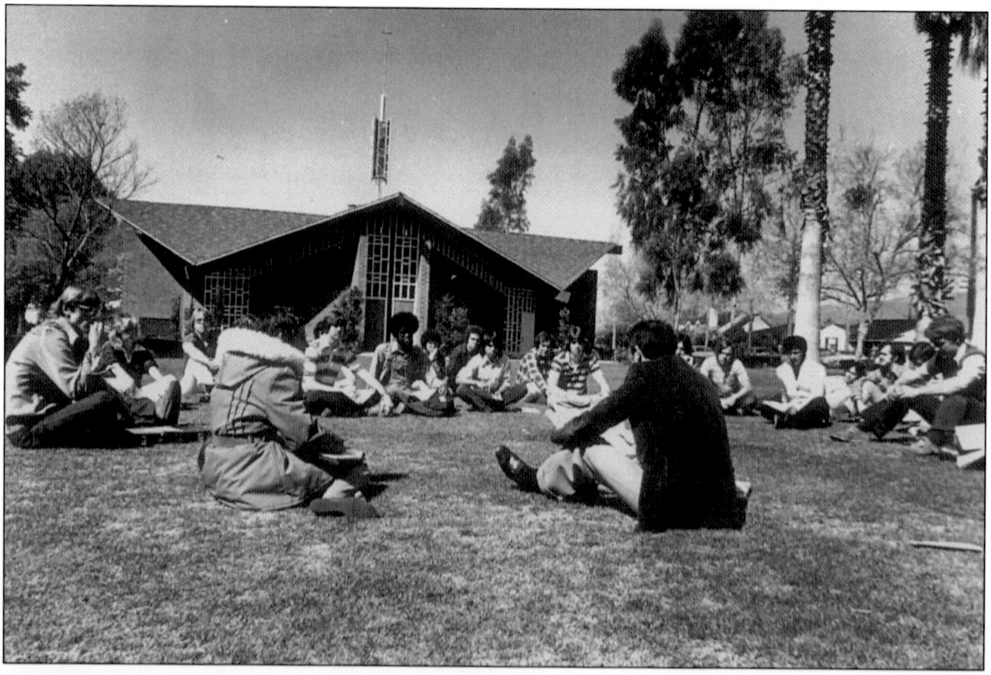

A 1970s class on the Lawn in front of the Chapel.

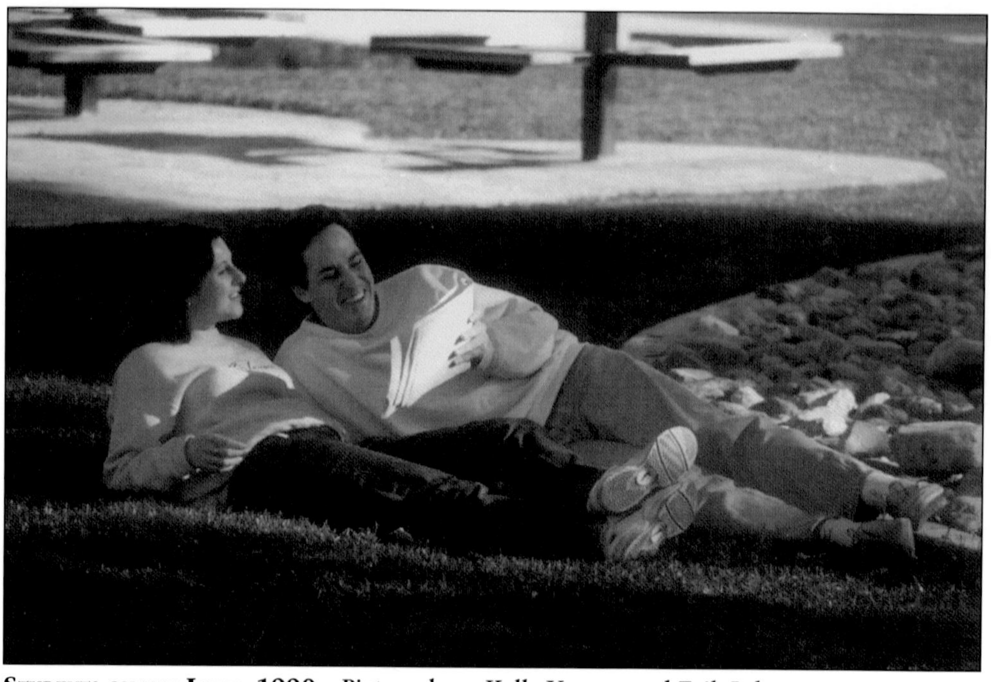

Students on the Lawn, 1990s. Pictured are Kelly Young and Erik Johnson.

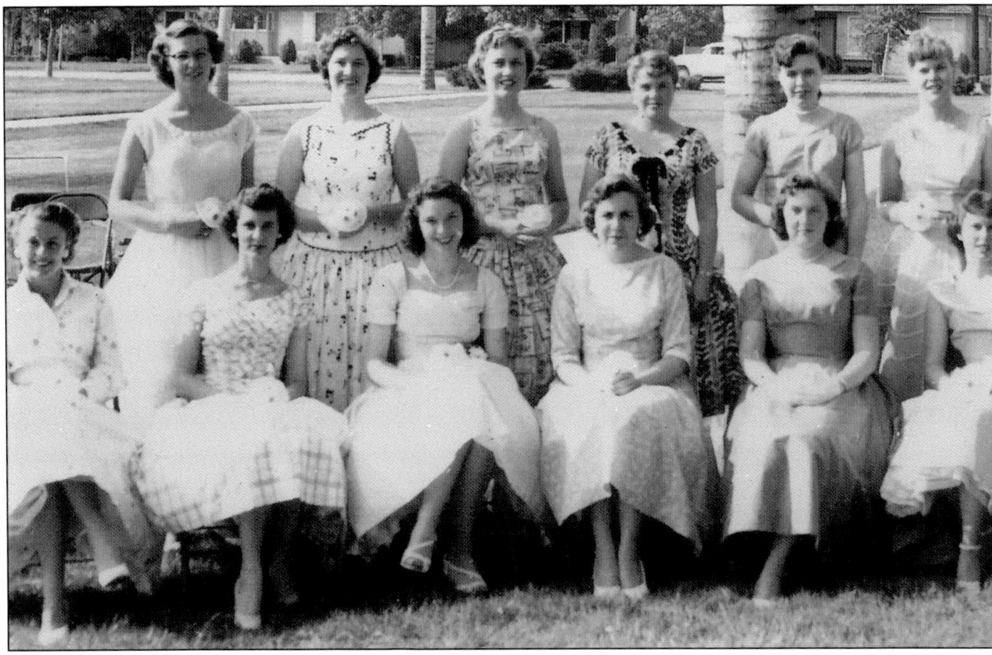

Daisy Ring Tea, 1956. This event was sponsored by the Home Economics Club. All participants had announced engagement during the year. Pictured left to right are: (front row) Jean Snyder, Joan Umscheid, Marilyn Kemp, Shirley Mummert, Wanda Weybright, Shirlie Steinberger (last to step through the Daisy Ring in a surprise announcement of her engagement); (back row) Evelyn Clifton, Marian Brandt, Myrna Wade, Sandy Shirk, Vera Stroup, and Evelyn Reid.

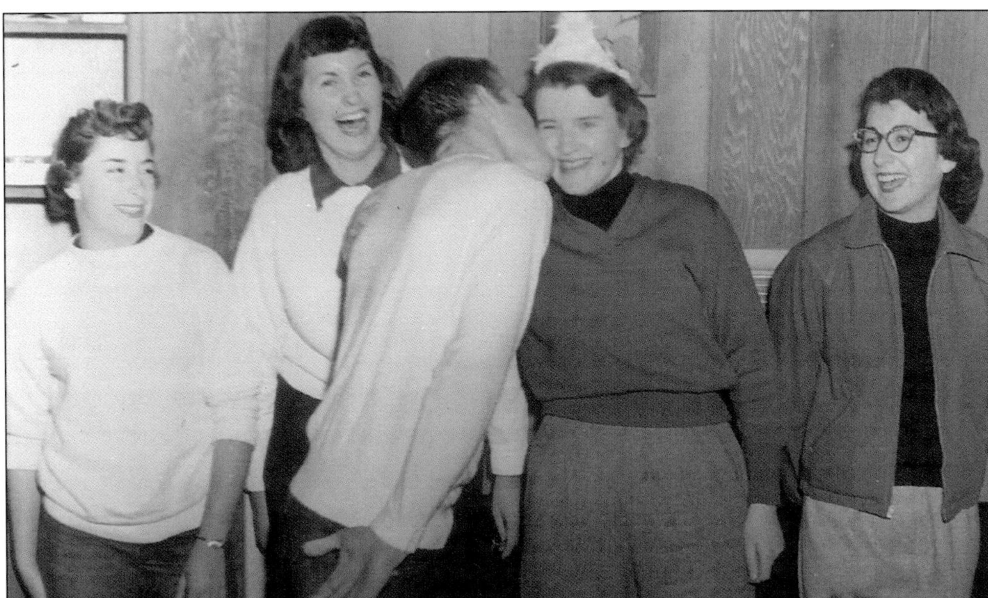

Snow Day Queen, 1956. Commissioner of Athletics, Maurice Flora, kisses the Queen, Gerda Hitzeman (German Exchange Student), as princesses Myrna Brubaker, Joan Lett, and Peggy Bohn look on.

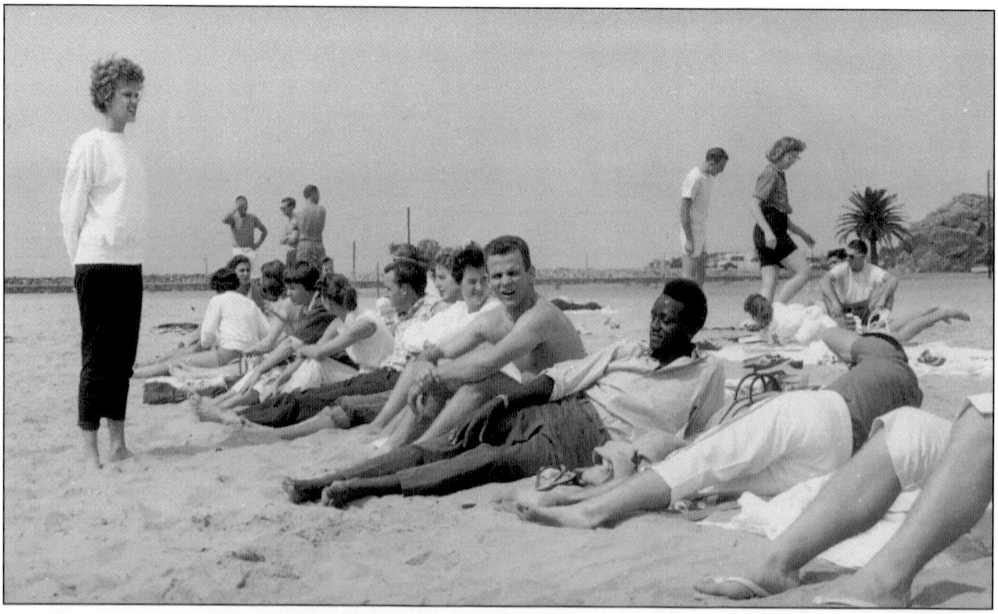

All College Beach Day 1959–60.

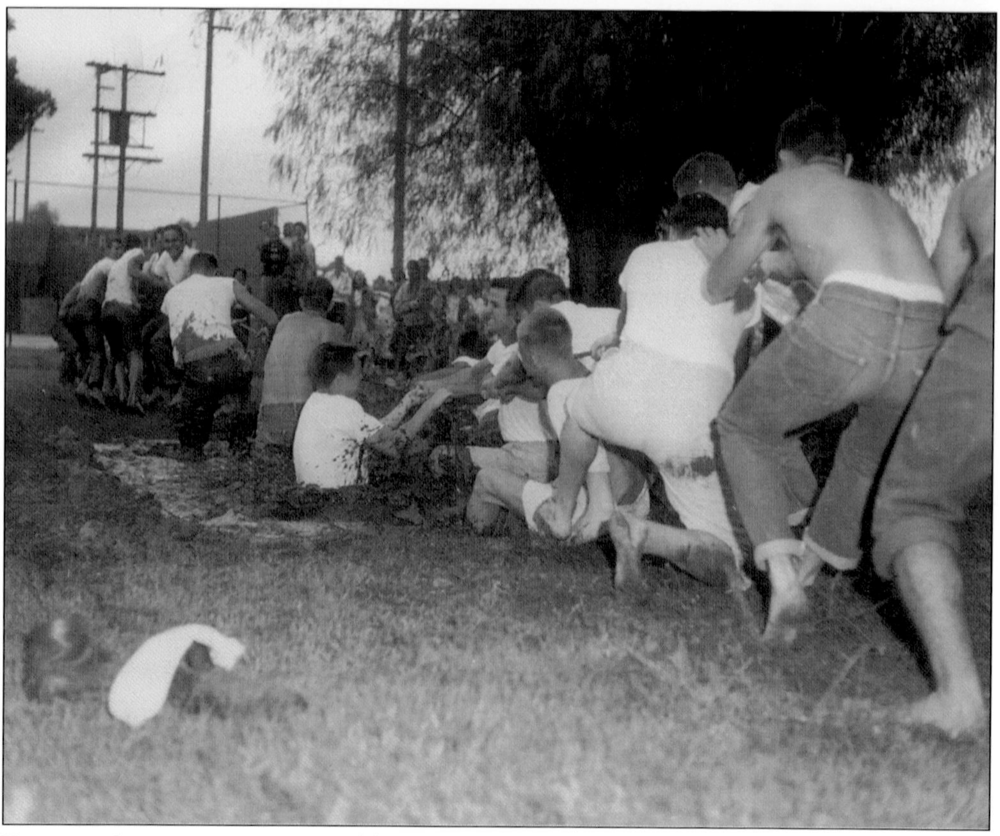

Freshman-Sophomore Mud Hole Tug of War, 1959.

BY THE 1980S, THE TUG OF WAR WAS OVER A LARGE AREA OF JELLO. The three men on the rope are Raphael Castellon, Richard Lopez, and Mike Estrada. (Photographer: Maria Gonzalez.)

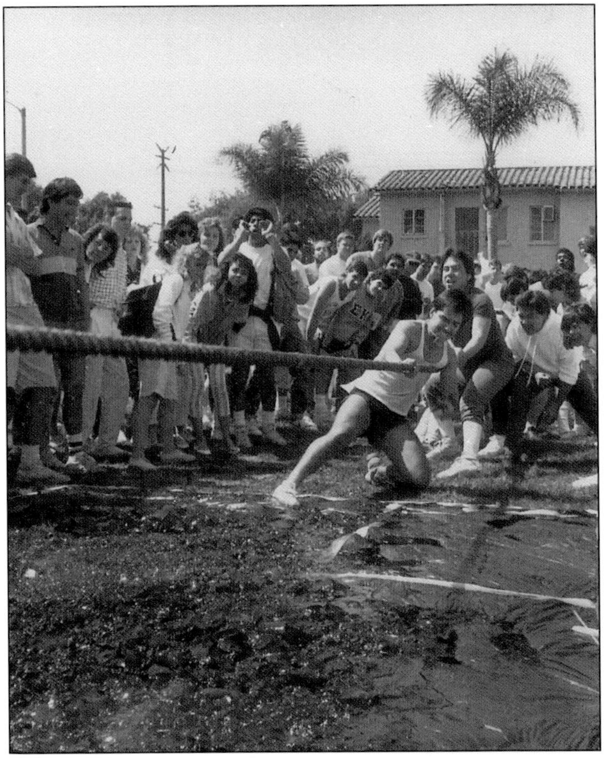

CLEAN UP DAY, 1939. This is the backside of Founders Hall, apparently before the days of OSHA regulations.

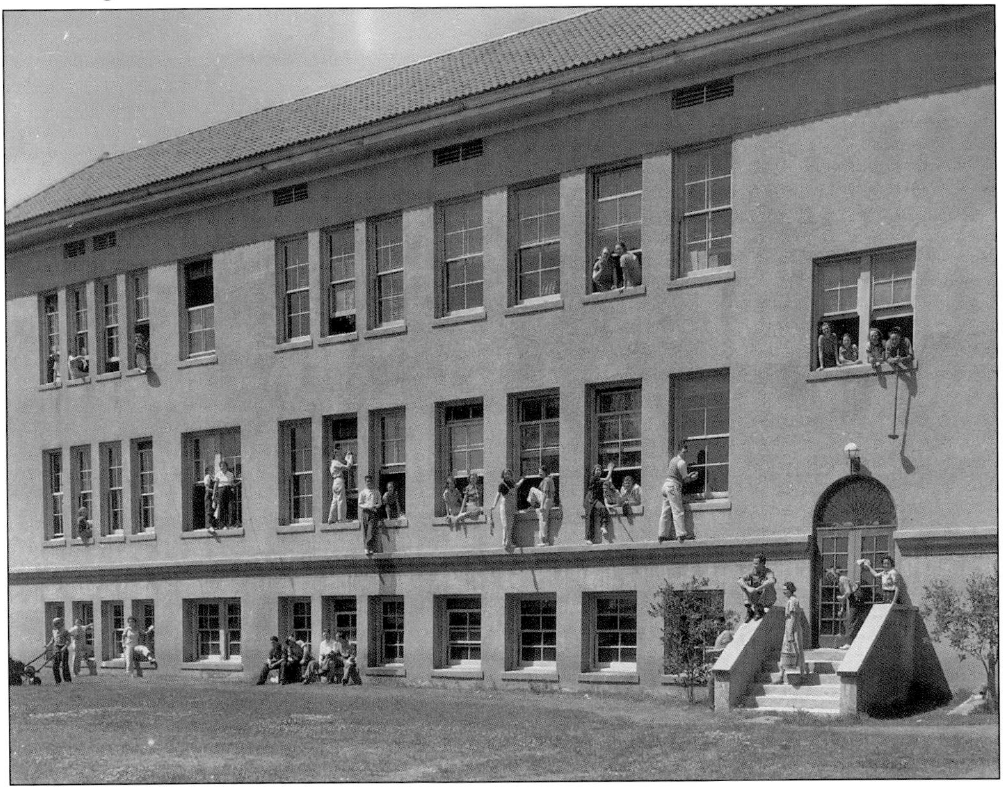

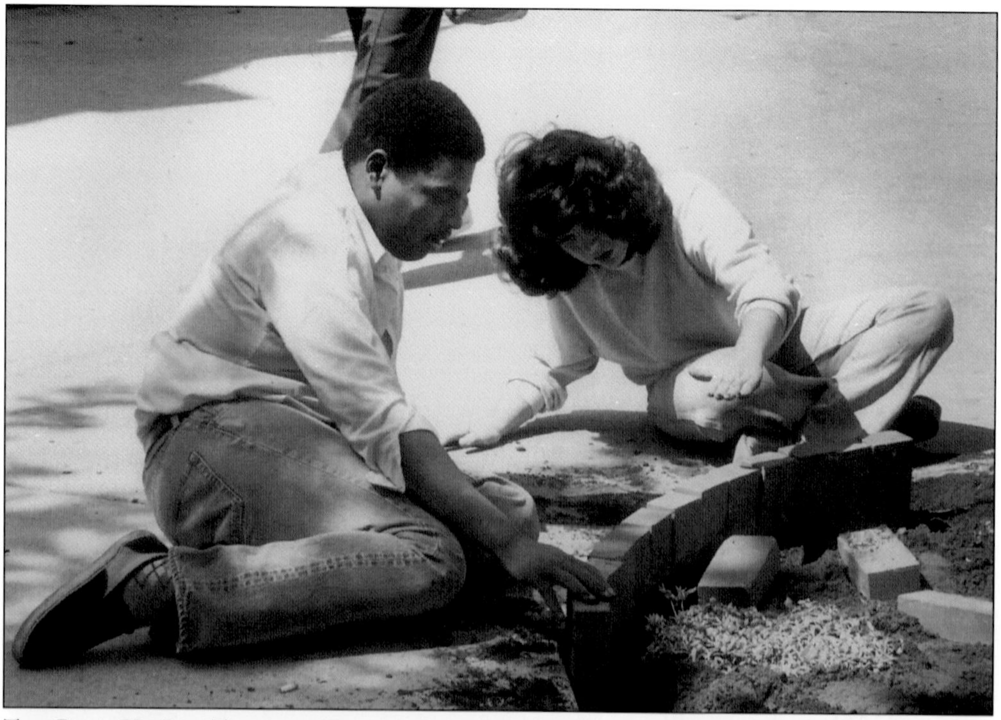

THE CLEAN UP DAY TRADITION REAPPEARED IN THE 1970S AND 1980S AS BUILD LA VERNE DAY. Derren Finks is being instructed in the art of brick construction by Ruby Montano Cordova. (Photographer: Christy Tyler.)

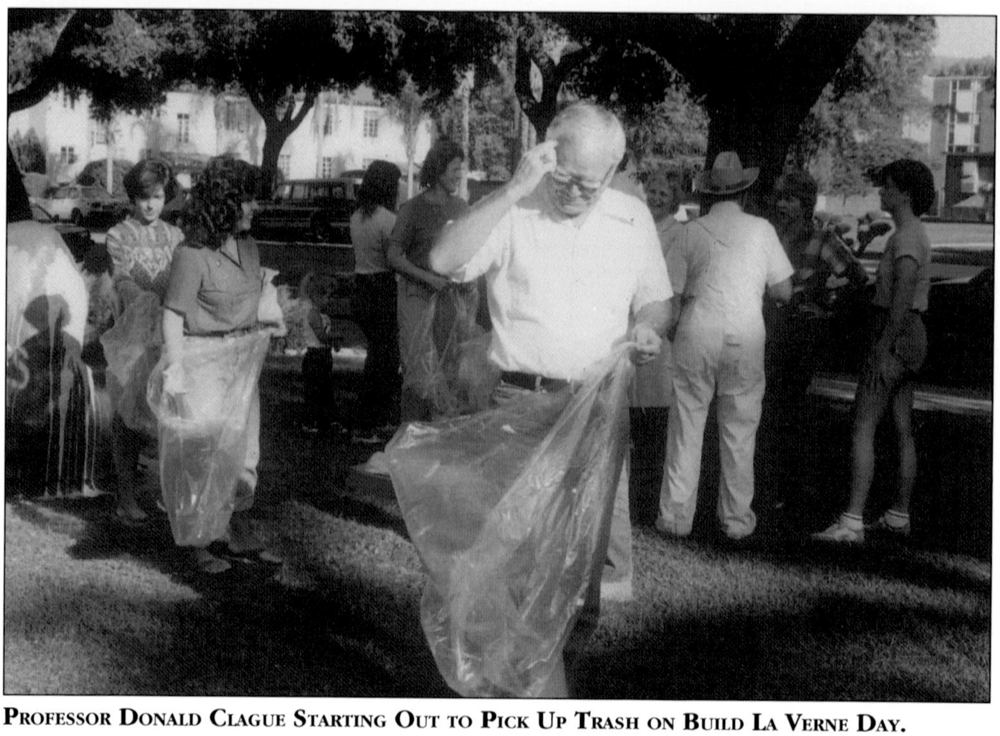

PROFESSOR DONALD CLAGUE STARTING OUT TO PICK UP TRASH ON BUILD LA VERNE DAY.

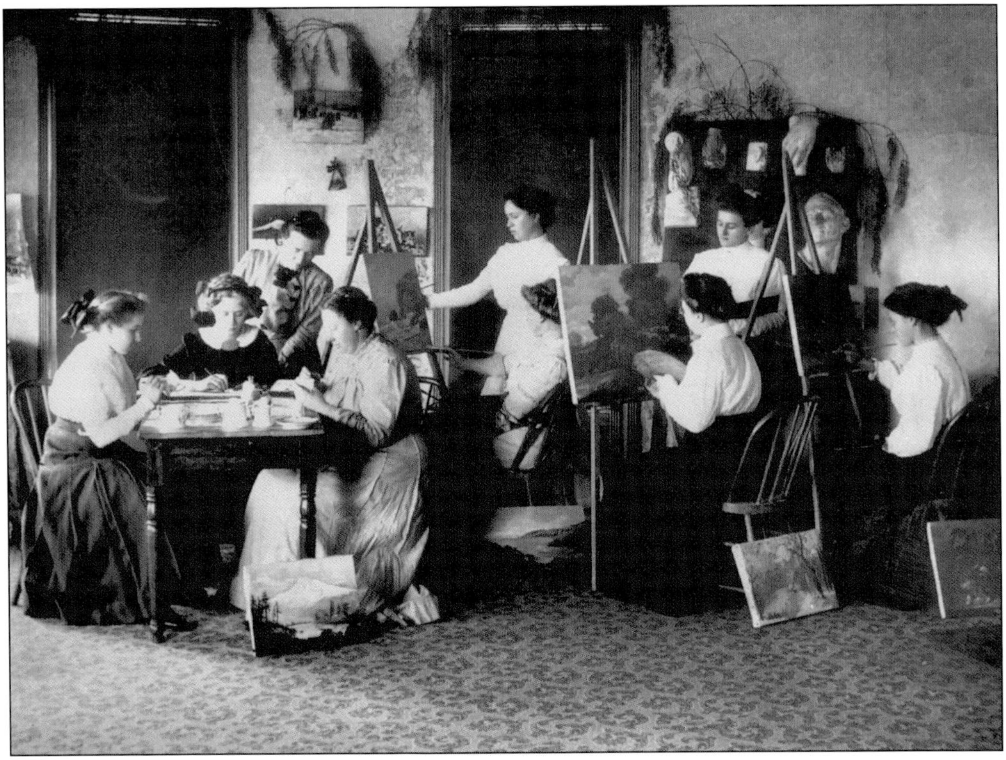

ART CLASS, 1890S; EVELYN KEISER, PROFESSOR.

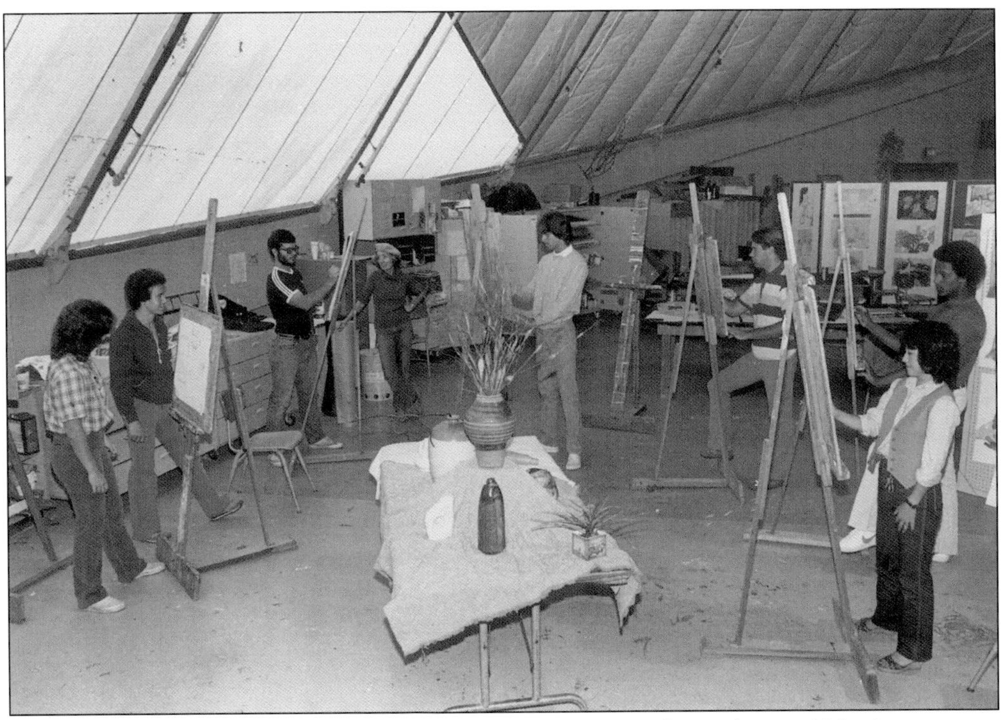

ART CLASS, 1970S; JOELLA MAHONEY, PROFESSOR. (Photographer: Christie Tyler.)

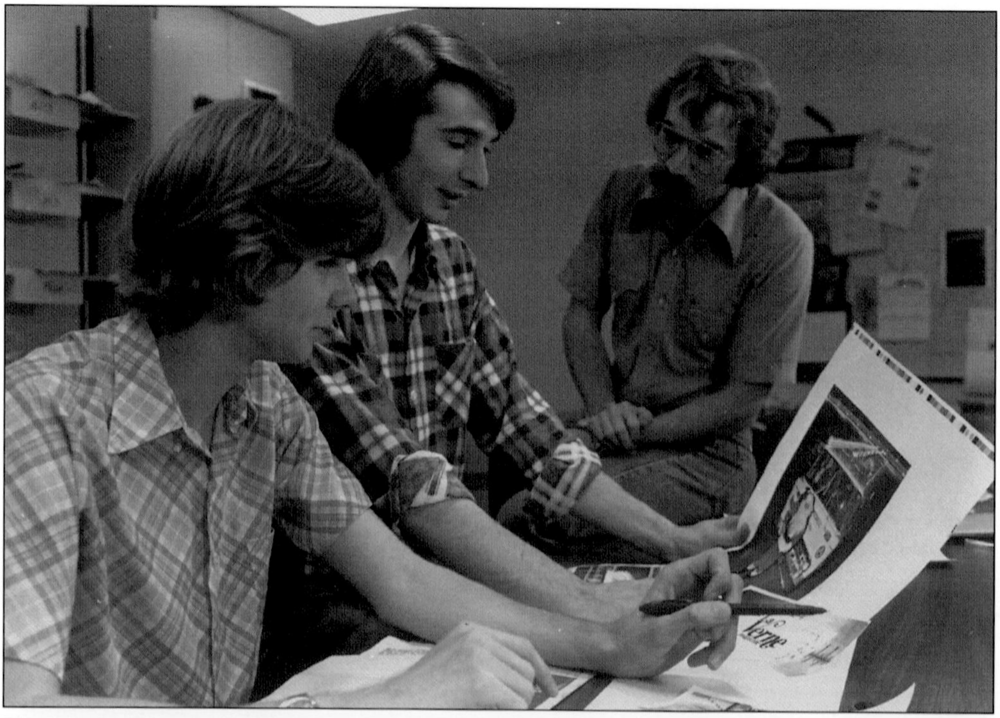

Editors and Professor Viewing Cover of the First Issue of *La Verne Magazine*, Fall 1977. Pictured are Steve Simmons, assistant editor; George Keeler, editor; and Professor Gary Colby.

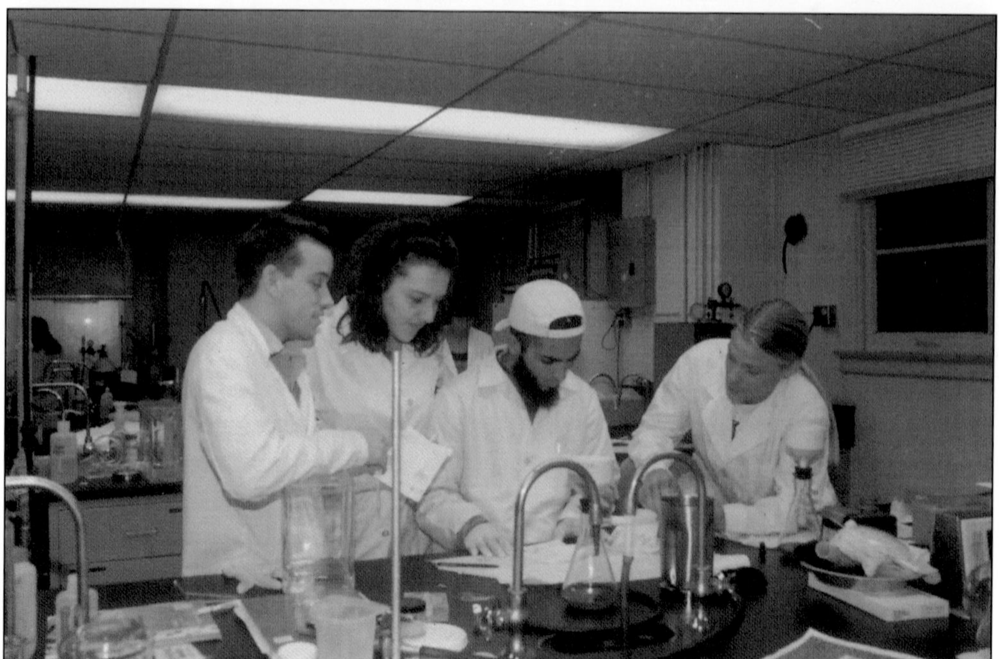

Bio–Chemistry Students, 1996. Pictured are Tyson Deutsch, Sonia Culjak, Ari Farayollahi, and Nate McConnell.

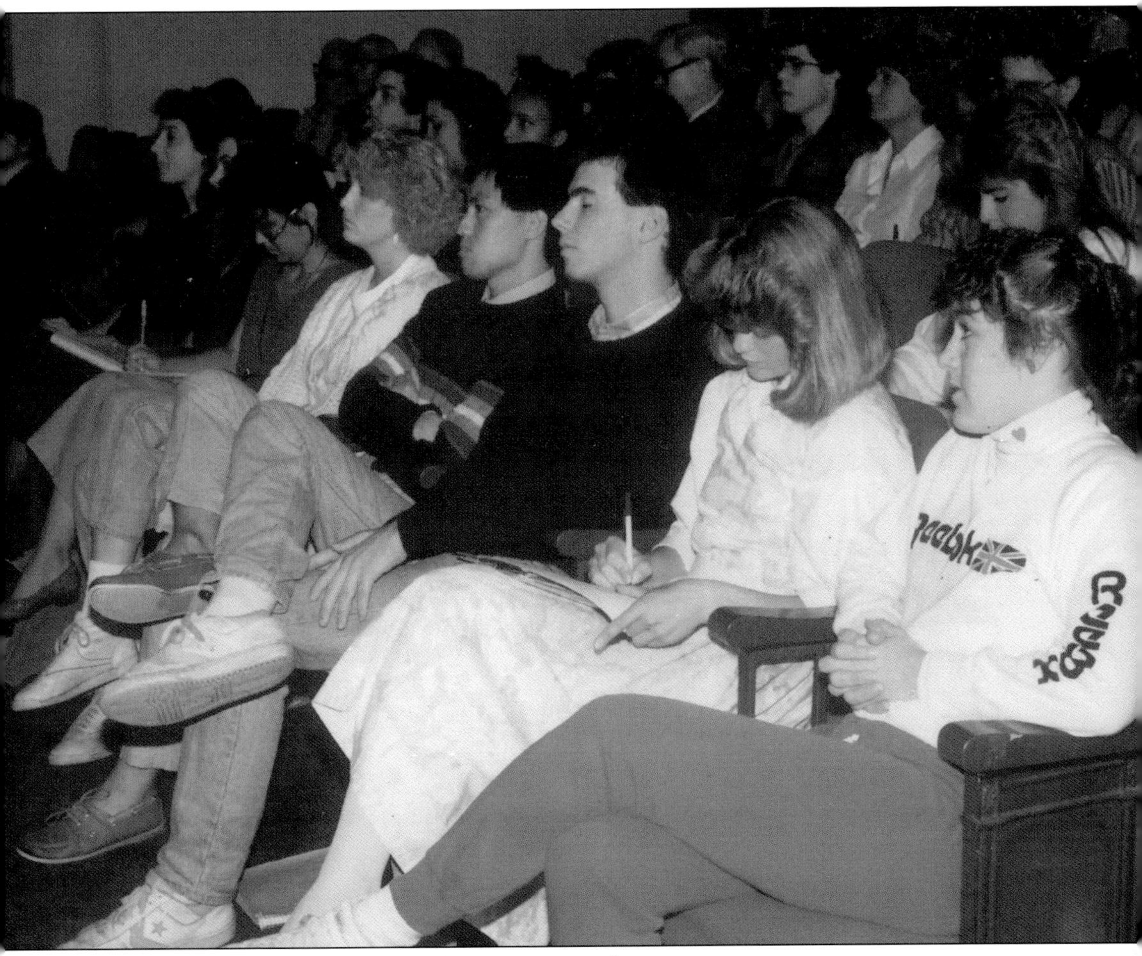

Mark Bagley, Third from Right, Enthralled by a Lecture.

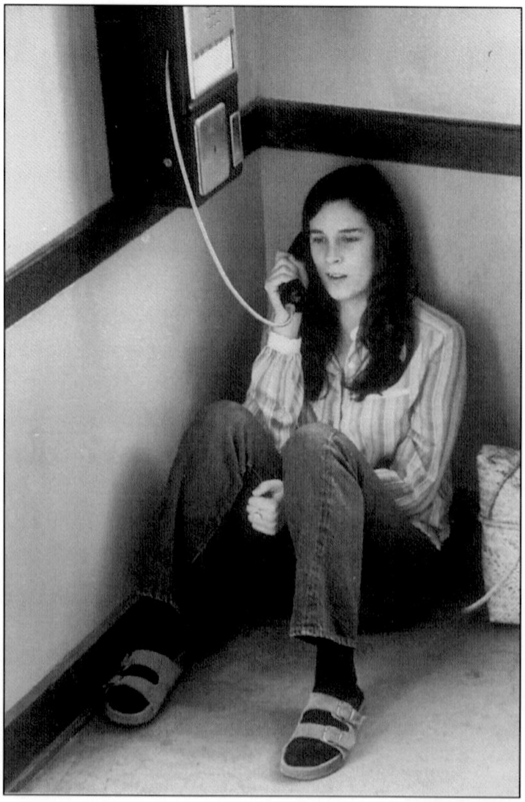

Carrie Lippold Engaged in an Important Conversation, 1981. This "campus" pay phone is a change from what students had in earlier years. "Two railroad depots, two telegraph offices, one express office, post office and public telephones are all within a few minutes walk of the college." (*Catalogue of Lordsburg College, 1899–2000*, p. 23.)

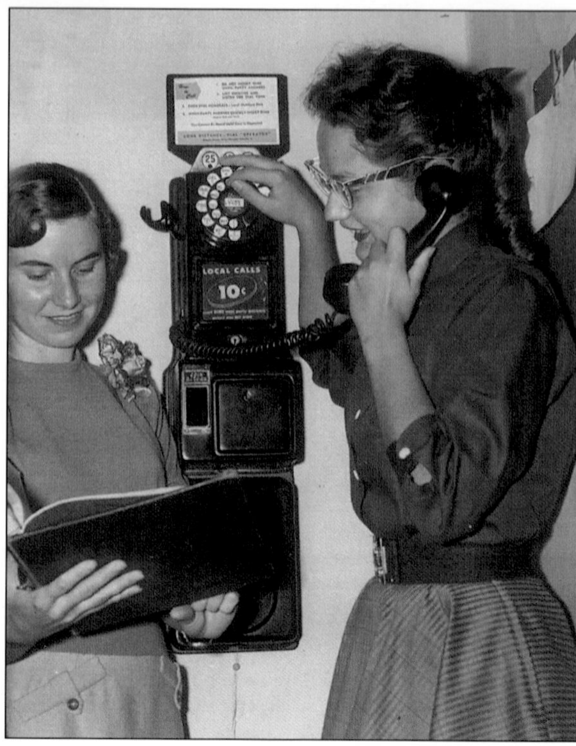

Unidentified Person and Carlyle Croisettier Place a Call. In the 1950s, local pay phone calls were 10¢. A notice at the Wilson Library entrance in 2001 reminds people to please turn off cell phones while in the library.

Benches are for Reading.

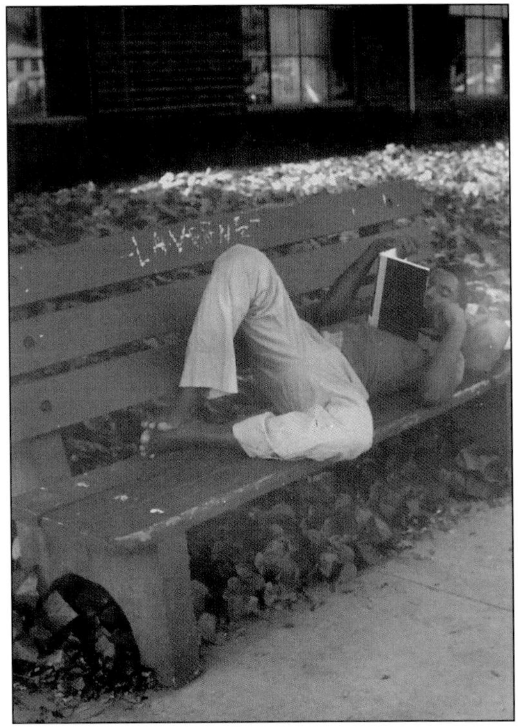

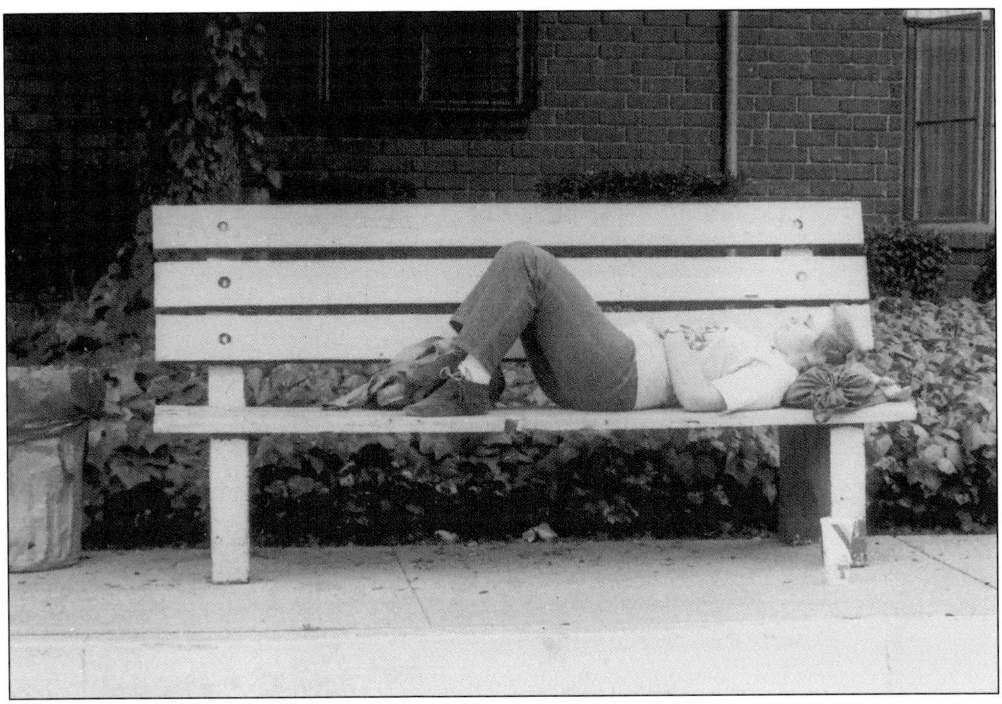

Benches are for Waiting for the Shuttle Van. Pictured is Ann Scherer, 1984. (Photographer: R. Chacon.)

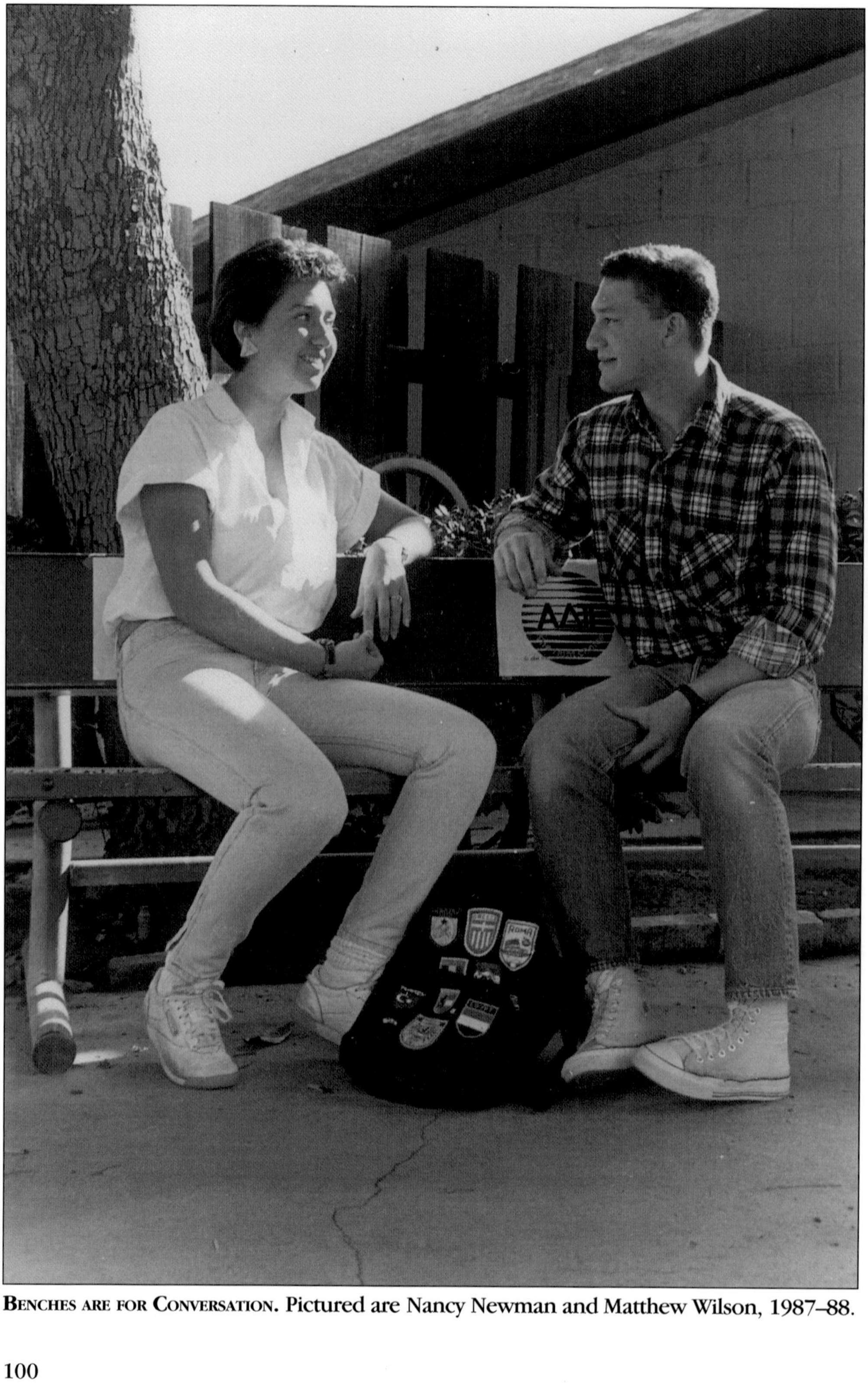

Benches are for Conversation. Pictured are Nancy Newman and Matthew Wilson, 1987–88.

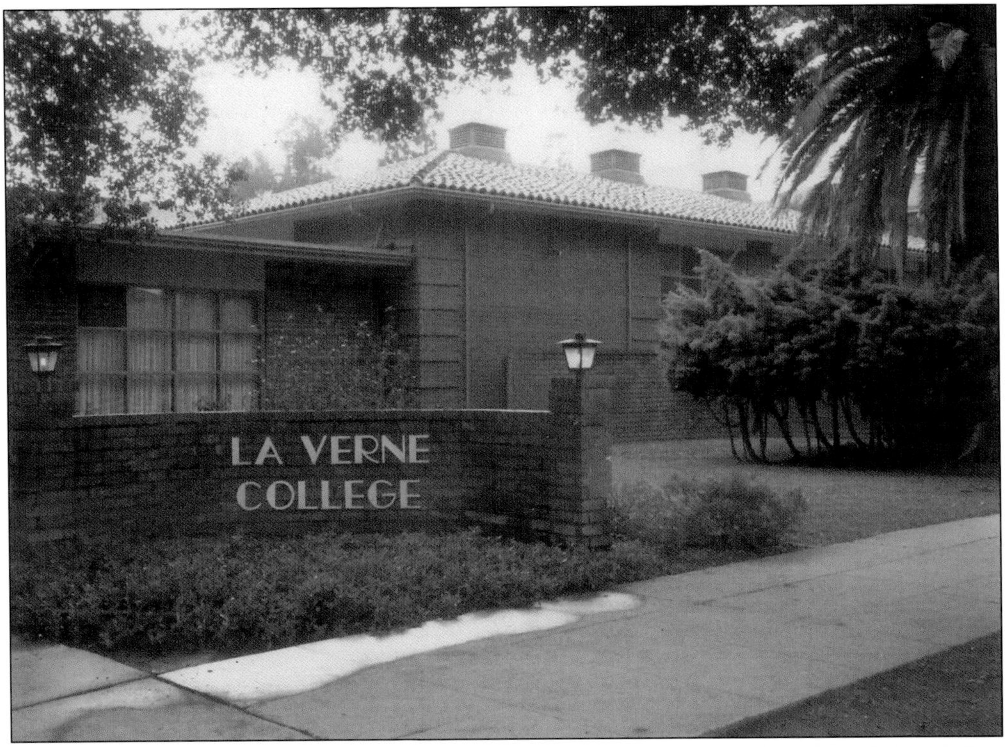

FOUNDED AS LORDSBURG COLLEGE IN 1891, THE NAME LA VERNE COLLEGE WAS IN USE FROM 1917 TO 1977. This sign was a gift of the class of 1962.

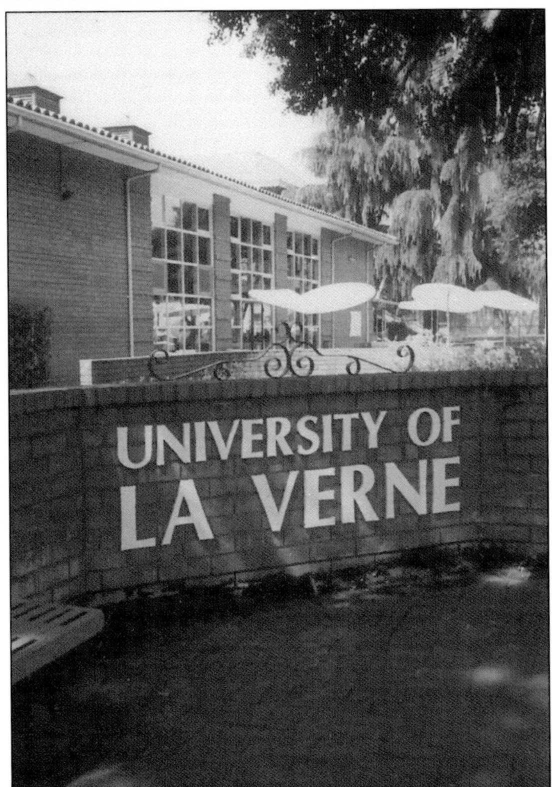

RECOGNIZING THE NAME CHANGE OF 1977.

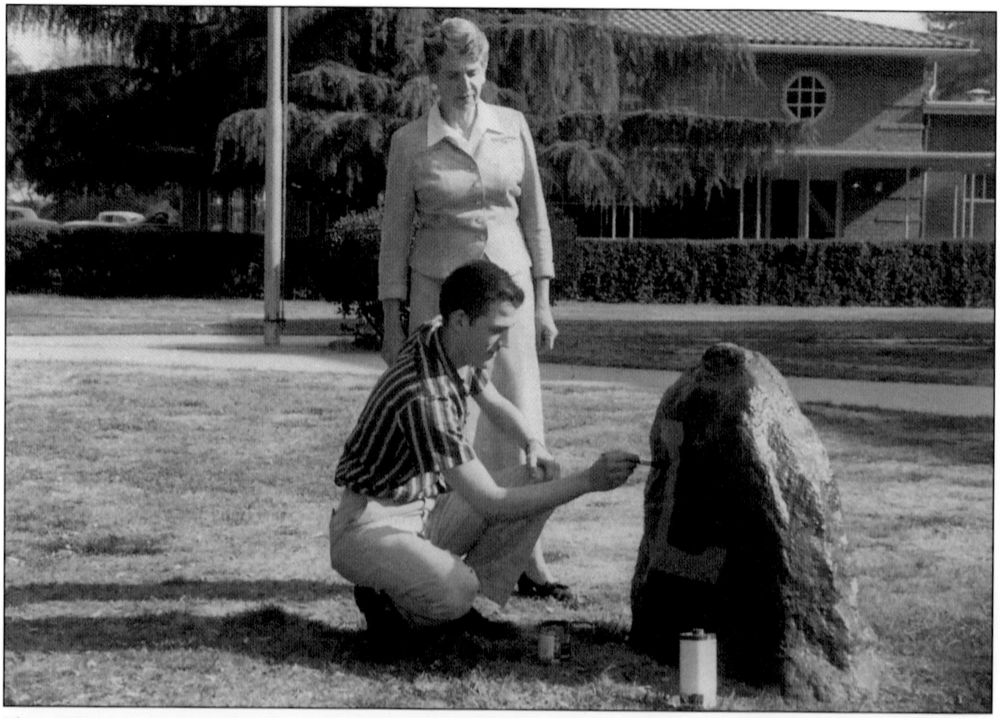

THE "ROCK" IN THE LAWN IN FRONT OF FOUNDERS HALL. Dean of Women and longtime professor, Dorothy Merritt, watches as Quinter Beery paints the block L on the Rock.

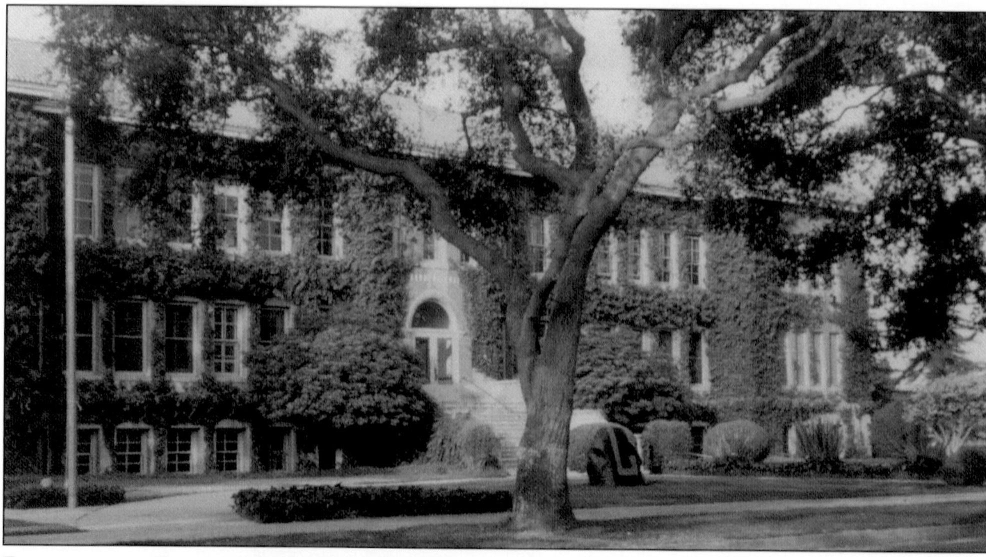

PAINTING THE ROCK. During its long history, the Rock was painted and repainted by freshmen and sophomores for about six weeks at the beginning of school. It was then returned to the green background with an orange L for the remainder of the year. Somewhere in the 1970s that tradition fell by the wayside, and now you might expect a different color any morning of the year.

A Club Decided It was Time to Fiesta.

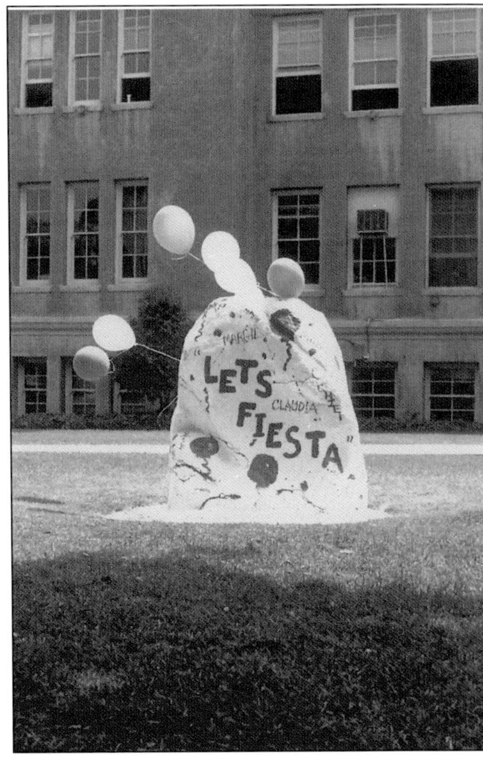

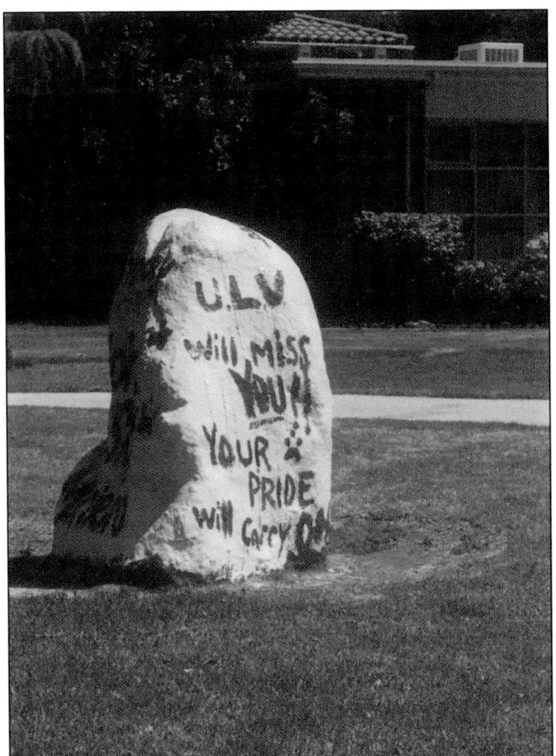

Upon the Tragic Death of Vice President Skip Mainiero in 1993, Someone Painted the Rock in His Honor.

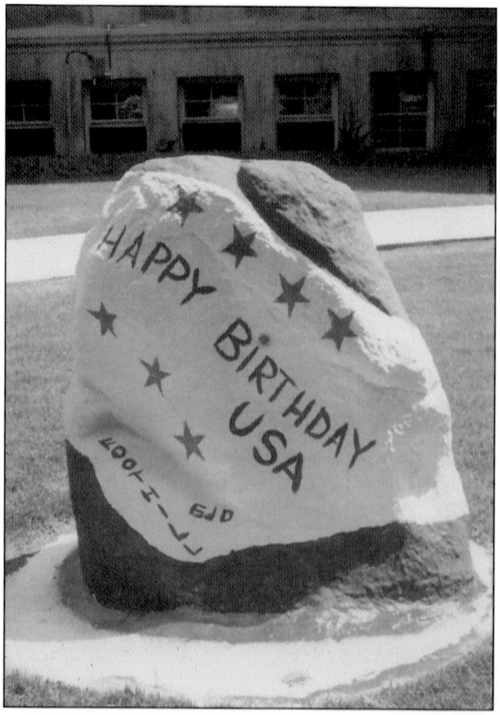

EVEN THE DOCTORAL STUDENTS HAVE GOTTEN INTO THE ACT DURING THEIR SUMMER RESIDENCY ON THE CAMPUS. This Independence Day theme was painted by members of the Foothill Cluster in 1989. (Photographer: Calla Smith.)

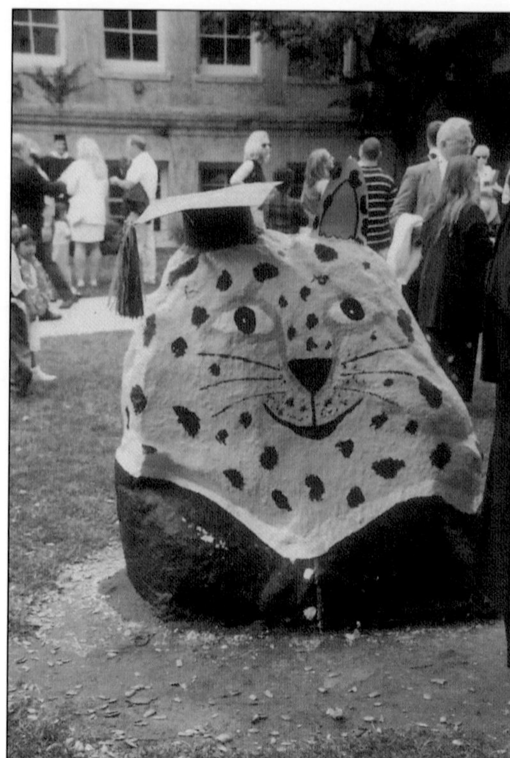

THIS COMMENCEMENT WEEKEND VERSION OF THE ROCK IS A FAVORITE.

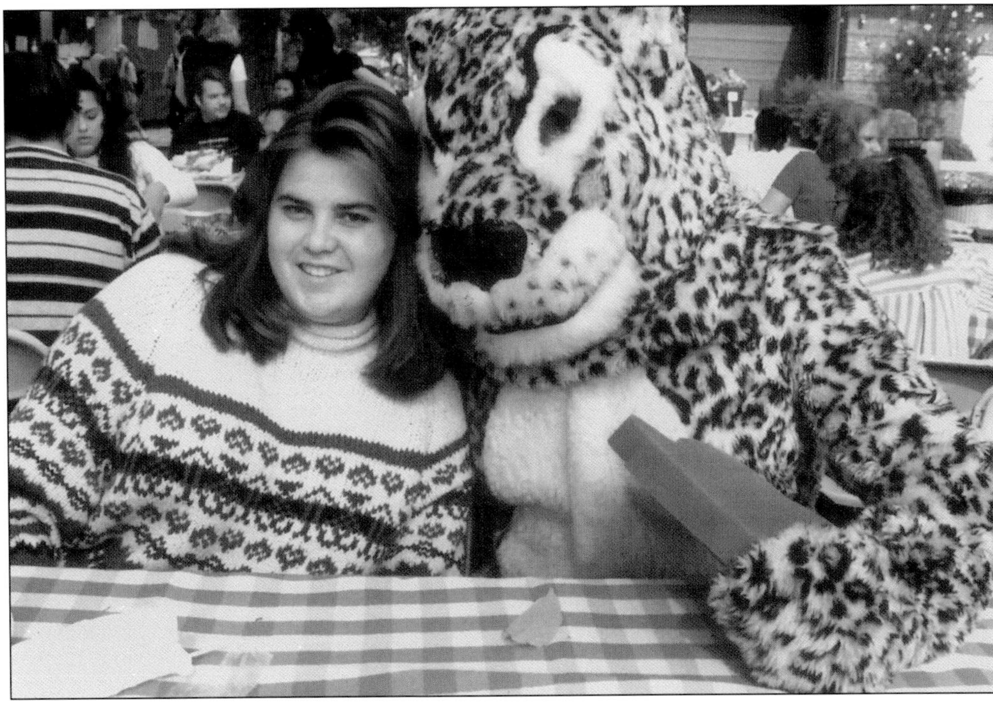

THE MASCOT, LEO, ARRIVES ON CAMPUS FOR FOOTBALL GAMES AND PICNICS.

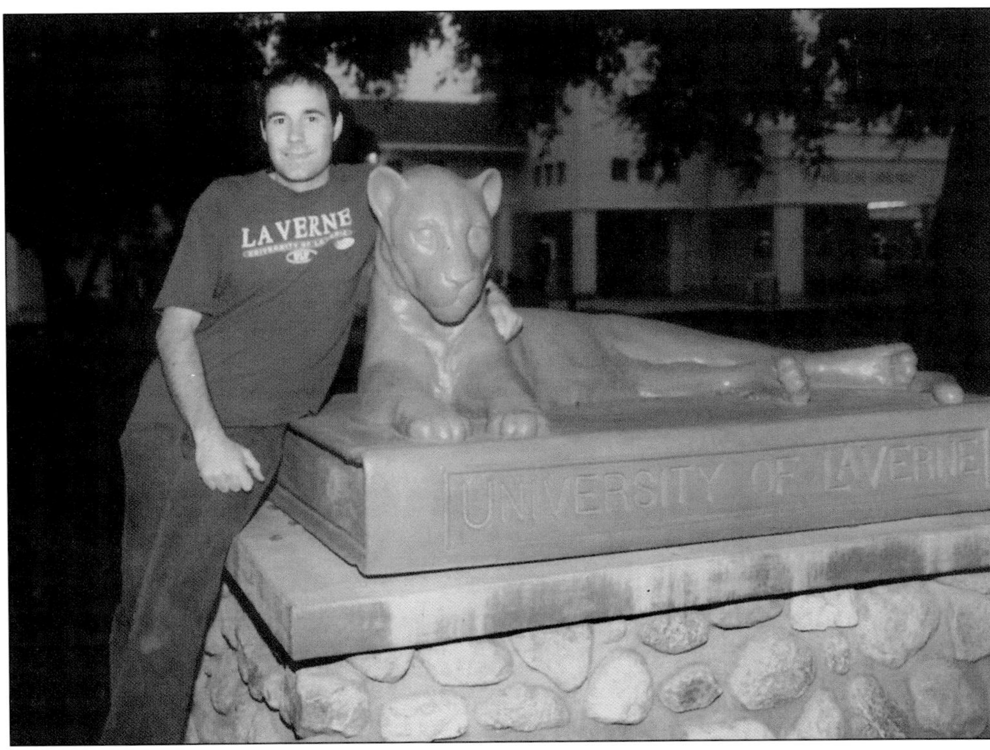

A MORE PERMANENT VERSION OF LEO IN THE PARK IN FRONT OF THE LIBRARY WAS A GIFT OF THE CLASS OF 1994. Pictured is Mike Morrow, Associated Student Forum President.

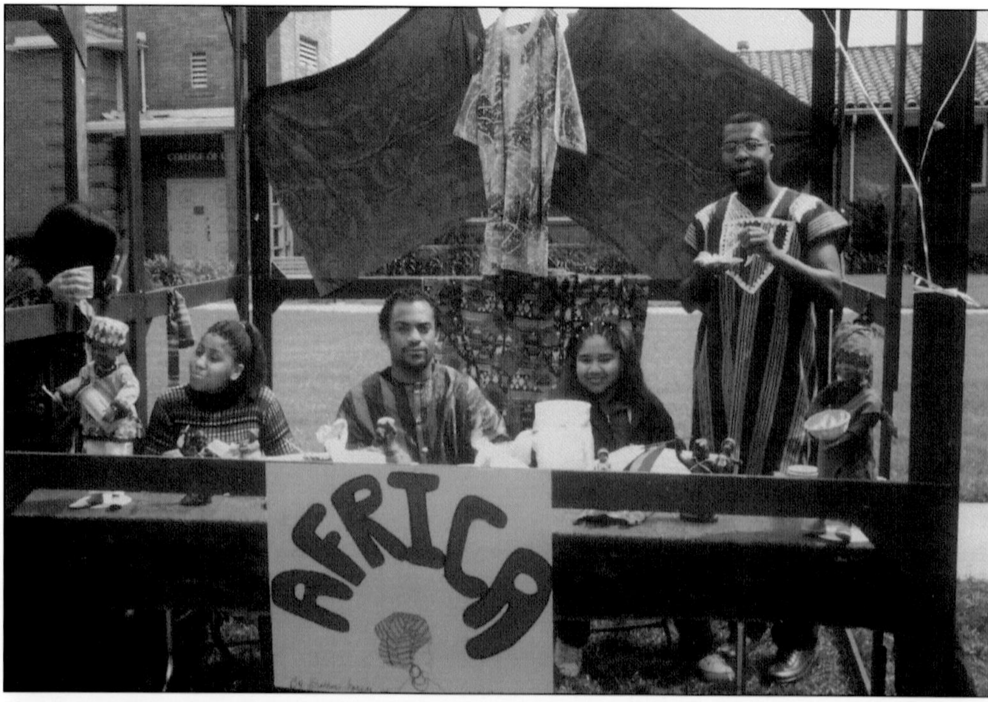

THE AFRICA BOOTH AT AN INTERNATIONAL STUDENT FAIR.

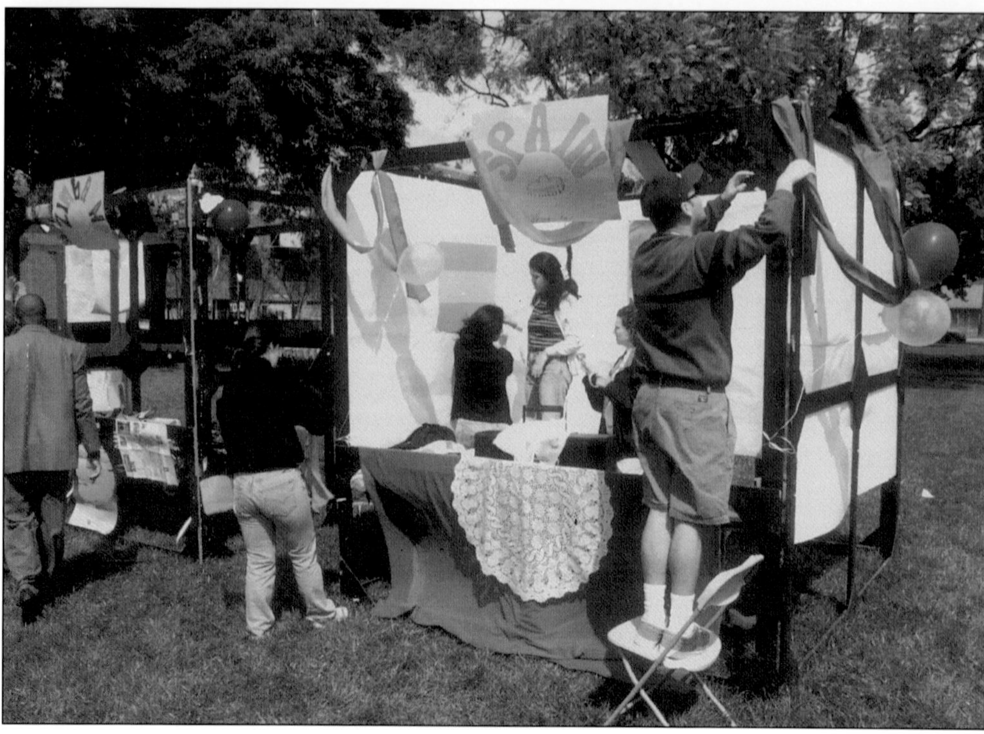

THE SPAIN BOOTH AT AN INTERNATIONAL STUDENT FAIR.

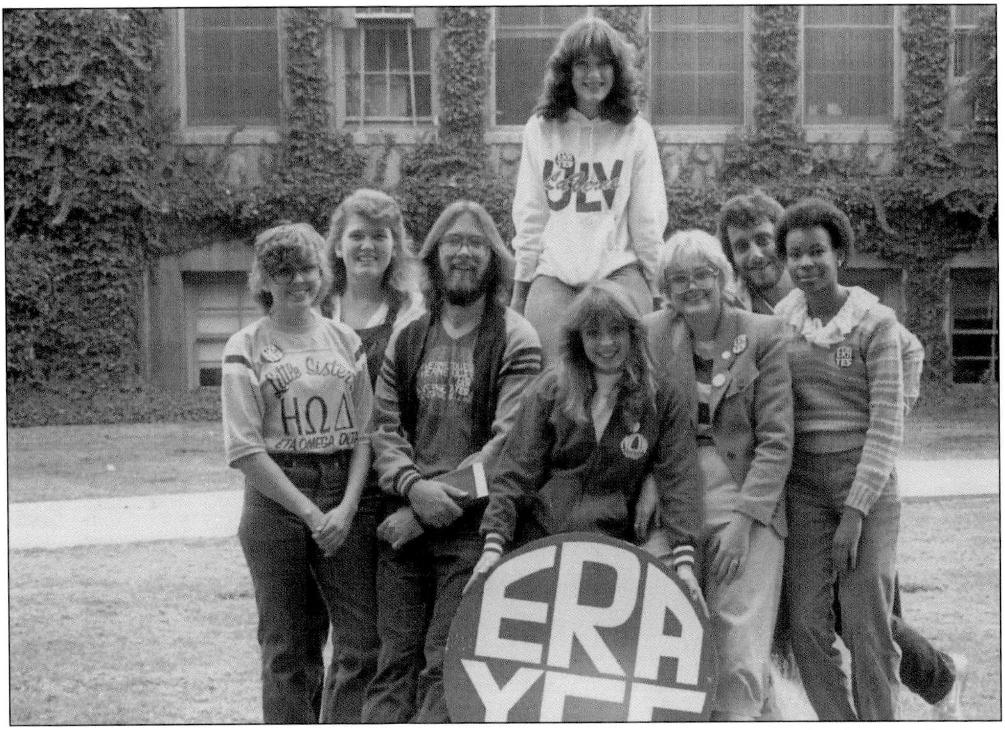

A Group Supporting an Affirmative Vote for the ERA, 1982. Pictured left to right are: (front row) Elaine Balanoff, Kim Palmer, Teddy Barber, Lori Nelson, Kathy Hauger, Tony Schaffer, Pam Swearingen; (back row) Jill Bittinger.

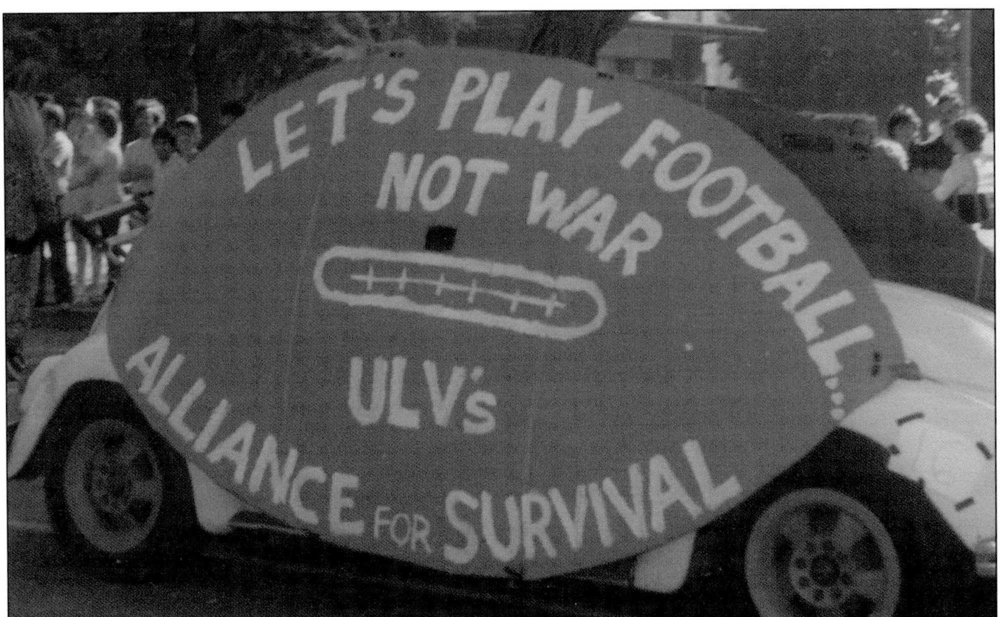

ULV's Alliance for Survival Sponsored a Float in the 1982 Homecoming Parade with the Slogan, "Let's Play Football, Not War."

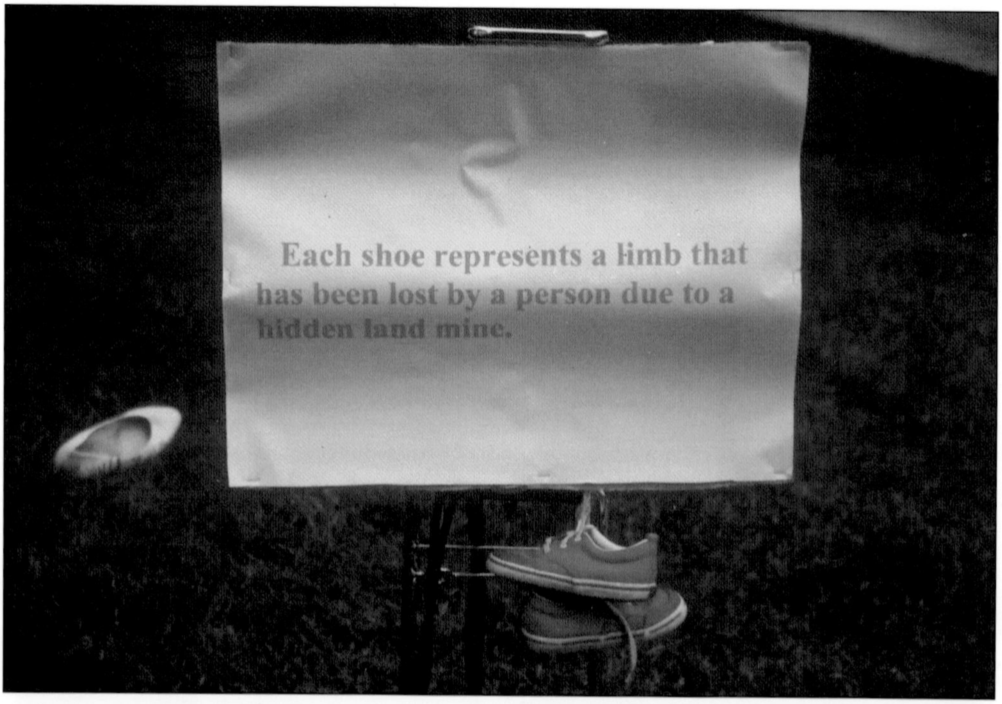

A Powerful Message was Presented by This Protest Against Land Mines.

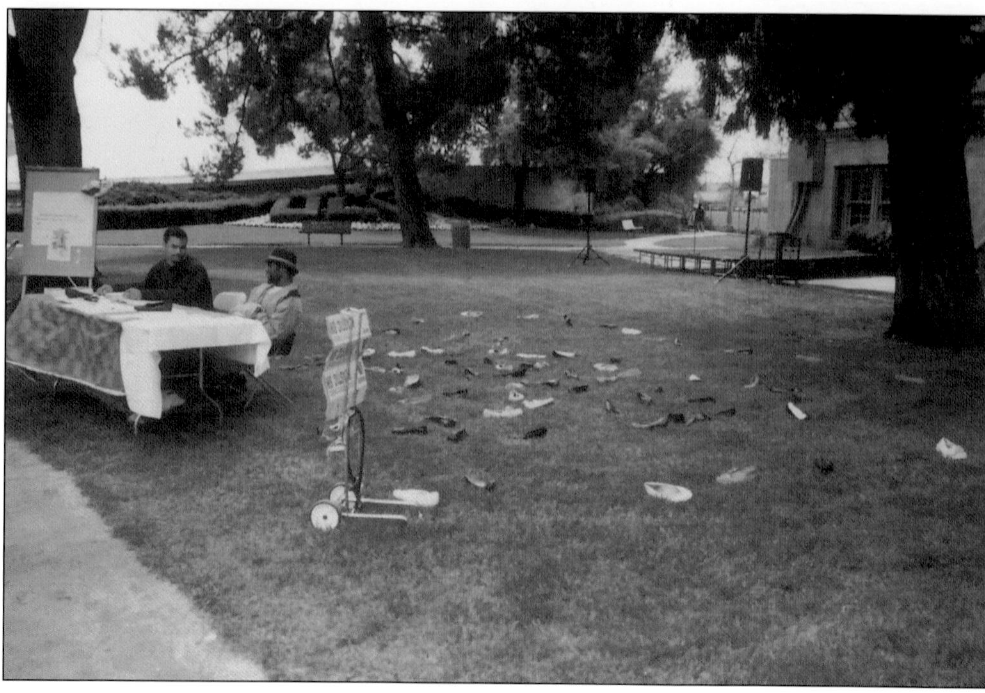

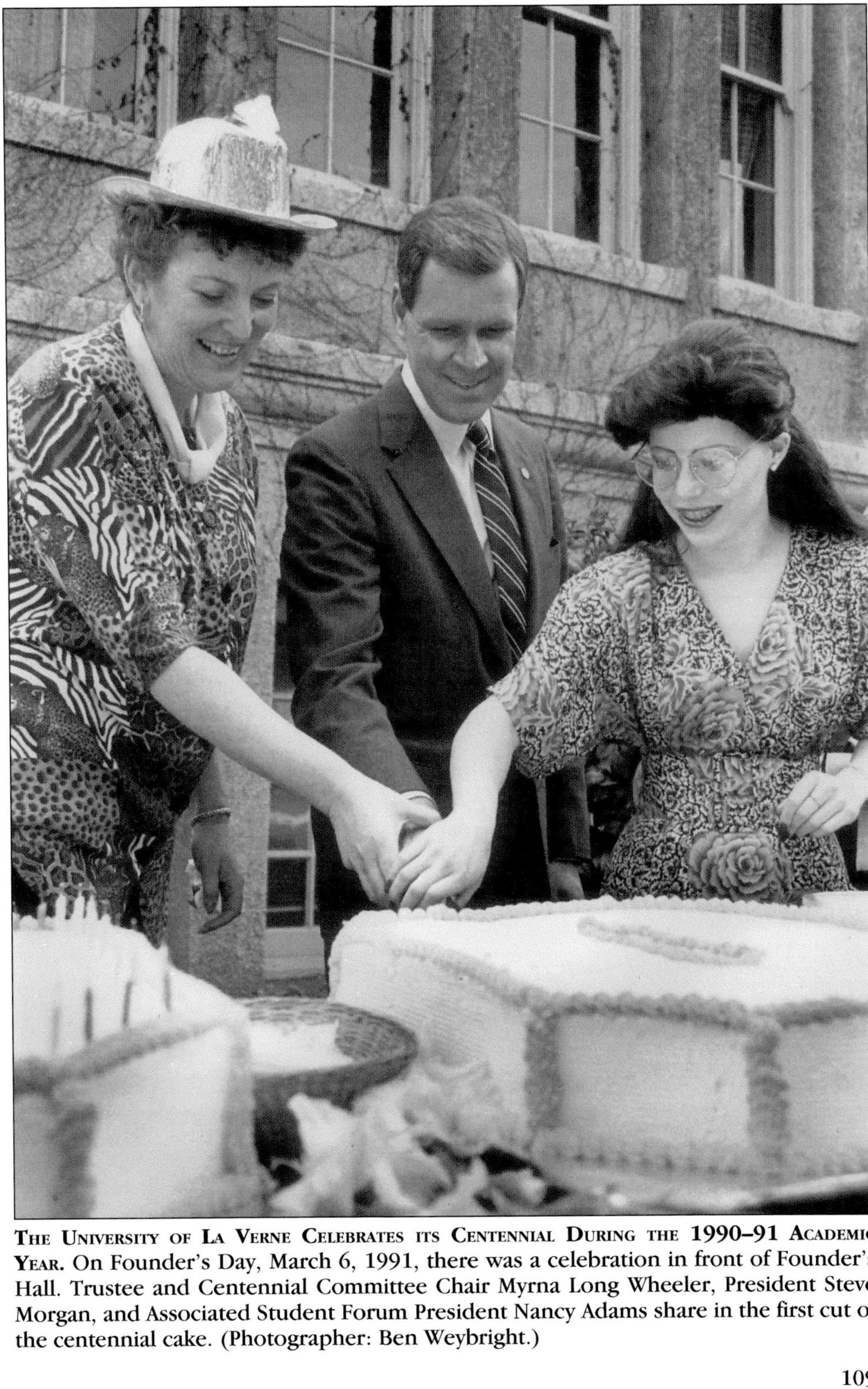

The University of La Verne Celebrates its Centennial During the 1990–91 Academic Year. On Founder's Day, March 6, 1991, there was a celebration in front of Founder's Hall. Trustee and Centennial Committee Chair Myrna Long Wheeler, President Steve Morgan, and Associated Student Forum President Nancy Adams share in the first cut of the centennial cake. (Photographer: Ben Weybright.)

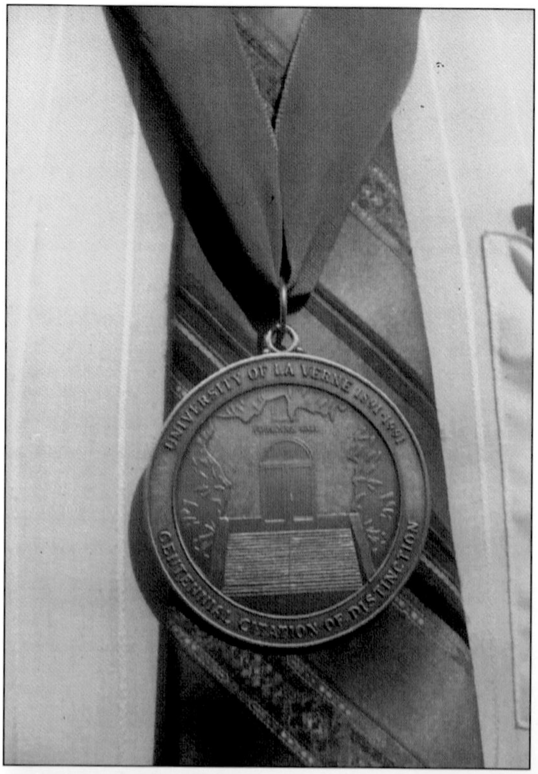

CENTENNIAL CITATION OF DISTINCTION MEDALS WERE PRESENTED TO ONE HUNDRED PERSONS AT VARIOUS TIMES THROUGHOUT THE CENTENNIAL YEAR.

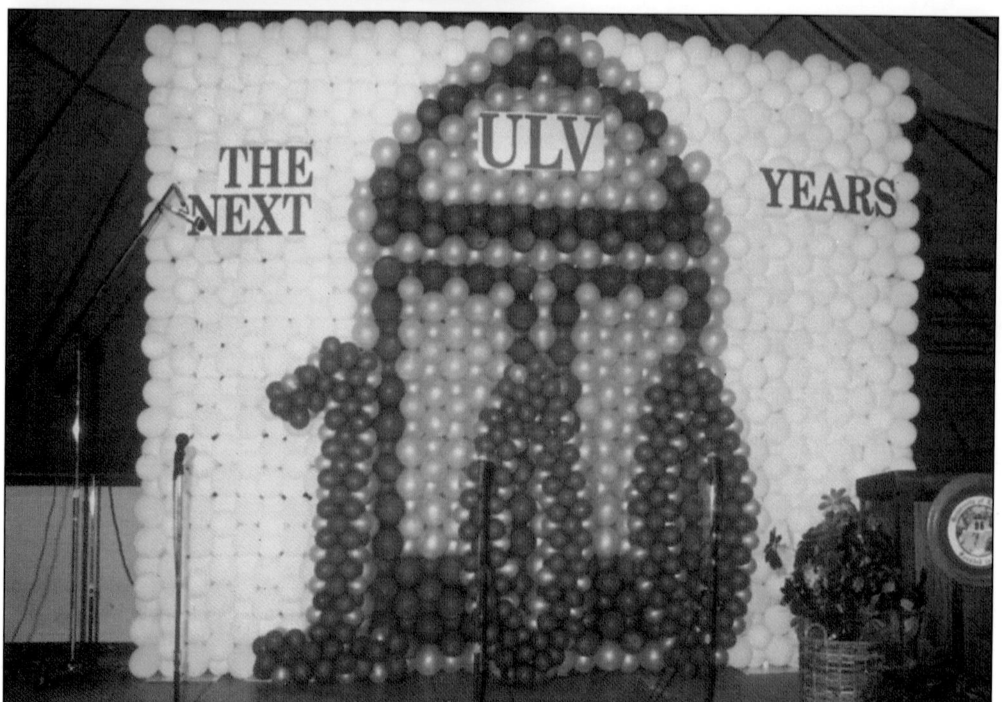

THE BALLOON BACKDROP FOR THE NEW ERA BANQUET IN 1991 HELPED LOOK TOWARD THE NEXT CENTURY.

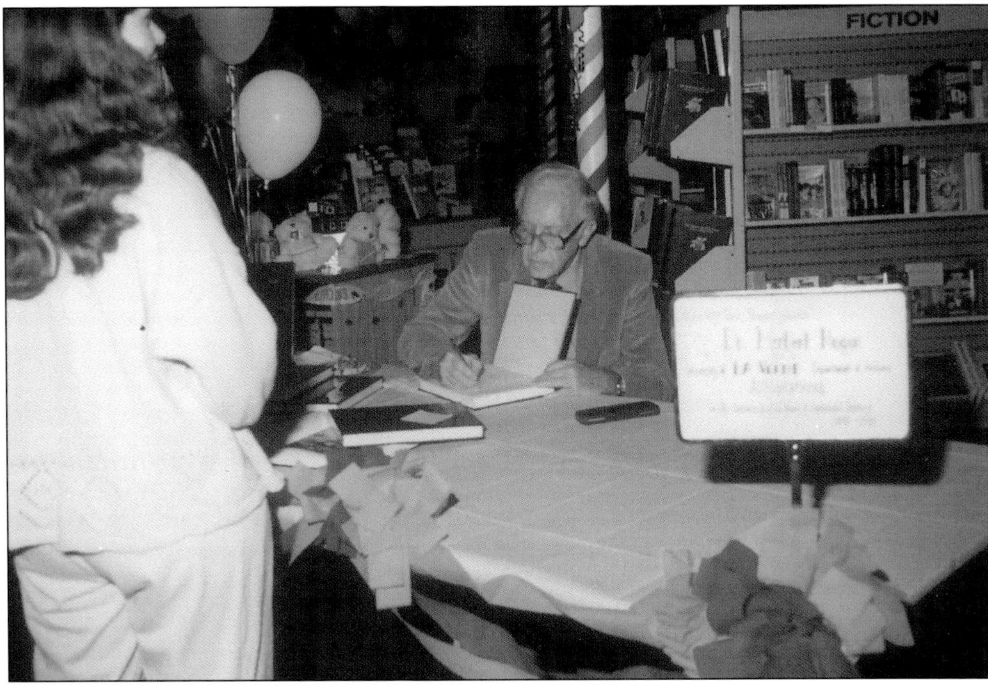

Dr. Herbert Hogan, Professor and Administrator for More than 50 years, Signing Copies of the Centennial History He Authored.

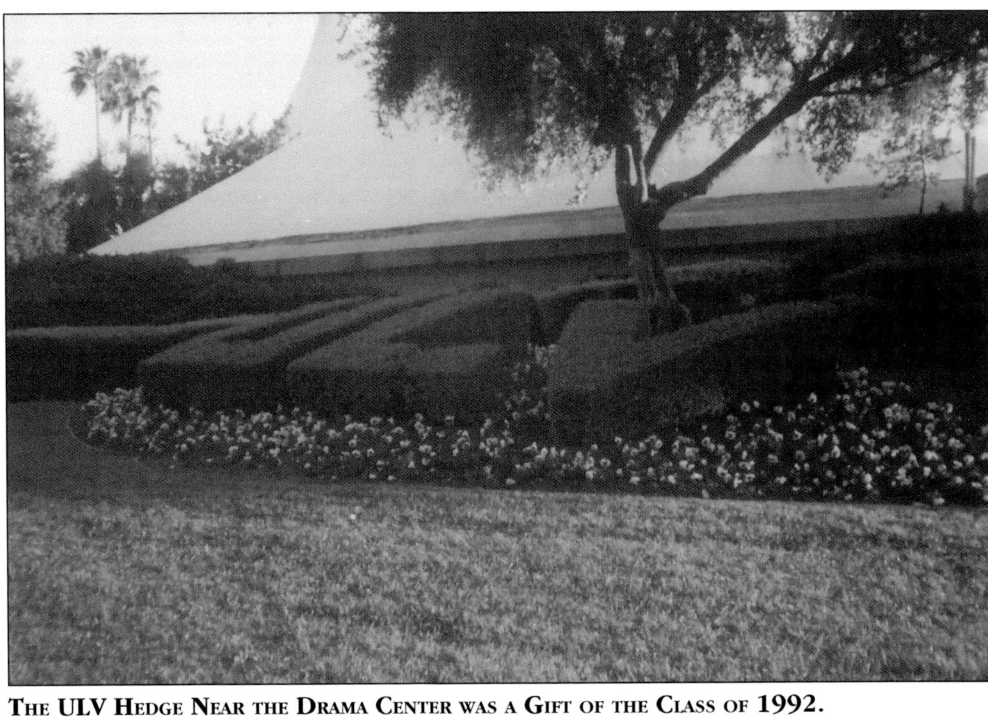

The ULV Hedge Near the Drama Center was a Gift of the Class of 1992.

Guide of La Verne

E. Raymond Root

How oft have you gazed at the mountains
That lie in the clear distant view
All clothed in their beauty and grandeur,
Set out by the vast sky of blue,
And gazing, you stopped in your wonder
To fasten your eyes on a place
Where seemingly carved from the ridge–side,
There glistens an "L" lettered space.

Chorus:
Guide of La Verne, You shall ever bring glory
To all who learn to revere and adore Thee.
Our L is the symbol of freedom
Of loyalty, faith and of love.
On! On! Upward with might Toward the light above.

When out in life's struggle we've drifted
And gloomy days come thick and fast
A mem'ry that lingers will lighten
The burden and toil of each task.
Then high like the "L" on the mountain,
An ideal of truth and of right
Will ever lean onward to vict'ry
And help us to win in the fight.

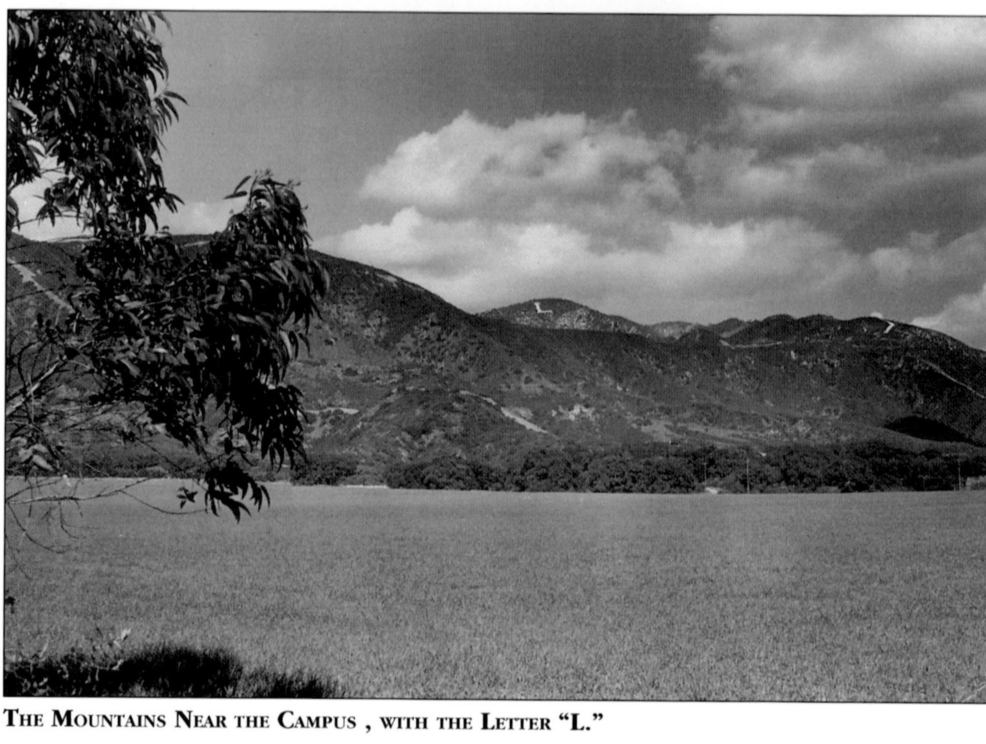

The Mountains Near the Campus , with the Letter "L."

Seven

The Library

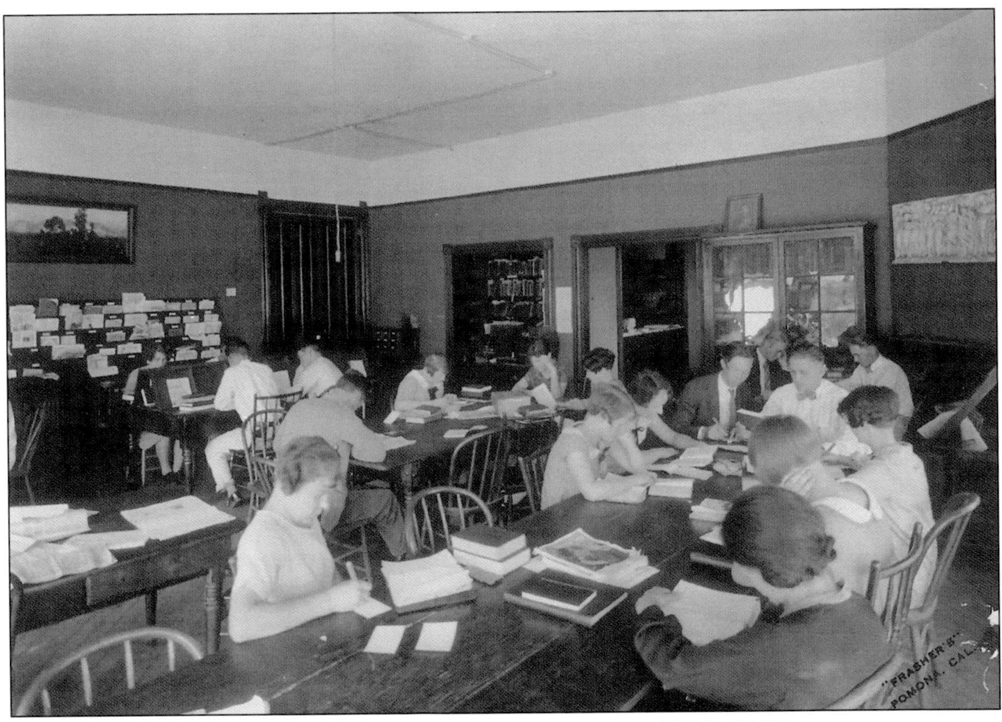

The Library in the Original Lordsburg College Building, 1891–1927.

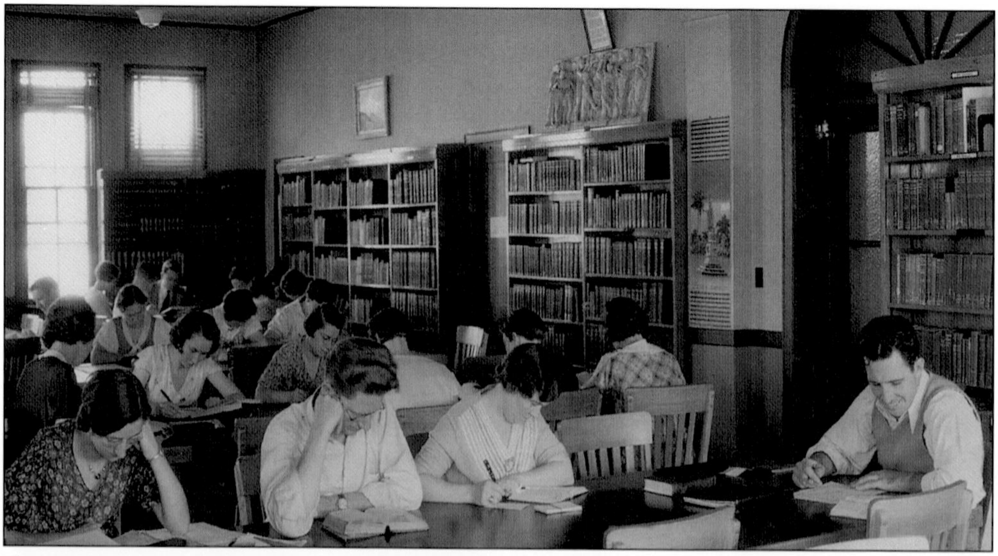

THE LIBRARY IN FOUNDERS HALL, 1927–1950.

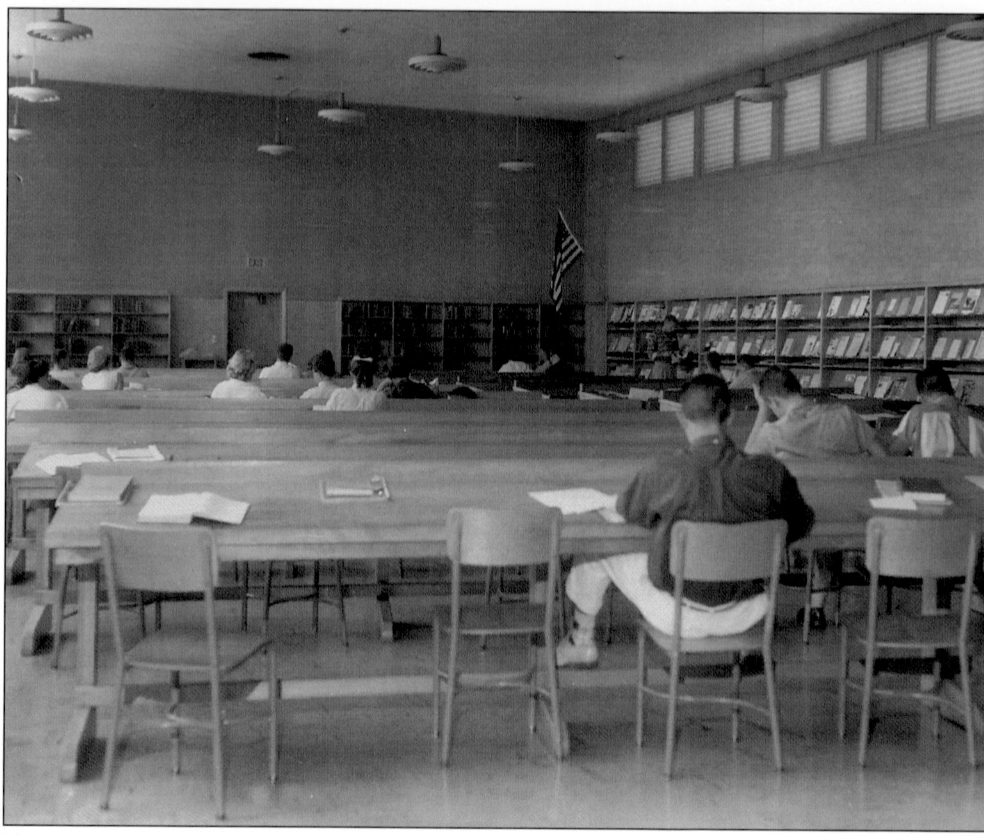

THE READING ROOM OF HOOVER MEMORIAL LIBRARY, 1950–1977.

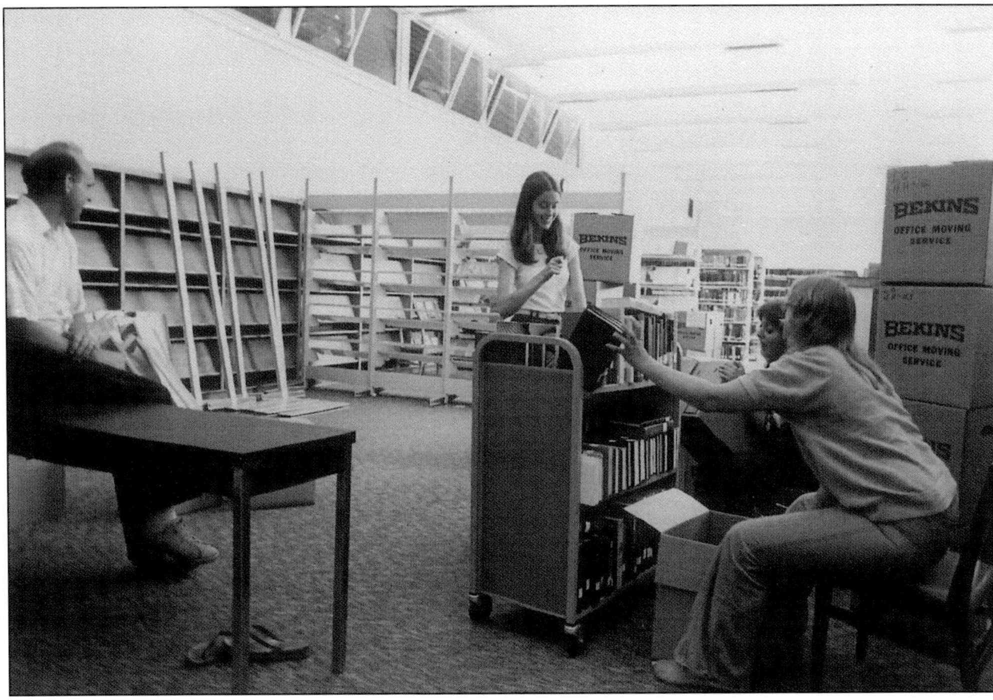

Preparations for Moving the Library Collection in 1977. Pictured are librarian Marlin Heckman, Sherrie Rand, Carol Bowman, and an unidentified person.

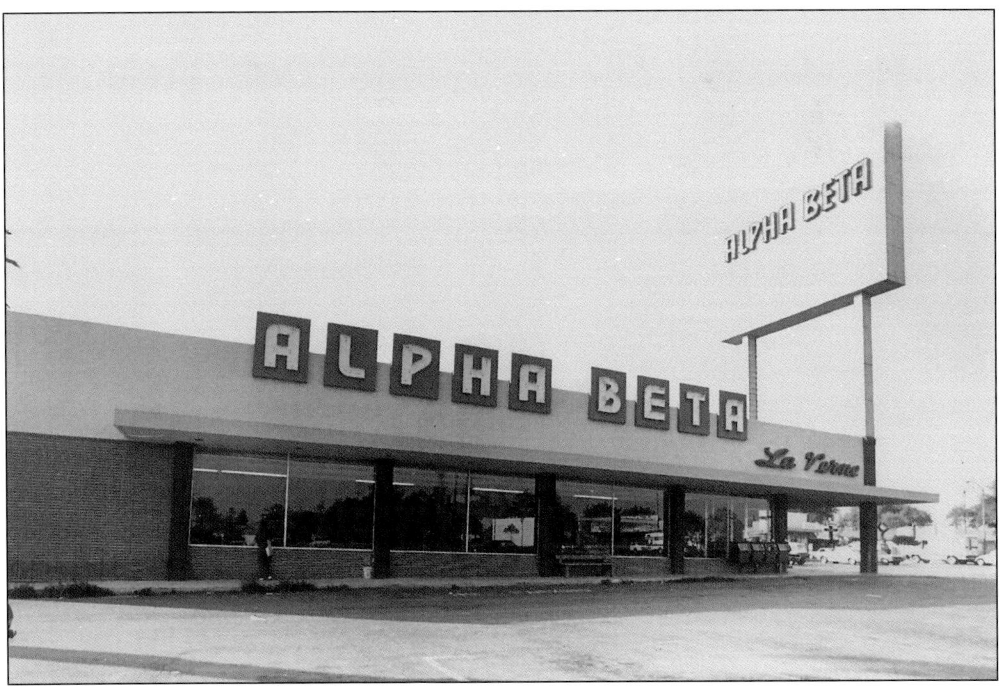

Alpha Beta Market, Prior to Renovation as the Library's New Home in 1977.

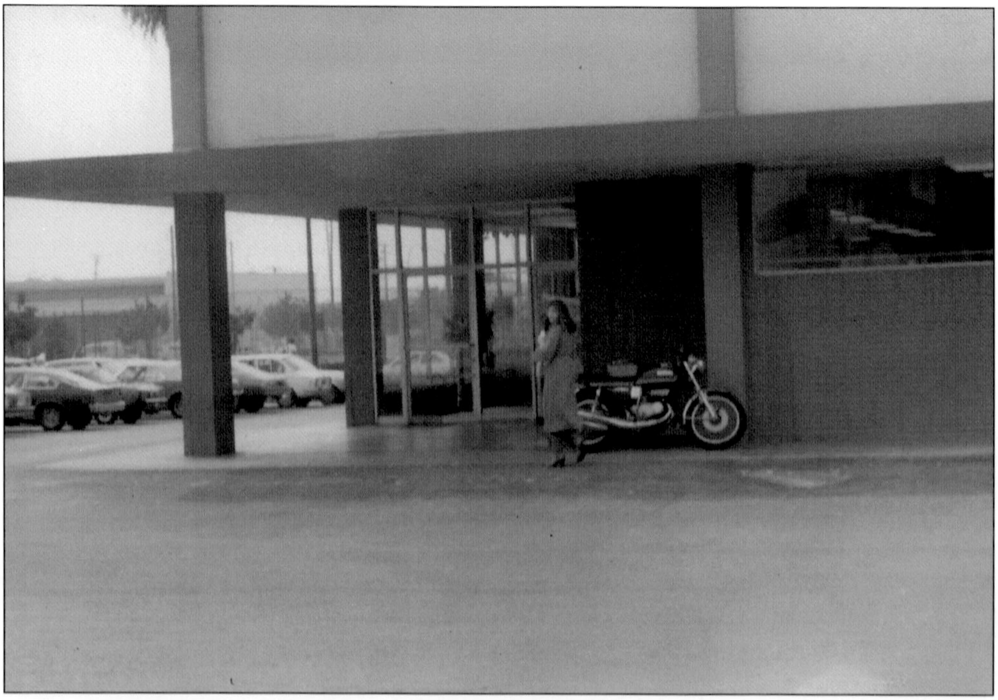

FROM A SUPER MARKET TO A LIBRARY IN ONE QUICK SUMMER.

UNPACKING BOOKS ONTO NEW BOOK STACKS, JULY 1977. Pictured are Jill Wilkinson, Sherrie Rand, and Carol Bowman.

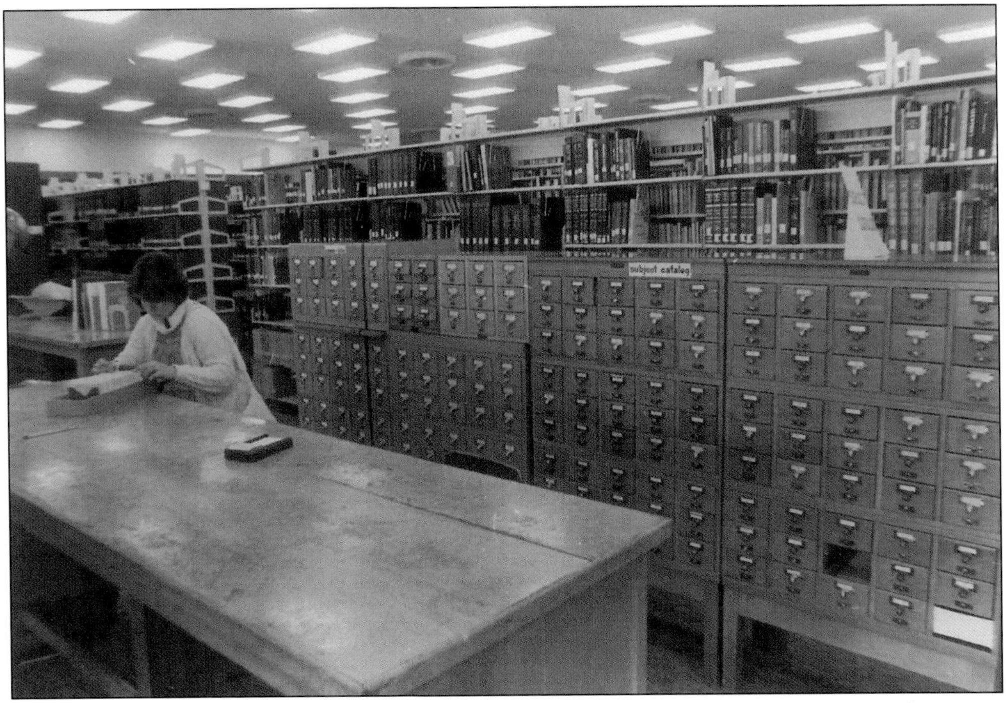

OLD FURNITURE, NEW BUILDING. Pictured is the serials librarian, Jacque Sunstrand, 1978.

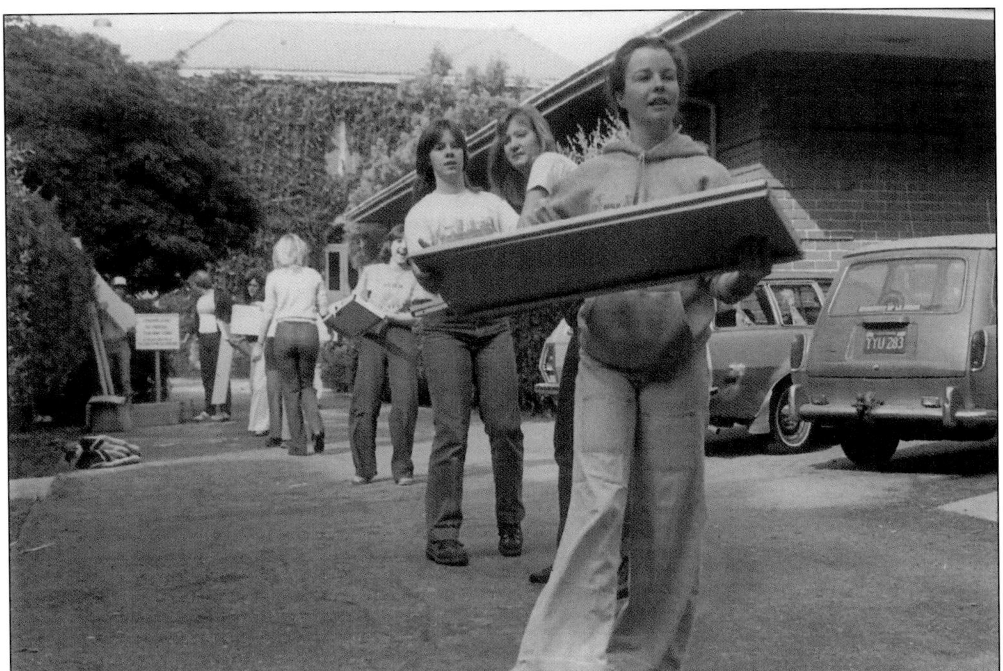

A HUMAN CONVEYOR BELT. Helpers move extra library shelving from storage in Miller Hall, across the park and over the wall to storage on the second floor of the library.

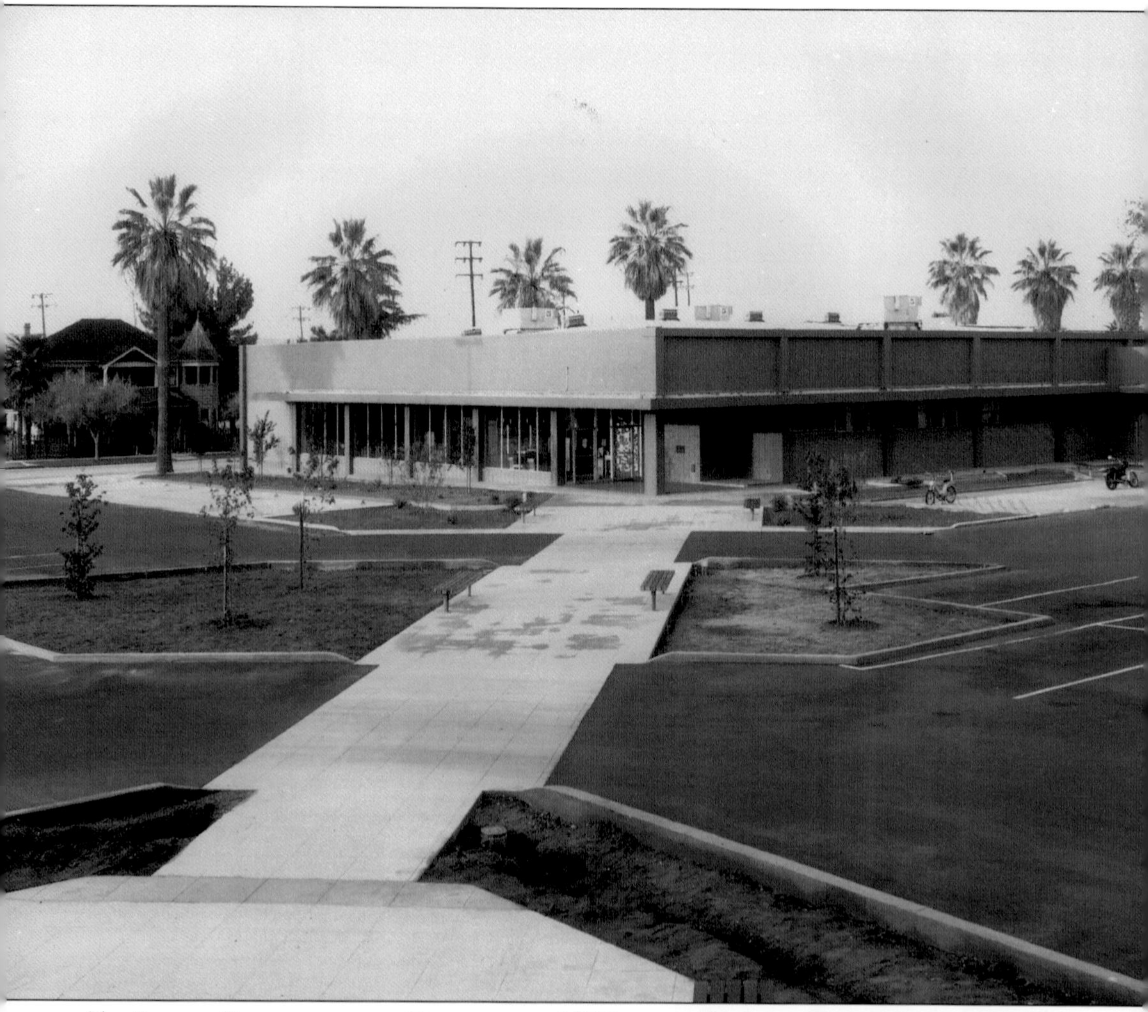

THE LIBRARY REFURBISHED AND DEDICATED IN 1982 AS THE ELVIN AND BETTY WILSON LIBRARY.

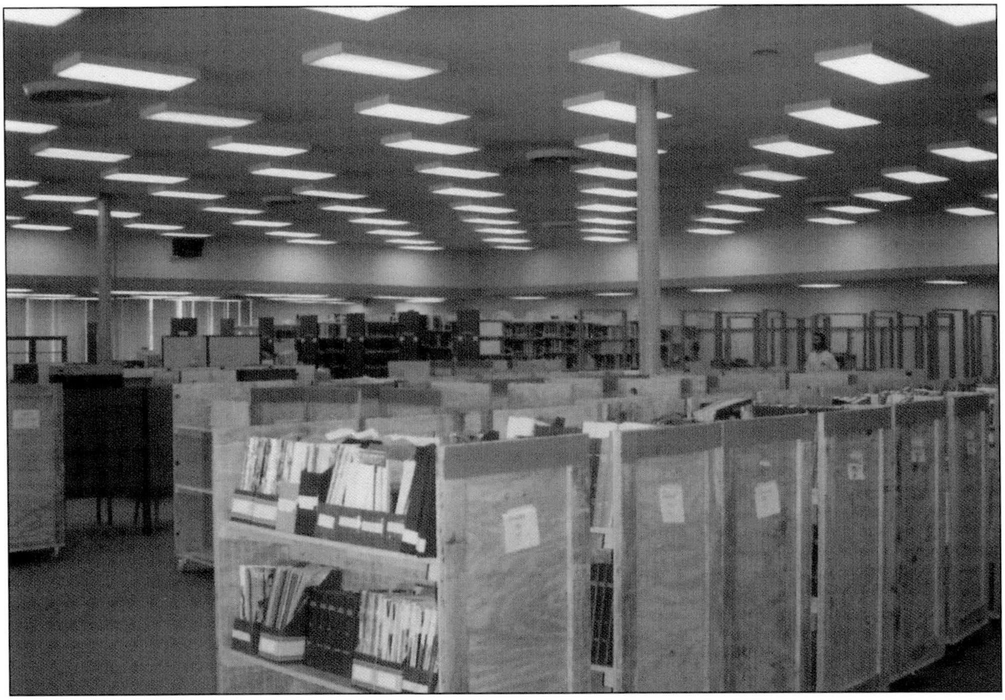

Time to Move Again! The collection was moved out in 1993 in preparation for the "New" Wilson Library. It was completed in 1996.

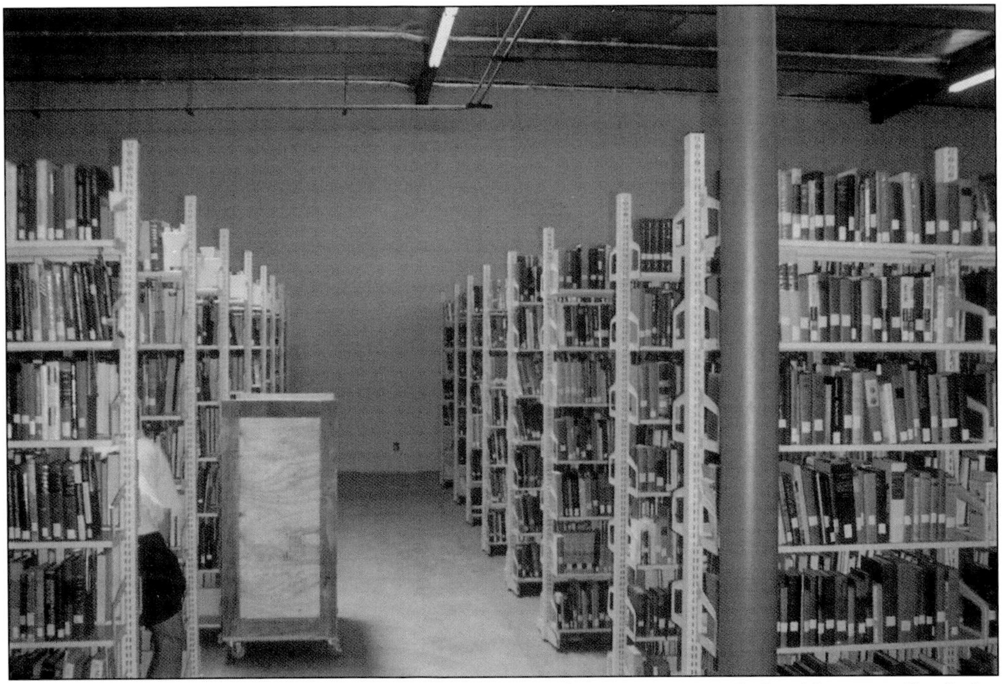

Renovation and Storage. During the 1993–1996 renovation of the library, all of the books where shelved in an off-campus warehouse, paged, and delivered four times each day.

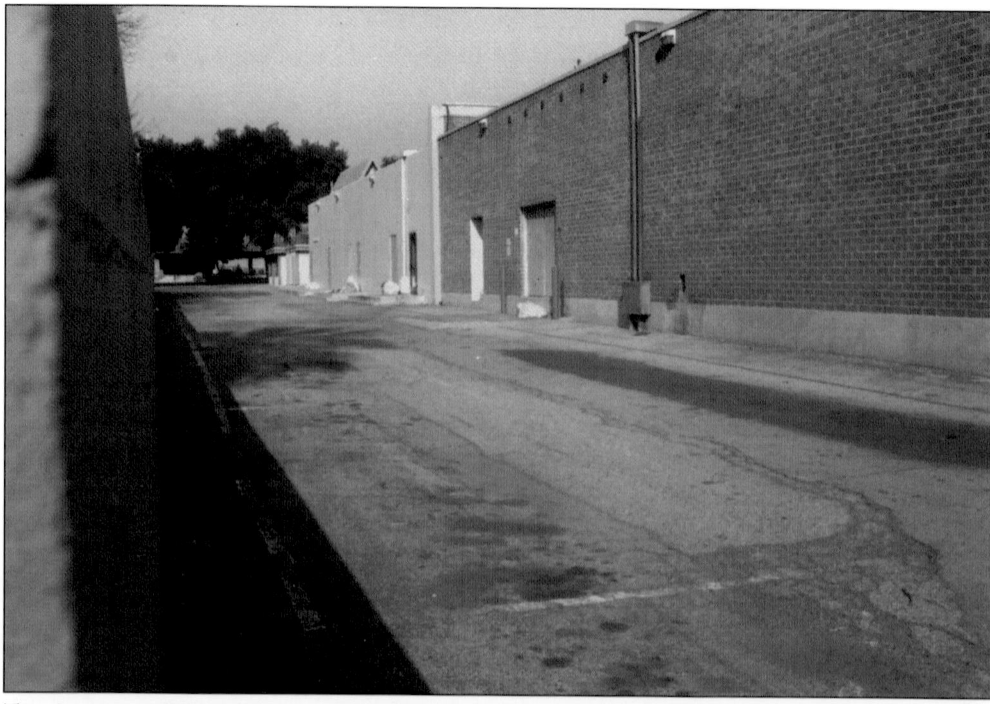

THE ALLEY AND "BACK WALL" OF THE WILSON LIBRARY BEFORE DEMOLITION IN 1994.

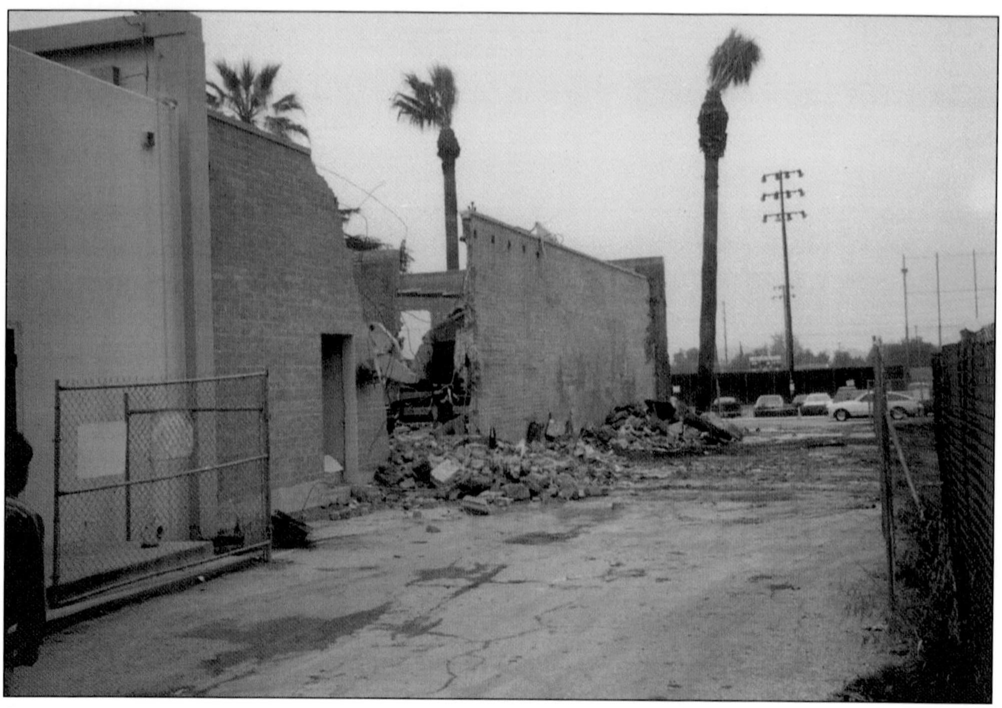

DEMOLITION AND CONSTRUCTION BEGAN MAY 1994.

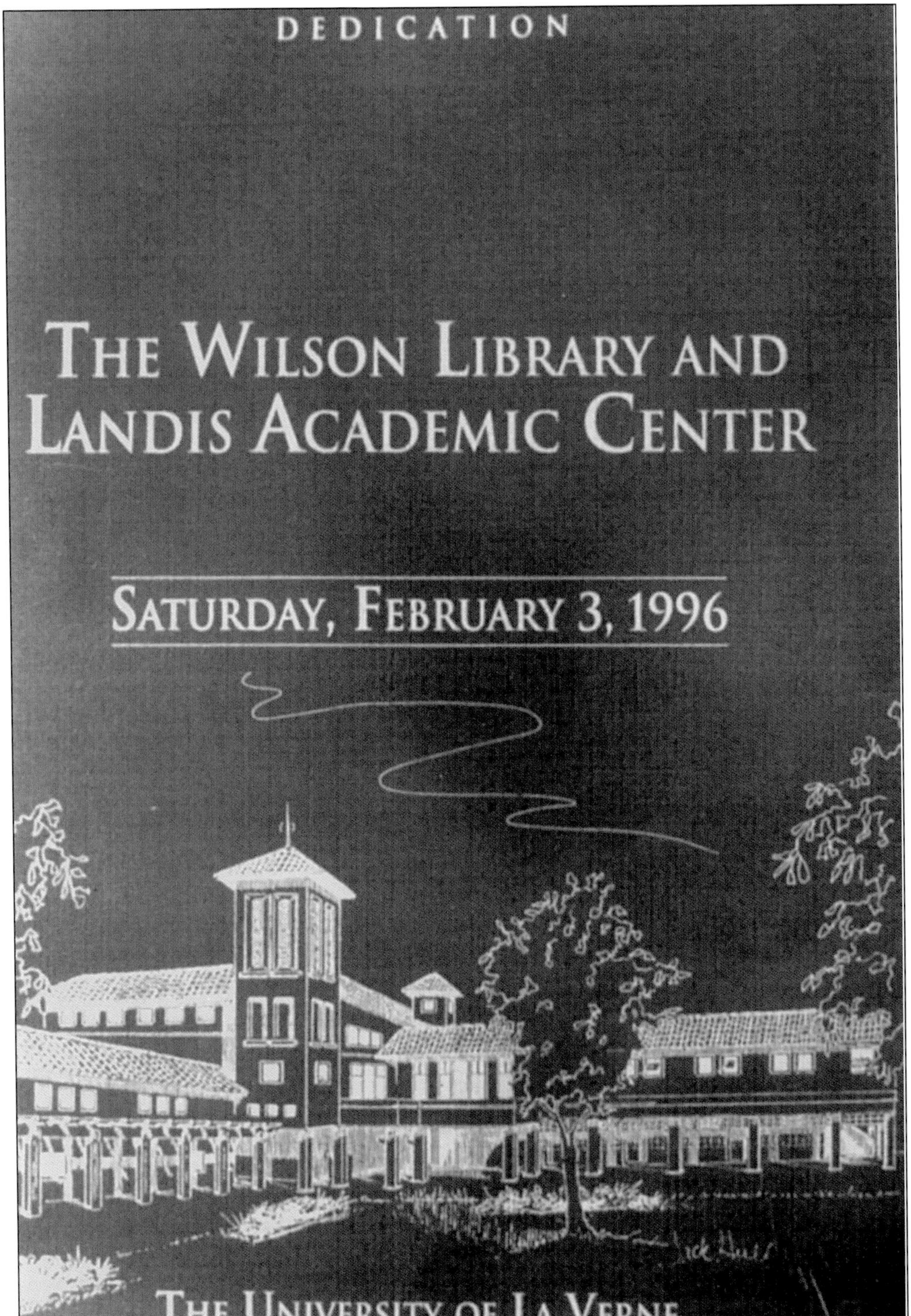

Dedication Day Program, February 3, 1996. Pictured are the Wilson Library and Landis Academic Center.

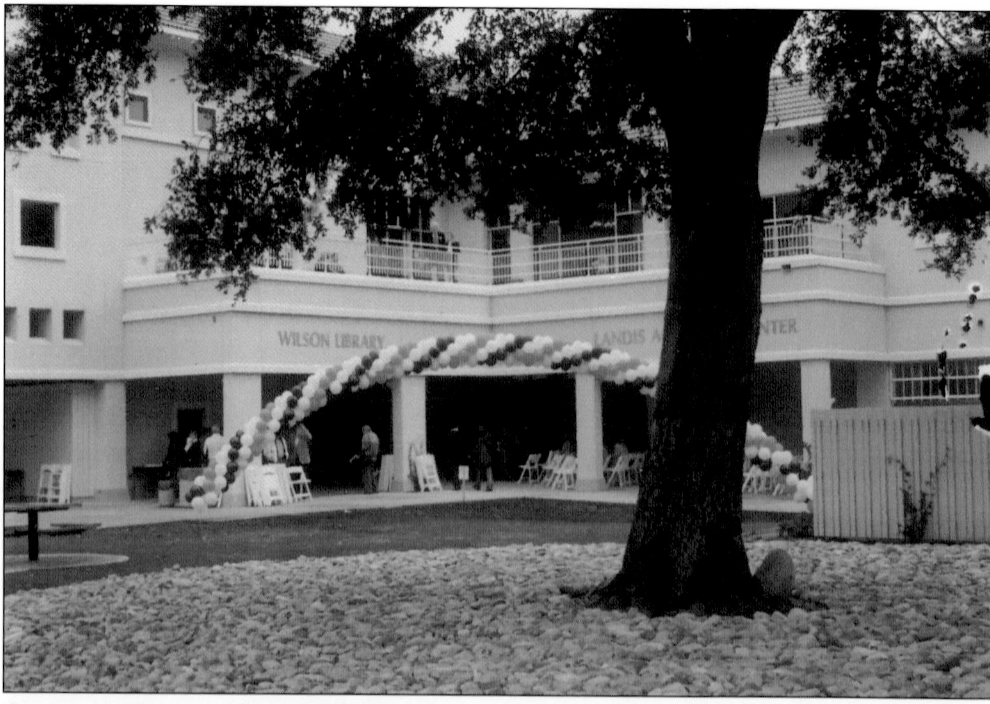

DEDICATION DAY WITH BALLOON ARCH.

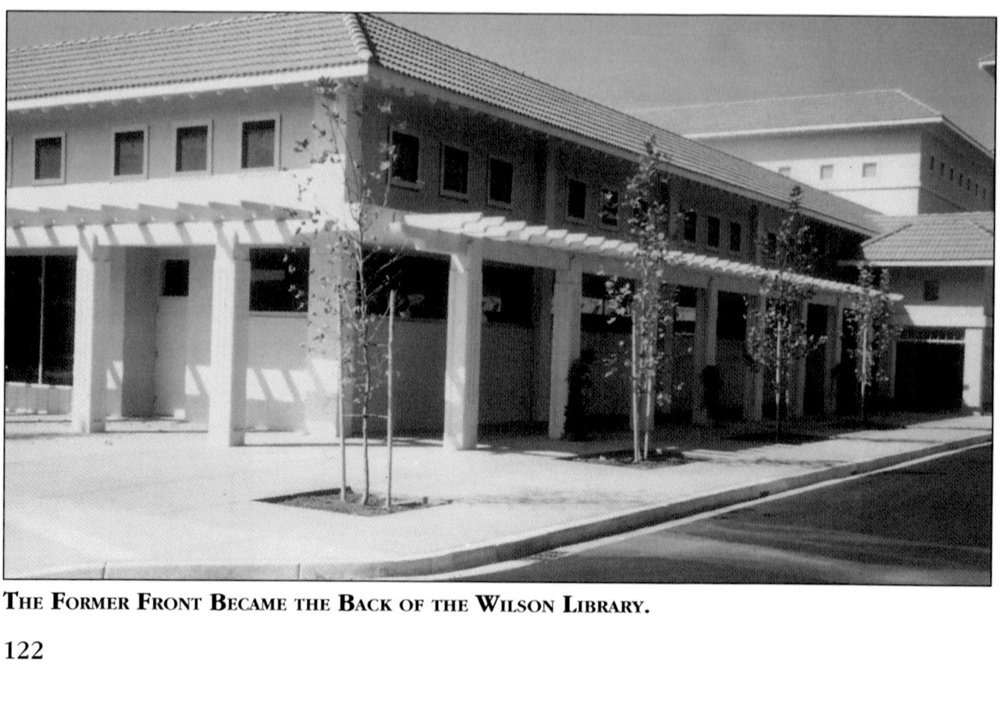

THE FORMER FRONT BECAME THE BACK OF THE WILSON LIBRARY.

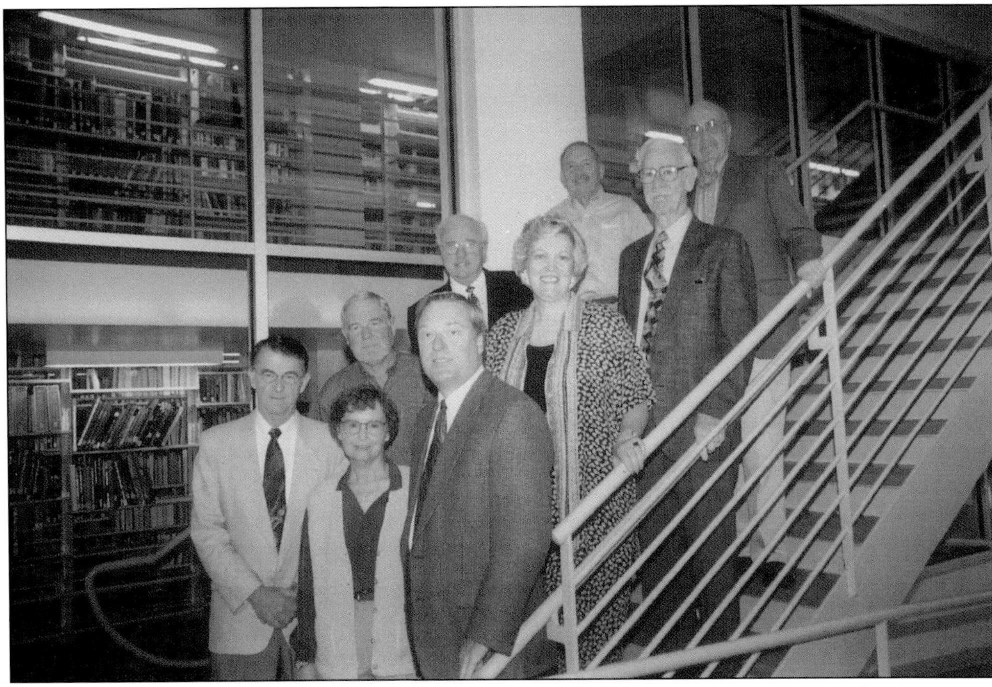

Executive Committee, Board of Trustees. Wilson Library can be seen in the background. Pictured left to right are: (front row) Don Wilson, Paula Stanley, Steve Renders; (second row) Jerry Laird; (third row) Roger Barkley, Myrna Long Wheeler; (fourth row) Jim Long, Chair, Lowell Brubaker; (back row) Kyhl Smeby.

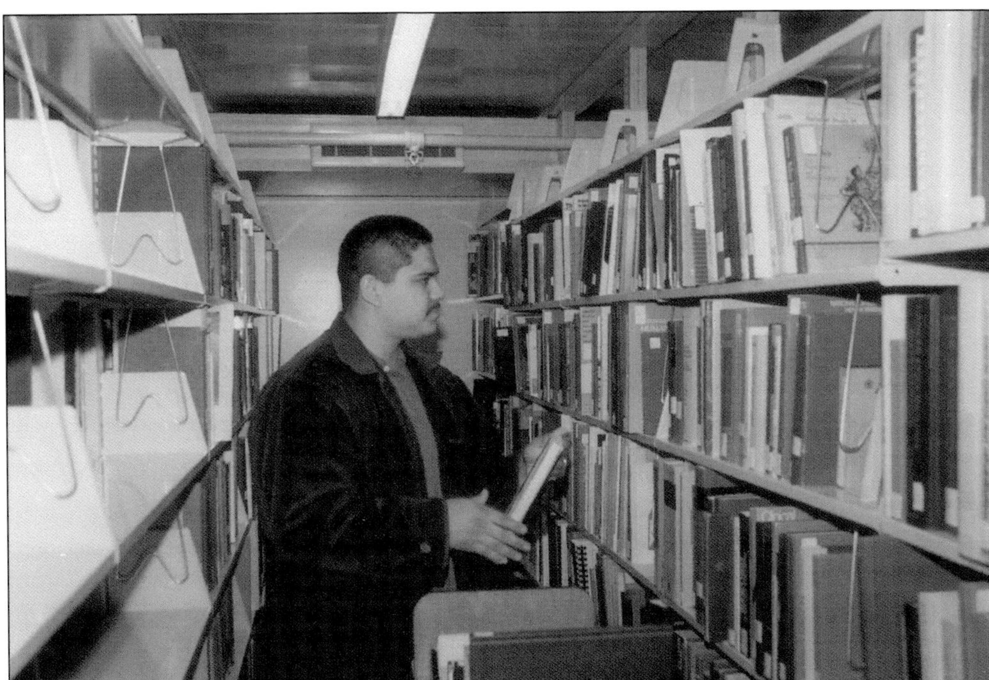

Jeffrey Soto, Shelving Books.

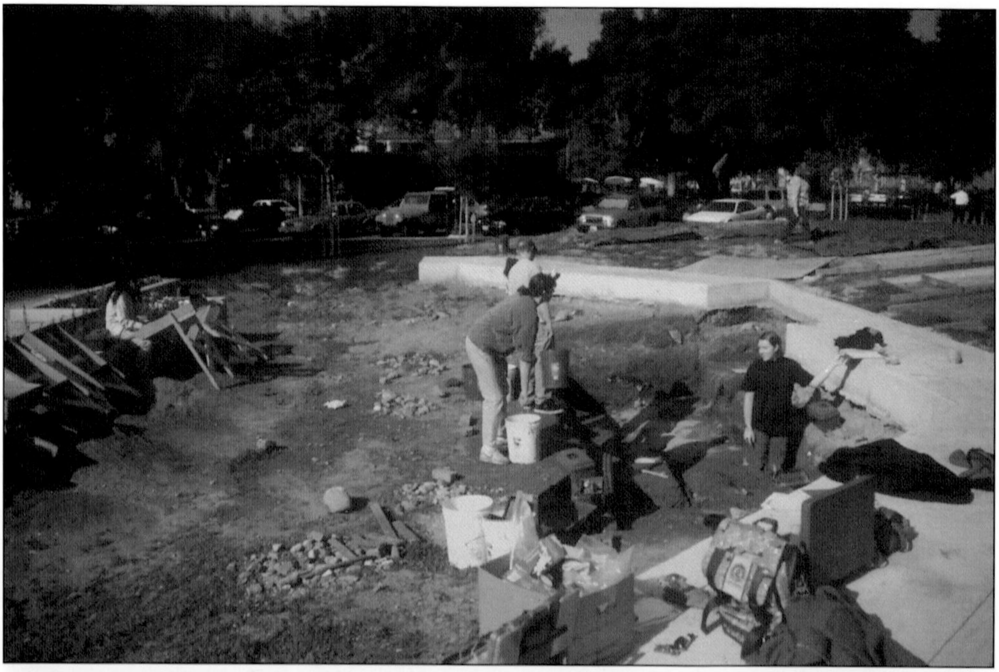

1996 Archeological Dig. Just as the library was being completed, some grading equipment uncovered the original trash dump of the Lordsburg College building. Ink bottles, dishes, eyeglass frames, and a pocket watch were among the hundreds of items excavated at the site.

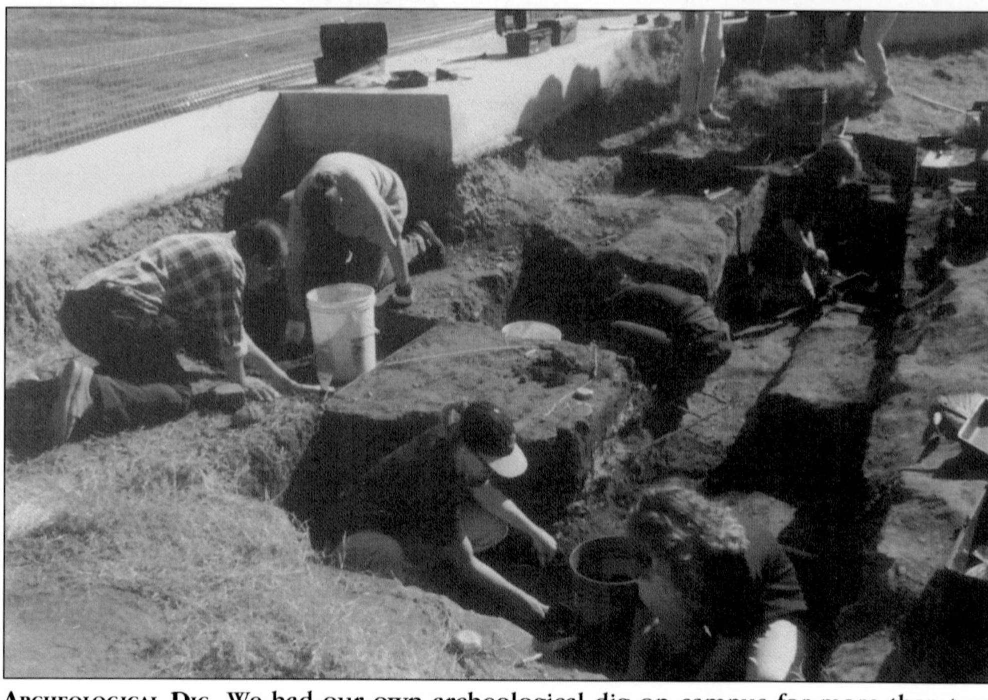

Archeological Dig. We had our own archeological dig on campus for more than two years, just outside the door of the library.

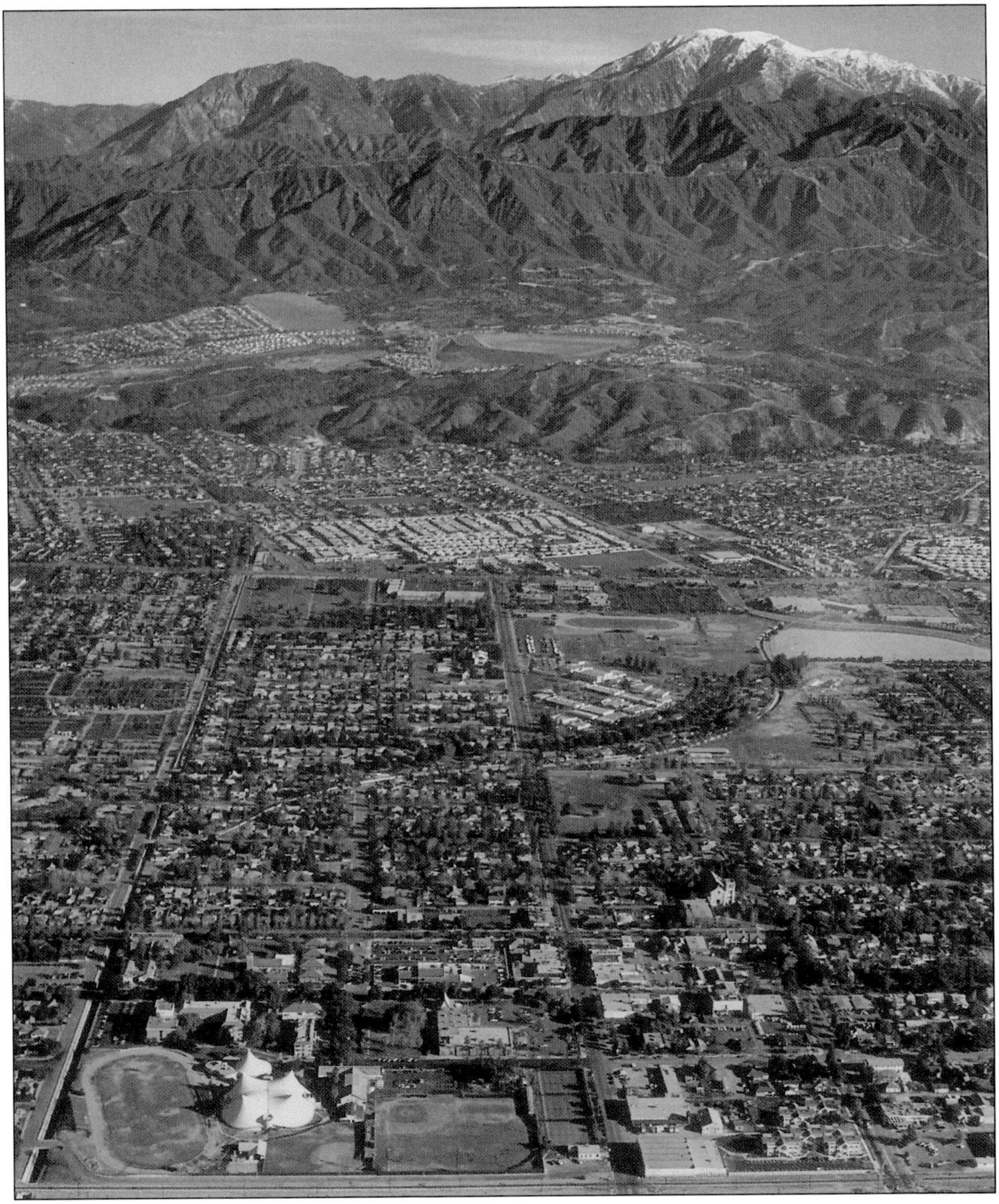

Aerial View of La Verne, 1978.

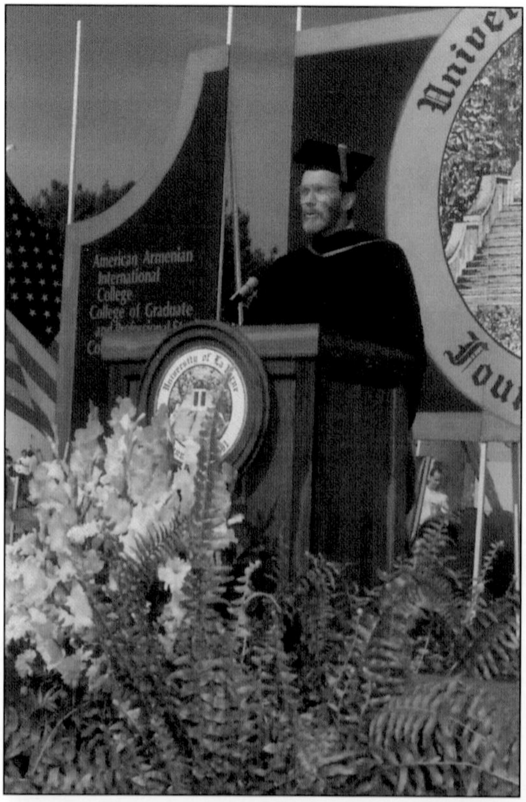

This Book is Dedicated to

Dr. Robert T. Neher

in Recognition of His Continuing

Service to the University of La Verne

as Professor of Biology, since 1958,

and

Acting Provost/Vice President,

Academic Affairs

2000–2001

Left: **Dr. Robert T. Neher, Commencement, 1998.**

Below: **Dr. Neher with a Student, Investigating Saber Tooth Tiger Skulls from University Collection.**

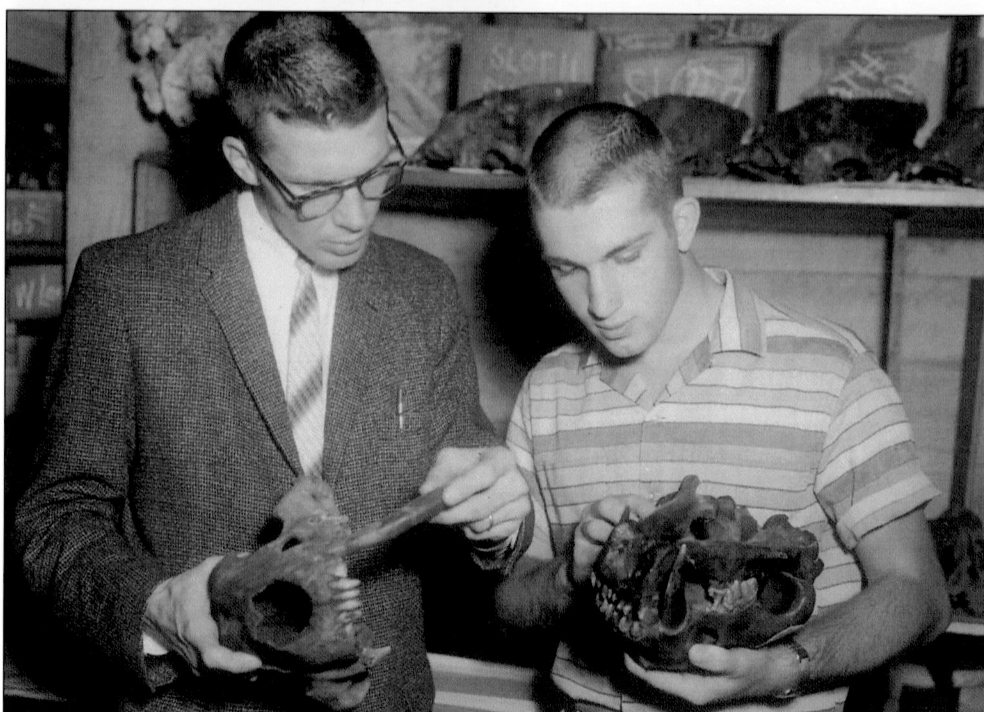

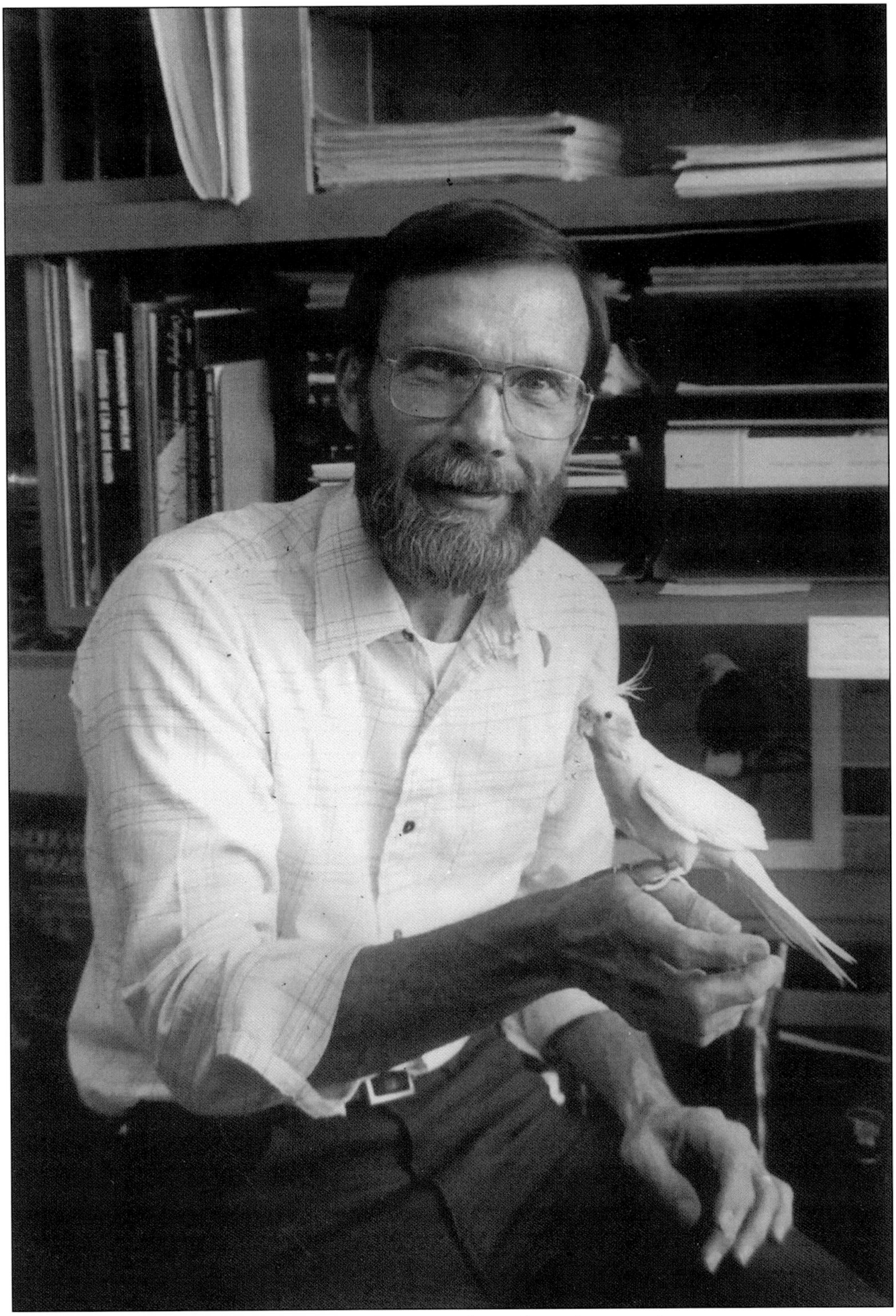

ROBERT NEHER WITH "TEAK," 1983. (Photographer: Tom Comeau.)

The Alma Mater
George Hollenberg

There's a dear favored spot That shall ne'er be forgot,
For its mem'ries will linger for aye.
Near the mountains it lies, Neath the bluest of skies,
Tis La Verne, with it friends true and gay.
In La Verne we believe, and a portion we leave that shall never depart.
For what e'er may betide there a joy will abide
In a dear favored spot in each heart.

Alma Mater, to you, each alumnus is true,
Ev'ry heart beats a tribute of love
As it goes but to give and in service to live,
For the truest and noblest above.
How we cherish your lore and your emblems adore
We'll be faithful and loyal to you.
With the shield of the right
There is courage and might
Alma Mater, La Verne, We are true to you.

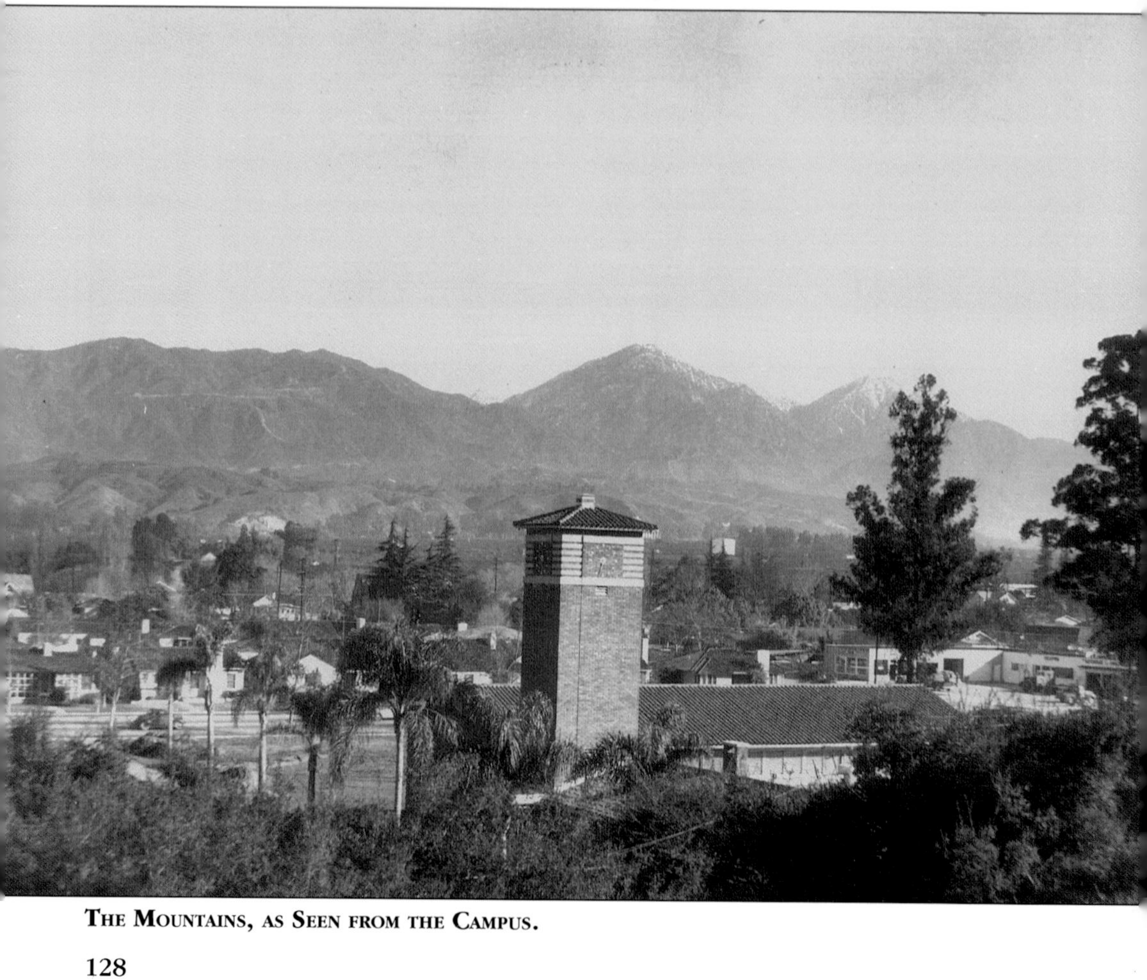

THE MOUNTAINS, AS SEEN FROM THE CAMPUS.